Praise for *Trial Practice Manual for Criminal Defense Lawyers*

"This is the most comprehensive, authoritative book on trial work I have ever read, understandable and encouraging to all, especially for new lawyers who do not yet feel they have permission to apply their creative skills and human understanding to trials. Bob Rose lays out a path that is truthful, ethical, and human, which will lead to good communication with juries and witnesses, and more victories for clients at trial."

—Charles Abourezk, Trial Lawyer, Rapid City, SD

"Robert Rose's book is much more than a training tool for criminal defense lawyers—it is also an ideal preparation tool for trial. Learn your case well and then use this book to help you structure your defense. Rose has taken all the testing, learning, and experimenting that many of us have engaged in and put it down in writing in a very valuable book. The combination of his book and the other sources cited by him will help you very finely prepare your case and present it in the best possible way. It will surely be of great benefit to you and your client."

—John Ackerman, San Antonio, TX

"Robert R. Rose has spent his career fighting for justice and the constitutional rights of people. He has written one of the best books ever to help criminal defense lawyers learn how to prepare for trial. Stressing the importance of thorough preparation and creativity, and how to reverse roles and stand in the shoes of the jury in voir dire, Rose demonstrates how to build unimpeachable credibility. This is the definitive guide on how to render effective assistance of counsel."

—Garvin A. Isaacs, Oklahoma City, OK

"From the first misdemeanor case to the last death penalty case, I have struggled with the desire for a precise checklist; a measure to ensure that all components were addressed and everything possible was performed for the human being whose future and life were in my hands. A lawyer armed with this guide and having the intestinal fortitude to stand up for the rights of the client will be prepared to become the warrior required for the fight for equal justice for all."

—Milton Grimes, Los Angeles, CA

"Bob Rose's *Trial Practice Manual* is proof that the apple does not fall far from the tree. He assimilates a lifetime of wisdom from his father and the legendary Gerry Spence, couples it with his own considerable experience, and distills it into two key principles (Trust the Jury/Tell the Truth) and two oft-neglected trial skills (Voir Dire/Opening Statement). On these four, one can weave a magical story and achieve the true miracle of justice."

—Andy Vickery, Houston, TX

"Few have taken on the Herculean task of writing a guide for trying a case from beginning to end. Bob Rose has put his heart and soul into this effort and the result is not only a scholarly work, but a look into what should be in every trial lawyer's heart and mind as they take on the task of representing the 'citizen accused.' Bob has given us a roadmap of how to tell our clients' stories and how to touch the hearts of the most important people in the courtroom—the jurors. This is a must-read for all lawyers aspiring to be better trial practitioners, as well as better people."

—Dale T. Cobb, Jr., Hanahan, SC

"Buicks and refrigerators have manuals; believers and readers have books. Despite its title, this is not a manual. It is a book: a humane work on the project of defending the accused, written with wit, honesty, and affection both for those who need defending and those who believe in defending. Use this book not just to learn how better to defend people—all people—but also to recommit and remember why."

—Dean A. Strang, Madison, WI

"I knew any trial practice manual by Bob Rose would feature his signature humility, decency, passion, erudition, courage, integrity, and meticulous thoroughness. What I did not anticipate was how funny he is willing to be, sharing the most practical truths of his experience, including some topics I've never seen addressed elsewhere, even wisdom on what a new criminal defense attorney need look at when negotiating fees. Savor this book and deploy repeatedly."

—Joshua Karton, Santa Monica, CA

"I highly recommend the *Trial Practice Manual for Criminal Defense Lawyers: A Field Guide to Courtroom Combat* by Robert R. Rose, III. This book is a trial lawyer's touchstone of clarity, steeped in strategy and insight, with skills and self-assurance for the trial lawyer working to win. I can feel Bob's years of experience and insight at my shoulder every time I read it. If you try cases, or want to learn how, this book belongs on your desk, dog-eared and coffee stained."

—T. Thomas Metier, Ft. Collins, CO

ROBERT R. ROSE III

TRIAL PRACTICE MANUAL *for* CRIMINAL DEFENSE LAWYERS

A FIELD GUIDE TO
COURTROOM COMBAT

AMERICAN BAR ASSOCIATION
ABA Publishing

Cover design by Kelly Book/ABA Design.

Printed in the United States of America.

26 25 24 6 5

Library of Congress Cataloging-in-Publication Data

Names: Rose, Robert R., III. author.
Title: Trial practice manual for criminal defense lawyers : a field guide to courtroom combat / Robert R. Rose.
Description: Chicago : American Bar Association, 2020. | Includes bibliographical references and index. | Summary: "So you want to be a trial lawyer. By reading this manual you have chosen not to fail. By choosing not to fail, you are seeing yourself as a trial lawyer. You have resolved to stand up for those whose light shines dim and whose voice is heard small. It is now time to get your head in the game. The ultimate goal in any trial is to win. You win by telling your client's story in such a way that it compels the jury to see and understand it and believe in it the same way you do. You accomplish that by establishing your credibility with the jury–by loving your client, telling the truth and being real"–Provided by publisher.
Identifiers: LCCN 2020012752 (print) | LCCN 2020012753 (ebook) | ISBN 9781641057028 (hardcover) | ISBN 9781641057035 (ebook)
Subjects: LCSH: Defense (Criminal procedure)–United States. | Trial practice–United States.
Classification: LCC KF9656 .R67 2020 (print) | LCC KF9656 (ebook) | DDC 345.73/05044–dc23
LC record available at https://lccn.loc.gov/2020012752
LC ebook record available at https://lccn.loc.gov/2020012753

Discounts are available for books ordered in bulk. Special consideration is given to state bars, CLE programs, and other bar-related organizations. Inquire at Book Publishing, ABA Publishing, American Bar Association, 321 N. Clark Street, Chicago, Illinois 60654-7598.

www.shopABA.org

For Ann, Ben, and Abigail

A real trial lawyer is rough, tough and hard to bluff.
—Garvin Isaacs

A good gun fighter picks the time and the place and doesn't let his opponent tell him when to draw.
—Gerry Spence

In life there is not justice. There is only "just us."
—Richard Pryor

Contents

Preface

So you want to be a trial lawyer.

By reading this manual, you have chosen not to fail. By choosing not to fail, you are seeing yourself as a trial lawyer. You have resolved to stand up for those whose light shines dim and whose voice is heard small.

It is now time to get your head in the game.

The ultimate goal in any trial is to win. You win by telling your client's story in such a way that it compels the jury to see and understand it and believe in it the same way you do. You accomplish that by establishing your credibility with the jury—by loving your client, telling the truth, and being real.

You begin the process by understanding who you are and what role you play in your client's story. You are the person whom the jury trusts to lead them out of the wilderness and into the light, the place where they are safe and they find what it is both they and you seek—justice for your client.

You are no longer a lawyer. Your client does not need a lawyer. Your client needs a *warrior* as big and as powerful as he can get. You are a *trial lawyer.* A true warrior for your client. And failure is not an option.

By following the methods set forth in this book, you may not always win, but you will never fail.

Acknowledgments

This manual is the result of nearly forty years of jury trial experience, encompassing employment as a state public defender, state prosecuting attorney, and private criminal and civil practitioner. Interspersed therein were stints as a Laramie County Circuit Court Magistrate, an adjunct professor of criminal law and procedure at Laramie County Community College, director of the Western Trial Advocacy Institute at the University of Wyoming College of Law, faculty member of the Summer Trial Institute at the University of Wyoming College of Law, instructor at the Annual Wyoming Trial Lawyers Association (WTLA) Robert R. Rose Jr. Voir Dire Competition, and jury trial consultant with the Wyoming State Public Defender's Office. Whether I ever displayed any significant prowess at any of it will be for others to say.

I was raised in a family whose generational focus was primarily representing the "little guys," those who were injured through the negligence of others and who were caught up in the criminal justice system. My grandfather, Robert R. Rose, left a comfortable law practice in Denver in the early spring of 1914 and moved to Kemmerer, Wyoming, having purchased sight unseen a tiny law practice from its owner, who availed himself of the next train to California as soon as possible after meeting my grandfather and handing him the keys. For the next two months, as the snow piled up in drifts, he sat alone at a small desk in a cramped little one-room office warmed by a rusting coal-fired stove. Not a single client walked through the door. From that precarious beginning, my family has since been involved in the practice of law in Wyoming, which, as of this writing, has comprised 106 years.

The debt of gratitude that I owe to those who have trained and guided me through the treacherous shoals of the legal profession over the years is simply overwhelming and one that I could never hope to repay. Space does not permit me to name all those patient souls here, but there are some whom I wish to single out for special recognition.

First and foremost, to my father, the late Robert R. Rose Jr., a practicing Wyoming trial lawyer for over fifty years, including ten years as a justice and chief justice of the Wyoming Supreme Court. There were few legal issues with which he did not have at least a passing acquaintance. Seemingly always at the right place at the right time, he enjoyed a career like few others. To me, he was the very embodiment of what a trial lawyer represented—smart, tough, and massively prepared. Infinitely patient and forgiving, loving and supporting, he never gave up on me and he helped shape my life in such a way that was almost mystical. I feel his presence daily.

Also of incalculable impact on my life and career was my father's long-time partner and best friend, Gerry Spence. From the moment I first met him when I was 13 years old to this day, he has remained a force of nature in my life. Together, their combined influence and guidance had, and continues to have, an inestimable and indescribable influence on who I am.

To my "second family," the core faculty of the Western Trial Advocacy Institute. Among the very best trial lawyers and trial advocacy instructors in the United States: Charles Abourezk, John Ackerman, Marilyn Bednarski, George Blau, Russ Born, Shawna Mackey Geiger, Stephanie Hewitt Bowen, Hon. G. Joseph Cardine, Dale Cobb, Milton Grimes, Garvin Isaacs, Hon. Joseph D. Johnson, Joshua Karton, Mary Kennedy, A. J. Kramer, Albert Krieger, Dallas Laird, Terry MacCarthy, Terry Mackey, Linda Miller, Bert Nieslanik, Steve Rench, James Shellow, Richard Tegtmeier, John Tierney, and Craig Truman. For thirty years, you selflessly dedicated part of each summer to teaching young trial lawyers in Wyoming how to be real, how to love their clients, and how to stand up for those whose light shines dim and whose voice is heard small. Giving all of yourselves, the very best you had to give, you gave it all away, never asking for anything in return. I was the luckiest man in the world to have had the privilege to know each of you and to work and learn side by side with you. I love you all.

I am forever indebted to attorneys Ed Moriarity, Bob Schuster, Gary Shockey, "Skip" Jacobson, and Doug McCalla, and to investigators

Chuck Herro, Chuck Wooden, and Mike Johnson, of the firm formerly known as Spence, Moriarity & Schuster. Spending my formative years with "SMS" had an extraordinary impact on me, and I call upon the skills and life lessons you each taught me in every case I try. Thank you for your abiding faith in me.

Thanks also to the Wyoming Trial Lawyers Association, and its executive director, Marcia Shanor. Your contribution to the improvement of the practice of law in Wyoming has been nothing short of heroic, and your unfailing support and steadfast belief in me and my family has been humbling and greatly appreciated.

I owe thanks to Diane Lozano, the Wyoming State Public Defender and true champion of the people if ever there was one. Because of her continuing friendship, support, and encouragement, I have had a home base from which to write this manual. Thanks for letting me pitch my tent and share your campfire.

I am particularly thankful to my good friend and colleague, and brilliant Wyoming trial lawyer and warrior, Tom Jubin, who graciously agreed to review the manuscript and assured me that someone other than my mother would wish to read it.

I am likewise grateful to John Palmer, executive editor at the American Bar Association Publishing Division in Chicago, for all of his enthusiastic support. His keen eye for balance, harmony, and accuracy in the creation and promotion of this manual was invaluable. A huge thank you also to Donna King, project manager at Progressive Publishing Services, for her considerable effort, patience, and outstanding guidance in the assembly and editing of the manuscript.

I would be remiss if I did not extend a heartfelt thank you to my close friend and frequent courtroom companion, collaborator, conscience, and touchstone, Mike Bennett. You are my trusted sidekick through these treacherous waters, and I would surely be lost without you. Stan and Ollie never had it so good.

Finally, and certainly most importantly of all, to my beloved wife, Ann, and my children, Ben and Abigail. You are the light of my life. I would never have been able to summon the courage to be who I am and achieve whatever success I have without your boundless love, forgiveness, and support. I will never be able to thank you enough. My love for you is eternal.

Introduction

Why We Do What We Do

> *One must, from time to time, attempt something beyond one's own capacity.*
>
> —Renoir

It was April 12, 1961.

In the pre-dawn darkness, NATO radar stations detected the launch of a Soviet rocket. At 5:30 a.m., Eastern Standard Time, Moscow News Radio announced that Yuri Gagarin, a 27-year-old Soviet Air Force pilot, had just become the first human being to fly into space. Americans awoke that morning to the news that they had lost the "race to space."

The impact of the announcement shook the world. President John F. Kennedy, barely three months into his administration, was already deeply immersed in the Cold War with the Soviet Union. Fiercely competitive by nature, Kennedy fired off a memo to Vice President Lyndon Johnson a week later, asking him if he thought America could achieve anything significant in space exploration that would trump the Soviets, such as sending a rocket to orbit the moon or even landing a man on the moon.

Although not that interested in space, and fearful that the staggering cost of developing and maintaining a federal space exploration program could easily capsize other more pressing social programs,

Kennedy nevertheless recognized that the United States could not afford to allow the Soviets to prevail. The very survival of the country depended on it, for the Soviets had convincingly demonstrated that they possessed the ability to strike a nuclear blow at the very heart of America.

On May 25, a mere six weeks after Gagarin's flight, the president announced the most ambitious and audacious goal ever undertaken by humans:

> *I believe that this nation should commit itself to achieving the goal, before this decade is out, of landing a man on the moon, and returning him safely to the earth.*

The declaration came as a startling surprise to everyone, especially the fledgling organization known as NASA (the National Aeronautics and Space Administration). At the time Kennedy made the speech, the task was impossible to achieve. It had never been done, no one knew how to do it, and virtually none of the technology or hardware that would accomplish it *had yet been invented.* Indeed, prior to that point, America's sole achievement in "manned" space exploration had been to launch a chimpanzee named "Ham" into space on a 16-minute sub-orbital flight, utilizing a rocket that was notorious for exploding on the launch pad.[1] The total budget for NASA at the time was $1 million for the entire year. By the time Neil Armstrong's boot sank softly into the powdery gray lunar surface barely eight years later, NASA was spending $1 million *every three hours.*

To say it was an extraordinary achievement is an understatement. Closer to superhuman, it required a level of singleminded national commitment and purpose of both government and private-sector effort not seen since the Manhattan Project developed the atomic bomb during World War II.[2] In the final analysis, what drove us to

---

1 The first American astronaut into space, Alan Shepard, was launched May 5, just 23 days after Gagarin. His flight was also sub-orbital, and lasted a mere 15 minutes. Ham therefore remained the more experienced of the two until Shepard flew again in 1971, this time to the moon aboard Apollo 14.

2 While the country was committed to winning World War II, only a relatively select few individuals were ever aware of the existence of the bomb project. In contrast, following Kennedy's announcement, the entire nation was not only aware of and

successfully land on the moon and fulfill President Kennedy's mandate amounted to far more than the sum of the parts it took to get us there. We simply *believed* we could. *We chose not to fail.* As NASA Flight Director Gene Kranz is famously credited for saying, "*Failure is not an option.*"[3]

As a criminal defense trial lawyer, and especially a public defender, your task is enormous, and the effort required to succeed seems no less daunting than undertaking a successful moon launch. You represent people who are in many ways "unrepresentable." The jury doesn't like them and doesn't understand why you represent them. The bias against your clients is almost palpable. The trial hasn't even begun and already you feel a sense of panic and desperation. Acquittal seems impossible. Their freedom, and sometimes their very lives, are in your hands. You are terrified of failure. You soon realize that

---

committed to the goal, but it was undertaken at a time when America was days away from the disastrous Bay of Pigs fiasco, fully involved in prosecuting the Vietnam War, and later reeling from bloody riots and student unrest on college campuses throughout the nation, suffering from violence and murders of citizens and civil rights workers throughout the South, the assassinations of President Kennedy, Malcolm X, Martin Luther King Jr. and Robert Kennedy, not to mention the horrifying deaths of three astronauts in a fire in the command module during a ground test of Apollo 1, which delayed the program for eighteen months. Yet, despite all of these events, the nation's steadfast determination and commitment to succeed at all costs remained undeterred. As one senior engineer wistfully noted, "If we had known at the time what it would actually take to do it, we wouldn't have done it."

[3] At the height of the Apollo program, NASA employed over 32,000 engineers. Including contractors and subcontractors, the total number of persons involved was around 400,000. There were few computers, and they used data punch cards for each inquiry, the answers to which took hours or even days. Many calculations were done with slide rulers. NASA thus developed the first "real-time" computing utilizing the newly invented solid-state integrated circuit in order to solve problems that required solutions instantaneously. The hard-wired memory loaded into the guidance computers aboard the Apollo command modules was hand-assembled, literally wire by wire, by women skilled at sewing. It took six weeks to complete each one, and it could perform over 87,000 calculations per second. By comparison, the 2018 i-Phone X can perform over *5 trillion.* The engineers and technicians at MIT and other laboratories were literally working out the mathematical calculations to solve the mystery of how to negotiate flying through space and land men on the moon, while simultaneously creating the very computers and other hardware that would use those calculations to get them there. The commitment to perfection was so ingrained at NASA that, during the entire Apollo program, including six lunar landings, *there was not one single failure of any software or hardware component.* They all worked perfectly the first time. They had to.

your clients do not need a lawyer—they need a warrior, as big as they can get. *More than that, they need someone who believes in them as human beings with value.* Failure is not an option.

In trial advocacy, it all comes down to your client's story and how well you deliver it. To put it bluntly, in this business you must "Go Big or Go Home." Whoever tells the best story wins. You cannot tell your client's story unless you believe in it. In order to believe in your client's story, you must first be able to believe in yourself and your ability to persuasively tell it. And you start believing in yourself by choosing not to fail.

By choosing not to fail, we begin to see ourselves as good lawyers—as warriors for our clients. It is entertaining to see good lawyering. We see so little of it in real life. But that's what gets juries excited. That's what wins cases: getting the jury to *believe*. It all comes down to theater—the presentation, the show. Give them their money's worth. Something to remember. A reason to believe that "justice" is not a sterile abstract notion, but a real phenomenon that we create when we need it most. Just like in the movies. We as trial lawyers must believe in it—and ourselves—that deeply in order to empower the jury to create it.

Much like the NASA engineers who must have gazed at the moon in 1961 and thought that it would take a miracle to get there and back, we have to believe in the miracle of securing our client's acquittal. That is why movies like *E.T.*, *The Natural*, *Field of Dreams*, and *The Verdict* work. That is why Christmas works and why Las Vegas works. We believe the magic is real because we suspend our disbelief, if only for a few hours. But it is more than just believing in a fantasy. The thing is, like Neil Armstrong's first tentative step off the LEM landing pad, it happens just often enough in real life to remind us that it's real.[4]

Being a trial lawyer is unlike any other profession. We do not create anything; instead, we are in the business of asking others to do it. To confound matters further, once created, it exists only momentarily

---

[4] Go on YouTube and watch Secretariat in the 1973 Belmont Stakes; the 1980 U.S. Olympic Men's Hockey Team in the semi-final; Kirk Gibson's home run in Game 1 of the 1988 World Series; or Kerri Strug's final vault in the 1996 Olympic Women's Gymnastics Championship. Do you believe in miracles?

and then vanishes forever, never to appear in that form again. Though fleeting in existence, its effect is immensely profound and everlasting. Priceless beyond measure, it changes people's lives and has even altered the course of history and shifted social consciousness. Eternally noble in concept and often impossible to describe, it is the very purpose for which we who call ourselves trial lawyers choose to live. It is known simply as "justice," and it is forged in the crucible of jury deliberation by those who, like you, believe in the miracle.

One of the most profound statements ever uttered by humankind is "tell me a story." Since the time we first huddled in caves and gathered around campfires, we have been telling stories. We were telling stories long before there was even a written language. We communicated history, social norms, the raising of children, news of the day, the passing of life, the great deeds accomplished by others, and the creation and enforcement of laws, all through telling stories. As a species, we need stories. We enjoy listening to them. Great stories are powerful; they have meaning. As children we crave them. A good story well told is one of life's sweetest joys.

Thus, it should be no surprise that jurors feel the same way. Yet, despite eons of human development, those whose chosen profession literally hinges on the ability to tell stories—trial lawyers—often seem incapable of doing so. A legal education or the "law school experience" have possibly made us doubt, or perhaps more accurately, forget, that we once *believed.* As does a child who, one day, no longer believes in Santa Claus. That sad day, marked so poignantly in the book *The Polar Express*, describes when we no longer hear the tinkling of one of Santa's sleigh bells, believing the bell has fallen silent because it is broken, not realizing that through our impatience to mature into rational and sober adulthood, we lost our faith in our ability to *believe in the miracle.*

A trial lawyer's power is derived from faith—faith in the power of our client's story and faith in our ability to tell it. The great trial lawyers believe in the power of that story, for great stories describe great truths. It is the passionate belief in the truth of the story that enables them—and most importantly the jurors—to hear once again the ringing of the bell. And to *believe.*

It is for those who believe, and those who once again want to believe, that this manual is written.

1
Introduction and Overview

Never give in. Never give in. Never, never, never, never—in nothing, great or small, large or petty—never give in, except to convictions of honour and good sense. Never yield to force. Never yield to the apparently overwhelming might of the enemy.

—Winston Churchill in a speech to schoolboys at Harrow, 1941

I started my career as a trial lawyer fresh out of law school in 1982.[1] I was never more of a danger to the public than at that moment. Another rookie and I were hired as public defenders to open a new full-time state office in the wind-swept, coal-rich boom town of Gillette, Wyoming. We arrived ahead of our furniture. My new partner and I stood in the doorway of the tiny space, located in the basement of the courthouse, and stared into an empty room, which contained nothing but a telephone lying on the carpeted floor. We stood silently for a few moments, not knowing what to do or even say. Then the phone rang. I knelt on the carpet and answered it. It was my first appointed

[1] It should have been 1979, but I took three years off between college and law school to work at a bank, thinking I would learn something important about money. According to my wife, I apparently didn't.

case—first-degree murder. Aside from an air-sickness bag, this is the manual I wish I'd had with me at that moment and every moment thereafter for the rest of my career.[2]

There are few professions more stressful than that of a criminal defense trial lawyer. Murphy's Law is in full force and effect for defense lawyers—anything that can possibly go wrong will and will do so in ways that are often indescribably and horrifyingly spectacular.[3] Law school prepares you for none of these adverse events, and more often than not we learn the craft by practicing on our clients. At least medical students have the luxury of making their mistakes on cadavers.

The purpose of this manual is, in part, to set forth basic guidelines for the inexperienced criminal defense attorney who aspires to be a top-flight trial lawyer. Specifically, it seeks to orient the attorney to the criminal jury trial practice and pleading process, from initial receipt of the case and client interview through post-trial, with a view toward, hopefully, avoiding costly delay and missteps, and ultimately toward obtaining an acquittal.

But what of those attorneys who, after perhaps five or ten or more years of practice, still feel adrift, lost at sea? Those who, despite attending seminars and reading the latest self-help books, are still losing many of their cases and are feeling as if they are not connecting with the jury—or their clients—at all? Or those attorneys who look at their friends and colleagues and ask, "*What am I missing? What am I doing wrong?*"[4]

A related purpose of this manual is to inspire practicing attorneys, regardless of their experience or skill level, to elevate their

---

2 While thinking of a title for this manual, I was reminded of the novel, *The Hitchhiker's Guide to the Galaxy* by Douglas Adams. In this work, Adams describes the *Guide* as having the words "DON'T PANIC!" written in "large, friendly letters" on the cover. Damn good advice.

3 If you've ever seen a video of a fireworks factory on fire, you know what I'm talking about.

4 Several years ago, an attorney friend approached me with that very question. He had been a practicing trial lawyer for nearly *fifty years*. He had a big civil personal injury trial coming up and asked if I would help him. He didn't know what to say to the jury. I spent a few days with him and trained him to use the principles outlined in this manual. He not only won the case, but the jury returned the largest verdict he'd ever had in his career.

skills to a much higher level. Becoming a master of any skill knows no pinnacle; it is always an exercise in becoming. The techniques set forth herein were developed, and are taught and practiced, by many of the greatest trial lawyers in America today. They have been proven to be extremely effective when applied correctly. The good news is that one does not have to be one of those "gold coast" attorneys in order to take advantage of them. These techniques apply to all trial lawyers, regardless of skill level. If you are willing to believe in them and to invest the time and effort necessary to master them, you, too, will see a dramatic increase in your ability to win jury trials and to settle more cases out of court on terms that are beneficial to your clients.

The information contained herein is by no means comprehensive and is not meant to address complex situations such as death penalty prosecutions or appellate litigation, as those situations are sufficiently unique unto themselves and would exceed the scope and purpose of this manual. However, to the extent that this manual would be relevant in such cases, it is hoped that the information contained herein will be of some benefit.

This manual contains little in the way of substantive law. It is also not intended to be a reference guide for the attorney who needs a quick response to an objection in the middle of a hearing, nor does it seek to show how to respond to an opponent's motion. Instead it is a guide to world-class jury trial advocacy. It is presumed that the reader is already well versed in basic criminal law and procedure; therefore, this manual is designed to put such knowledge to practical use as much as possible. Where appropriate, however, references and citations are included.

Not all states are uniform in the manner in which they charge individuals with crimes. Some states utilize the grand jury indictment system, whereas others employ the prosecutor-charged information and preliminary hearing model.[5] The effect, however, is essentially the same. This manual will note the differences where applicable.

The reader will notice that a significant amount of this manual covers just two particular subjects—voir dire and cross-examination/impeachment. These two areas comprise the heart and soul of a

---

[5] The federal system employs the grand jury indictment process exclusively.

criminal defense case, the most important of the two being voir dire. Knowing how to conduct an effective voir dire is paramount to any trial lawyer's success. You are selecting the people who will decide if you win or lose. You must get it right. It is by far the most complex and difficult part of a trial because one is dealing with human nature, emotions, and behavior.

Credit for the voir dire section is due largely to the extraordinary, groundbreaking efforts of Wyoming attorneys Gerry Spence and his long-time friend and law partner, my father, the late Robert R. Rose Jr. Utilizing Spence's intensive study of the works of humanistic psychologist Carl Rogers, together they developed a human-centered "assertive empathy" approach that enabled them to tap directly into the deep subconscious psyche of each juror in order to identify the "common denominator" that links each juror's humanity to the client's humanity. The result of this effort is the creation of the one factor that becomes the critical bedrock of the attorney's case, from opening statement through delivery of the verdict: the attorney's credibility.

Their approach revolutionized the practice of trial advocacy in the United States. This system continues to be taught today at the Trial Lawyers College at Thunderhead Ranch near Dubois, Wyoming, and at the National Criminal Defense College in Macon, Georgia, in addition to numerous other programs and seminars.

Cross-examination and impeachment comprise the other "load-bearing" pillar of the present manual, the importance of which cannot be overstated. The materials and techniques set forth in these chapters were developed and taught for many years by Terence F. MacCarthy Sr., the former federal public defender for the Northern District of Illinois, in Chicago. Long considered the "guru" of cross-examination and one of the nation's greatest instructors of trial advocacy, Terry MacCarthy created a system that employs the "Looking Good" cross-examination, which is centered on the formula *Short + Statements = Control,* discussed later in Chapter 14. This system enables the defense attorney to hone his or her focus to a razor's edge, allowing the examiner to excise only what is needed and thus avoid the pitfalls of self-inflicted injury. I am grateful for Terry's gracious permission to allow me to base this section, Cross-Examination and Impreachment, on his two seminal works,

MacCarthy on Cross-Examination and *MacCarthy on Impeachment: How to Find and Use These Weapons of Mass Destruction.*[6]

The reader may ask what it is about this book that sets it apart from others. More than anything, perhaps, is its emphasis on mastering voir dire. Voir dire is the gateway to victory. Learning how to conduct a great voir dire is meaningless if you don't understand *why* you have to ask certain questions in certain ways. Understanding the philosophy of this method is the key to its mastery and thus the key to victory.

Just as each of us who aspires to be a great trial lawyer needs to find our own unique voice, it is important to understand that this manual brings no message from the "burning bush" as to what that voice should be. We can only truly be ourselves, and in that regard the style that you develop in the courtroom should be uniquely yours and no one else's. Many defense attorneys may disagree with the styles and techniques advocated in this manual. However, while the styles and techniques may vary, in my opinion there is only one sound method for trying cases, and that is the method set forth herein. Regardless of whether you are a public defender or a private counsel, the principles set forth here are universally applicable, and the greatest trial lawyers in this country utilize them.[7]

Before I am accused of being unrealistic, naïve, and otherwise completely out of touch with the reality of criminal defense work, let me say at the outset that in no way do I believe all cases should be tried, nor do I discount the critical importance of guilty pleas. They account for well over 90% of the total number of convictions in the criminal justice system.

A portion of this manual is dedicated to the preparation of your client for entering a plea of guilty. Having practiced as a public defender for a number of years, I am well aware of the realities of a crippling caseload, overwhelming evidence, and difficult clients. The vast majority of cases filed by prosecuting attorneys in this country are

---

[6] T. F. MacCarthy, *MacCarthy on Cross-Examination* (2007); T. F. MacCarthy, Sean P. MacCarthy, & Hon. Terence F. MacCarthy, *MacCarthy on Impeachment* (2016).

[7] The methods discussed herein were developed and taught at the National Criminal Defense College, the Trial Lawyers College, and the Western Trial Advocacy Institute.

quite provable. By that I mean it is very difficult to convince a jury of a defendant's innocence. Most trials end in convictions. For that reason, the vast majority of criminal defendants prefer to negotiate the very best resolution possible through plea negotiations rather than go to trial and risk conviction on greater charges and incarceration for lengthier periods of time. I learned many years ago that all things being equal, it is always better to settle a case than to go to trial.

The point is, however, that all things are *not* equal. In this business, we must, from time to time, go to war. Negotiations fail. The state's evidence is weak. Clients are uncooperative. Therefore, we cannot expect to have a favorable resolution of a plea negotiation if we have the reputation of being afraid of the sting of battle, of being unwilling to die fighting for our clients. After all, there comes a time when, despite our best efforts to avoid trial, we must face our adversary and say, *"Pull that pistol and go to work."* This manual is written for what happens next.

A. Dealing with Fear

> Why is it us? Why us?
> *Because we're here, lad. Nobody else. Just us.*
> —Nigel Green as "Colour-Sergeant Bourne"
> to a terrified private. From the movie *Zulu.*

> *Reality is never as fearful as the fear of reality.*
> —Robert R. Rose Jr.

The most important thing a trial lawyer must learn to confront is fear. Fear is the constant companion of the trial lawyer. We are afraid of the magnitude of our task in each case. We are afraid of the "bad news" our case contains. We are afraid of making mistakes and of not having prepared well enough. We are afraid of not being able to understand our client and to tell his story. We are afraid of the jury and of their silence when we try to talk to them. We are afraid of not knowing how to talk to them so that they will trust us and talk to us. We are afraid of the judge. We are afraid of our opponents, who appear to be smarter and more experienced than we are. We are afraid of losing, and we are afraid of the shame that accompanies it. Most of all, we are afraid of *rejection.*

We must not be afraid of our fear. Fear is good. It is good to be afraid of things that can hurt you. You learn to respect their power. Fear feeds oxygen to our brains so that we think and react faster, more clearly, more decisively. By acknowledging that we are afraid of things, we learn to understand them and thereby to master them. We learn that the best way to neutralize the paralysis that often accompanies fear is thorough preparation. The more prepared we are, the more confident we are. Fear makes us stronger. It becomes our trusted companion. It is alright to have fear. But we will not be *intimidated.*

The best way to manage your fear is to get your head in the game. Learn as much as you can about the problems in your case, as well as your opponent's case.[8] The prosecutor puts his reputation on the line in every trial. As the top law enforcement officer in the district, he represents the community's notion of "justice." He has at his command all of the law enforcement resources of the state, and he controls when, where, and how to charge every case. He enjoys the respect and admiration of almost everyone in the community (all of whom seem to be on the jury), and thus he is always expected to win. He must be perfect. *He therefore has everything to lose.*

By contrast, the defense attorney represents persons charged with a crime. They are usually in jail (the clients, that is), clad in something that looks as if it were pulled out of a trash bin at the homeless shelter. The charges allege behavior that is reprehensible. The clients are disheveled and incapable of coherent thought, and to add insult to injury, they have no money to pay us. In the jury's eyes, we occupy a space not only below the prosecutor—if not most life forms—in terms of status, not only below just about every other profession on the planet, but in a deep trench somewhere. From the moment we

---

[8] NASA astronaut Chris Hadfield put it this way: "Fear is not the only defense mechanism you have. You choose to be afraid of things. Things are not scary. Fear is your reaction to the thing. Fear is an indicator that you haven't learned what it is you need to do yet. The best antidote for fear is competence. The more you know the less you fear. Boil the entire case down into a 'one-pager.' You've got to be able to solve your problems in one breath. When you are competent, you not only can do it, but you can relax while you're doing it and enjoy the experience."

appear in court we are behind. We lack time, resources, and ideas. We are not expected to win. Accordingly, *we have nothing to lose.*

The prosecutor needs all twelve jurors to agree on a verdict; the defense team needs only one to disagree. The prosecutor is not unlike those entertainers on the old television variety programs, who would scurry about the stage, frantically juggling balls and keeping the dinner plates spinning on top of the sticks. The entertainer couldn't afford to have one fall, lest the audience consider the entire act a flop. All we have to do is trust the jury and tell the truth. And love our clients.

When one's back is against the wall and all hope seems lost, a curious phenomenon occurs. We are freed from the paralyzing restraint of the fear of loss. We can only improve our situation.

B. Always Tell the Truth

In jury trials, as in much of life, perception is reality. We like people we trust, and we trust people we like. And we trust people who at least appear to be honest. There are two ways to appear honest: (1) go to great lengths to tell elaborate lies; or (2) tell the truth.

If there is any message that is to be gained from this manual, it is to tell the truth about your case at all times. Throughout this manual, you will see repeated references to being honest and being yourself. Admit your weaknesses and be up front about what concerns you. Study your cases carefully enough so that you understand that each case, when boiled down to its very core, has a "truth" about it that is irrefutable. It rests upon solid bedrock and cannot be toppled by your opponent through any argument or proof of facts, no matter how powerful. Your task as the trial lawyer is to know your case well enough so that you can distill the "truth" of your case for the jury, whatever it may be. You must be able to do this in order to convince a jury that the truth of the case, *as you see it*, is the truth of the case that they must also determine with their verdict. This sounds simple enough, but it is very difficult to do.

The reason it is difficult to do is that it first requires that each of us, as trial lawyers, be honest with ourselves—about who we are as persons, as individuals, as fathers, mothers, sons, daughters, brothers, and sisters; that we know our limitations and believe in our potential.

We must first know who we are before we can effectively establish our credibility with the other human beings who in our case matter the most: the jurors. It is for this reason that the primary focus of this manual—and that of every great trial lawyer—is on understanding and developing the skills to communicate with the jurors as real human beings, so that we can make our journey through the trial together as trusted friends instead of strangers.

Being a good trial lawyer has very little to do with knowing the law. The great trial lawyers are not great because they are able to quote chapter and verse from the statutes or rules, or citations from case law, although many can. The law is important only to the court, and with the exception of the jury instruction conference, it is confined almost exclusively to the pretrial process. The jury couldn't care less about the law. They don't have to since they don't rely on it to reach a verdict. As you will later understand, the jury will use the instructions to justify their decisions, not determine them. What distinguishes a great trial lawyer is her ability to effectively communicate her credibility to the jury.

A great trial lawyer is a great storyteller. A good story well told is compelling and persuasive. And the jury is looking for someone who can communicate with them. That is because the jury is composed of individuals who don't know each other and don't know your client, but they are being forced to form themselves into a group in order to make extremely important decisions involving your client's life. They know nothing of the law or the legal system, and indeed, they are wary and somewhat frightened of it. They're intimidated by the attorneys and the judge, and they don't know who to trust. They don't know who is right or wrong or what is expected of them. They certainly don't want to communicate with anyone. They are most afraid of making a mistake—of not doing the right thing. They therefore instinctively seek a leader, someone in the courtroom to whom they can turn who will show them who to trust and who and what to believe. They need someone who will answer their questions and someone they can always rely on to guide them through the evidence and help them make the right decision.

At the outset, the judge fills this role, being the obvious authority figure in the room, though only briefly. She cannot provide what the jury needs most: knowing which side to trust. If the jury does not know who to trust, they will not be able to decide the case correctly. And if there is one thing a jury wants to do more than anything else, it is to do the right thing. That means knowing they have reached the right decision with their verdict.

The great trial lawyers who win the big cases are those whom the juries instinctively trust. They become the "go-to" persons for the jury. When the jury is confused or uncertain, they turn to those attorneys for the answer. That is because those attorneys have established the only asset that matters in a jury trial: credibility. A lawyer's credibility is his or her stock in trade, and in a jury trial it is the coin of the realm. An attorney can wear the right suit, the best shoes, have the perfect hair style, radiate Hollywood good looks, possess a well-modulated radio announcer's voice, boast of the highest bar exam score, and cite case law with the precision of the executive editor of Westlaw. But if he or she lacks credibility, it is all meaningless.[9]

Prior to trial, "justice" is whatever the prosecutor says it is. All of the power rests with the prosecuting attorney. At trial, however, all of that power and authority are transferred to the jury. It is when the case is presented to the jury—when, essentially, the jury has settled in and said, "*Tell me a story . . .*"—that our unique skill set is put in motion. For that precious "golden moment," we must make our presence known in the biggest way possible. And we only get one shot at it.

The concept of "justice" is elusive. It is not a corporeal thing. It is ethereal, a notion, *an idea.* The attorneys do not create it, but they empower the jury to find it. It comes into being during the jury's deliberation process, and it exists only as long as it is necessary. The jury's collective conscience alone determines the "justice" of every case, be it conviction or acquittal. It is a creation unique to that circumstance, that case, that time and place, with those individuals. And when its purpose has been served, it vanishes forever. Because those who create it will never again be summoned together to re-create it, it assumes different qualities for each jury. Defense attorneys must be able to recognize what qualities are required for each case, and then they must trust the jury to determine its form. Thus, the "justice" of a

[9] Or, as Dale Cobb would say, "You're done. It's time to call in the dogs and put out the fire."

case becomes whatever the jury determines it to be. And that is why the jury is always right.

This manual, then, is designed with one thing in mind: to help you successfully tell the truth of your client's story by enabling you to be the best trial lawyer you can be—the warrior you need to be—and by showing how to establish and maintain your integrity and credibility throughout every phase of the case, including trial.

C. Integrity

> *I am not bound to win, but I am bound to be true. I am not bound to succeed, but I am bound to live up to what light I have. I must stand with anybody that stands right; stand with him while he is right and part with him when he goes wrong.*
>
> —Abraham Lincoln

> *I tried never to forget who I was, where I came from, and where I was going back to.*
>
> —Harry S. Truman

Credibility is based on your integrity. Certain aspects of this profession will test your integrity daily in subtle but significant ways. Every aspect of your practice, from your relationship with your family and colleagues, with your clients, the manner in which you treat your support staff and draft your pleadings to the arguments you make in court—all showcase your integrity. The ability to stand your ground when the pressure is on is crucial in trial work. You must recognize these challenges in order to avoid damage to or even loss of your credibility.

As a defense attorney, your goal is to obtain an acquittal through zealous representation of your client. How you carry yourself and the manner in which you relate to your client and others in your profession are on display at all times, both in and out of court. Here in Wyoming, the state bar roster is small enough that we in the legal profession are fortunate to know on a personal level many of the attorneys with whom we deal on a regular basis. That includes the prosecuting attorneys.

Maintaining a close personal relationship with the prosecuting attorney can carry some risk in that it is potentially corrosive, particularly in a smaller community. Since the prosecuting attorney initially possesses all of the power in the case and the defendant none, it is natural for the defense attorney to seek a relationship with the prosecutor, so that there is often no need for constant formality and strict adherence to the rules of discovery, or for the sharing of confidential or privileged information.

A defense attorney may, after initially receiving the case and interviewing the client, wish to meet with the prosecuting attorney as soon as possible to discuss what is "really going on" with the case, what the client "really did" that resulted in the charges being brought, and how the attorney "really feels" about the client or the case in general. These types of conversations are often the result of the close relationship you may have with the prosecutor.

Although it is important during certain phases of the development of the case to meet with the prosecutor and engage in discussions as to what direction the case should take, the problems with having such informally "real" discussions at the outset of the case are twofold: first, as defense counsel, you know virtually nothing about the state's case (not to mention your own case) or about what your ultimate defense may turn out to be; and second, sharing any such information with the prosecutor may violate the attorney–client privilege and improperly reveal to your opponent otherwise highly confidential and potentially prejudicial information regarding your client. Moreover, it often sends the message to the prosecutor at the outset that you are seeking a quick resolution to the case and are not interested in or, worse, are afraid of going to trial and putting the state to its proof.

On a deeper level, it also suggests that you do not respect your client and that you have no desire to do your best to fight for your client. Rather, you are tired or frightened and are looking for an easy way out of the case. These meetings are typically concluded with the defense attorney soliciting the prosecutor for some type of negotiated plea agreement that can be entered into quickly, so that the attorney doesn't have to invest any more time or effort in the case than necessary.

This approach is bad enough for public defenders, but it is at least understandable, if only from the point of acknowledging how massively and desperately overworked they are. Having been there myself, I know I would sometimes be willing to do just about anything to resolve a case without having to work on it a moment longer. But it is much worse for a private attorney to take this approach, since the client has likely paid the attorney a substantial fee to represent him. That fee may or may not take in preparing and trying the case, but it at least covers all pretrial work. That pretrial work includes maintaining client confidentiality and investigating the facts and circumstances of the case to the point where the attorney is satisfied that she has a competent understanding of where the case should be headed and whether seeking a plea agreement with the prosecutor is in her client's best interest. It is only after that stage of the case has been reached that *any* discussions with the prosecuting attorney concerning resolution of the case should be undertaken.

All of this is not to say that you should not seek to maintain a positive working relationship with the prosecutor. But there is a difference between enjoying a relationship with the prosecutor that is based on mutual respect versus one that is based on fear, that is, currying favor with your opponent simply because he or she is holding all the cards.

There is another reason that any discussions regarding case resolution should not be held until you have thoroughly investigated the case. If you engage in such discussions at the outset, any efforts you make thereafter to investigate the case will be affected by your desire to settle the case rather than contest it. This means that you will be subconsciously looking for evidence of your client's guilt that you can point to and use to rationalize your desire for a plea agreement (and thus no hard work), while ignoring or downplaying evidence of innocence. In short, you will be looking for evidence to convict your client rather than acquit him. Whose side are you on?

Do not allow your familiarity with the prosecutor to disarm and distract you from your dedication to your professional standards. It is better to maintain a courteous and friendly—but at all times professional—relationship. In other words, know when to leave the room. You should strive at all times to maintain the highest professional standards and safeguard your reputation so that it is unimpeachable. You want to be remembered for being not only a good attorney, but a good and honorable person.

Make no mistake about it; criminal defense work is demanding, exhausting, unforgiving, often discouraging, and at times depressing. You represent people who often do not care about themselves or others, and thus it is sometimes difficult to generate any desire to care about them yourself. They are often accused of acts that are reprehensible and vile and are universally scorned by the public. As their representative, you tend to be painted with the same brush. Your friends, and sometimes even members of your own family, may not understand why you do this for a living. You may be asked how it is that you can defend someone who has been accused of doing such things. Therefore, you will need to arrive at an understanding with yourself from the outset that will enable you to stay in this game and keep your focus.

Criminal defense attorneys are sometimes viewed as not only smart, but "clever," in the sense that they seem to be willing to do anything to manipulate the truth, twist the facts, shift the blame, lie, hide important evidence, and in general do anything possible to ensure that the "truth" of their client's case never sees the light of day. In other words, they are sometimes seen as "snakes": deceitful, dangerous, slippery characters with shady ethics and no soul, who will take advantage of any honest situation and turn it to suit their nefarious purposes. Slithering out from within their dank, slimy subterranean caverns only when enticed by the promise of large fees, they are considered by many to be the "used car salesmen" of the legal profession; they are the attorneys that people love to hate. Under no circumstance should they be trusted!

The fact of the matter is, however, that the truly great criminal defense lawyers in this country are among the most ethical, principled, decent, loving, dedicated, selfless, courageous, and fearless professionals alive.[10] They have to be. The jury will be able to tell if they're not.

They are gunfighters in the purest sense of the word. They stand and fight for those who can't. They possess and exhibit skills in the

[10] Not to exclude certain prosecutors as well. My great friend, colleague, and Western Trial Advocacy Institute (WTAI) and the Trial Lawyers College (TLC) faculty member John Tierney, former district attorney of Hennepin County (Minneapolis), Minnesota, is among them. These prosecutors are the very embodiment of "integrity."

courtroom far above those of their contemporaries. They are not intimidated by either the professed power of the state or the stain of the accusations made against their clients. They tell the truth and they communicate it honestly without mincing words. They say what they mean and they mean what they say. They are sometimes feared but are always respected. They believe not only in the rights guaranteed by the Constitution, but also in their clients as human beings with value. They are incorruptible and absolutely unstoppable. In short, they have integrity. And out of that integrity is born unimpeachable credibility.

Interestingly, law schools seem to be missing the boat in this respect:

> Recent studies have shown that prestige and income, law school debt, class rank, law review and law school ranking have little or no correlation with well-being. To the contrary, the group with lowest incomes and grades in law school—public service and legal aid lawyers—had stronger autonomy and purpose and were happier than those in the most prestigious positions with the highest grades and incomes. What appears to be missing in law school is the concept of *serving people*. The skill sets law schools teach are tools with no overarching purpose. True satisfaction in law comes from what Harvard legal philosopher Lon Fuller described as "the prevention of indecencies in the use of power." In representing people who are suffering through adverse and extreme life experiences, you are defending them against the indecencies in the use of power. The pride one feels in the legal profession and the satisfaction one derives from practice are demonstrated and reflected in the lives of the people you guide through those experiences. [11]

To succeed in this profession, to have a sense that you are accomplishing something worth fighting for, achieving a sense of

---

[11] Excerpted from "Swan Song," the keynote address to the Colorado Trial Lawyers Association Spring Dinner by Hon. John L. Kane, Senior Federal District Judge, United States District Court for the District of Colorado. Wyoming Trial Lawyers Association (Winter 2016). *Swan Song*, COFFEE HOUSE MAGAZINE, at 2-3, 7. (Reprinted with the kind permission of Judge Kane and the WTLA.)

meaningful purpose not only as a defense lawyer but also as a person, in order to revel in it—in other words, to secure a sense of "well-being"—you must have fire in your belly. Criminal defense attorneys are often asked why they represent persons charged with crimes. To the average citizen unfamiliar with the legal system, it is unfathomable that we would ever wish to represent someone who may be guilty.

Perhaps most discouraging of all is to hear a defense attorney respond with something like this:

> *My job is simply to make sure that the defendant has an attorney, an opportunity to present a defense, and receive a fair trial. If I lose, it's no big deal. It's not like he was innocent to begin with.*

With an attitude like that, no wonder he is likely to lose. The client would be better off representing himself. At least he'd have someone representing him who believes in him. If you have that attitude toward your criminal clients, you should do yourself a favor now and close this manual and seek another field of practice immediately. You don't get it. You are wasting your time, and you will be forever miserable and resentful of your clients.

The Hon. John L. Kane, United States District Court Senior Judge for the District of Colorado, put it this way:

> The first step in the process of achieving a sense of well-being is to recognize the suffering—the experience—of those who are subjected to injustice. The word "deprivation" in its literal sense is the key to understanding this. To deprive is to "deprivatize." To take away that person's sense of being as an individual, a self that is unique. To deprive means to sap a person of his or her individuality, his personhood, his mattering, and to reduce him or her to a number or the product of an algorithm. Justice is achieved when an individual's unique value is recognized and his life is restored to balance so that he is not pushed around by indecencies in the use of power.[12]

---

[12] *Id.*

The great defense lawyers in this country do what they do not because it is easy but because it is hard. They routinely undertake those cases that others would never consider. They take great pride in fighting on behalf of those who cannot fight back. They send the clear message to prosecutors that they had better prepare for battle. They never think, "How can I settle this case quickly?" Instead, they think, "Go ahead. Skin it. Skin that smokewagon and see what happens."[13] Gerry Spence was once asked how he negotiated a guilty plea for his clients. "I don't know," he replied. "I've never done one."

Integrity also reveals and showcases the depth of your professional commitment. The artistic and creative genius of the great film director Stanley Kubrick was reflected in the fact that he framed and shot every scene as if his entire career depended on it. Practice law the same way. Prepare every hearing as if your entire career depended on it.

A final word on integrity must be added regarding the treatment of your support staff. While they may not possess the advanced degrees and certifications you do, you must never forget that you would not be able to function at all, either in court or out, without the loyal support of your staff. Your paralegals, investigators, clerks, interns, etc., all play a vital role in the functioning of the office and ultimately contribute to your success as a trial lawyer.

Despite what your GPA, class ranking, or bar exam score may have been, it is your staff that makes you look good. They consider themselves professionals as much as you do yourself. Take care of them. A kind word, praise for work well done, encouragement on a rough day, and recognition of achievement will go a long way toward helping your staff feel valued and part of the team. They will want to work for you. They will want to help you succeed. In short, they will make you *look good*. And looking good is the name of this game. When mistakes are made, as they invariably are, correct but do not scold. Your staff is well aware of your authority; you need not remind them.

Instead, take the opportunity to teach and guide. Be mindful of your deadlines, and NEVER, EVER blame your paralegal or anyone else for missing one. The case was assigned to *you*. It is therefore your

---

[13] As Kurt Russell's character, "Wyatt Earp," snarls in the motion picture *Tombstone*.

responsibility to make sure that whatever needs to be done gets done on time. Clean up your own mess. One of the first steps in coming to grips with who you are as a person—and thus establishing your integrity and credibility—is to accept responsibility for what belongs to you.

Stress adversely impacts performance, both yours and your staff's. If you are the type of person who leads by instilling fear in your employees, such that they are reluctant to communicate with you, that can have devastating consequences. Staff members who are frightened and intimidated by you are also reluctant to reveal problems. In a law office, that can be catastrophic. We all make mistakes from time to time, and often time is of the essence in correcting them. Maintaining a calm, professional, friendly, and supportive environment in your office will help ensure that your staff is willing to notify you promptly in the event of a problem. It is therefore wise to remember the words of President Harry Truman: "Always be kind to the people who can't talk back to you."

2
Getting Started

A. Getting Familiar with Your Case

Every great success needs two things: a goal and not quite enough time to finish it.

—Leonard Bernstein

There are no other cases. This *is the case.*

—Paul Newman
as attorney Frank Galvan in *The Verdict*

In order for you to do a good job for your client, you must become familiar with his case. Getting familiar with the case takes time. You must carve out what time you can to do it. As early as possible, you must be able to get a sense of its strengths and weaknesses, to prepare you for deciding whether and how it should be tried.

By far the most common complaint voiced by those engaged in the practice of public criminal defense is lack of time. There simply isn't enough of it. There are too many cases and not enough hours in the day to address them fully. And it will never get any better. The most important thing you can do is learn to manage your time and resources efficiently. You must develop a method of triage that enables you to size up a case quickly, so that you can get a sense of what kind of case it is, whether or not it is likely to resolve short of trial, and what it is going to require to successfully resolve it. This is critical, for it will help you to avoid a typical pitfall of many trial lawyers: not being able to distinguish a good case from a bad one.

Pleading out your good cases and trying your bad ones is a common malady in this business. Unaddressed, it can lead to ruin. Before long, you will find yourself losing more of your cases, so that your opponents would rather force you to trial than negotiate a plea. Things will begin to snowball and get ugly real fast. With more cases to get ready for trial, you will end up with less and less time to work your other cases. You will then become so overwhelmed that you will become frightened of your cases and lose confidence in your ability to win them. You will then fall into the worst trap of all: not being able to properly prepare cases that you do try, so that you are not prepared for trial. Your confidence will erode. You will find yourself working longer hours, later into the night, and on weekends. You will then panic and look for a way out. You will seek a continuance or offer last-minute deals capitulating to the demands of your opponent just to end the case and take some pressure off of you.

Except the pressure is not off for long. The next unprepared case is sitting on your desk, staring you right in the face. With your weakness having been exposed to your opponents, they will exploit it. You'll hate your job and begin to fantasize about taking time off, or even quitting and going into private practice, or entering an entirely different profession.

So, to repeat, start by knowing a good case from a bad one. Work with as many experienced colleagues as you can. Once you develop those skills, you will have gone a long way toward avoiding unnecessary stress on your physical and mental health.

No matter how simple or obvious a case appears to be at first glance, every case you undertake has the potential of blowing up into a complicated mess that ends up in a lengthy jury trial, complete with numerous pretrial motions, expert witnesses, and media coverage. And more often than not, it's that simple little case that landed on your desk at 4:45 p.m. Be careful. Don't be overconfident. Do not underestimate the ability of a seemingly insignificant case to transform into a disaster of biblical proportions before your very eyes.

This also means never accepting a case that you don't intend—or are not willing—to try.

Never approach a case cavalierly. Never forget whose interests are at stake, the power you are responsible for, and the care with which you must discharge that responsibility. Your clients' legal rights, freedom, and sometimes their very lives are on the line. You must be vigilant at all times and mindful of the consequences of your actions.

While interning for a firm during law school, I failed to appreciate the gravity of that duty while working on a case. One day one of the partners pulled me aside and said, "Listen to me. We are trial lawyers. We operate at levels most other attorneys can't even comprehend. We are like professional racing drivers driving Ferraris at top speed. We must have total concentration at all times. If we take our eyes off the road or our hands off the wheel for even a split second, the consequences will be catastrophic. Now pay attention, goddammit."

B. Private Attorneys and the Fee Agreement

As private counsel, you have the enormous luxury of deciding whether to accept or reject any case that comes through your door. That decision is typically driven by several factors: (1) whether your schedule permits you to take on a criminal case (understanding, of course, that criminal cases are on a "fast track" with the court docket and thus take priority in scheduling. This means that the clock is usually ticking, and deadlines are fast approaching); (2) your willingness and ability to represent the client in light of the particular charge; and (3) the amount of the fee you require and the client's ability to pay it.

As a private attorney, one of the reasons you are in business is to make money.[1] This means being mindful of the kinds of cases you accept and the amount you charge the clients for your services. You will quickly learn that when it comes to criminal defense, few clients can afford large fees. Even fewer can afford to pay them in full in advance, which is what a private attorney must insist upon. Despite this, some criminal lawyers will agree to discount their fees and delay full payment, simply because they want to help the client or because

[1] Believe me, there will be days when this becomes unclear.

accepting a reduced or partial fee is at least something, whereas the feared alternative is to have the client walk out the door and hire someone else.

One of the most difficult and important words that a private criminal defense attorney can ever learn to use is "No." While it is true that there will be days (hopefully not many) when the payment of even a small fee will seem welcome, discounting your fee out of fear that you need the money and the client will leave and hire someone else is one of the worst traps an attorney can fall into. For it takes just as much time and effort to undertake the defense of a criminal case for a small fee as it does for a large one.

You will find yourself working yourself to the bone for a pittance. Moreover, you will quickly gain a reputation in the community as a criminal lawyer who will work "cheap." This usually means that you will attract a number of criminal clients who will want you to work yourself to death on their behalf and will be unable or unwilling to pay even the reduced rate that you have reluctantly agreed to quote them. You will have a growing list of clients who owe you money and who will seldom, if ever, pay. Worst of all, you will not be able to get out of the case you have undertaken. The court will not care whether or not you have been paid. You have entered your appearance on behalf of your client, and the fact that you haven't been paid is of no concern to the court. A motion to withdraw from the case will usually be denied. You are in it until the bitter end.

It is far better to set your fees according to how busy you wish to be and what the competitive rate in the marketplace is, and then stick to your guns. When a client calls and asks you or your paralegal whether you will accept a reduced fee or partial payment, be ready to politely—but firmly—respond that you cannot do so. The fee is what the fee is, and it is payable in full at the outset of the case. No exceptions. Be ready with a list of referrals to other competent counsel.

To be sure, there will be some fees that you will see walk out the door, but let them go. You will earn a reputation as a quality attorney with class. Your commitment to the cases that you do undertake will yield noticeable results. You will begin to get the big cases with correspondingly bigger fees. That is because the more trouble people find themselves in, the higher the fee they expect to pay for legal help. Look at it this way: it is far better to reject ten cases, each of which would have paid you $1,500, and to accept the one case for $15,000. You will end up doing a much better job on that one case than you would on those ten others.

C. Public Defenders

As a public defender, you are mercifully relieved of the hassle of negotiating a representation fee with each client, as well as the stress of worrying about paying monthly bills, overhead, malpractice insurance, payroll, advertising, and a thousand other expenses. In return for a monthly income that would not support a goldfish, you enjoy the privilege of working 38-hour days, representing the most despicable people imaginable, with no viable defense, and no help.[2]

When you receive a file, do not set it aside and tell yourself, "I'll review that when I have a few minutes." You will never have a few minutes. Other matters will interrupt you and distract you, with the result that the file will be buried under a pile of other files and papers (which you've also set aside to review "later"), and before you know it you are in serious trouble. Instead, take ten minutes, grab a cup of coffee, and review the pleadings. Schedule a time as soon as possible to meet with your client. If he is out on bond, arrange to meet him in your office. If he's in jail, go see him as soon as possible. If the case is a misdemeanor, you will need to meet him in court at the initial appearance to enter an initial plea of "not guilty."[3] If it's a felony case, he may have a preliminary hearing coming up in a few days. You will need to determine whether you will attend and cross-examine the state's witnesses or waive the hearing. You cannot make that decision without first meeting with your client.

---

[2] And that's just your first week!

[3] Almost without exception, a plea of "not guilty" is entered. You need time to obtain and review all of the state's discovery materials and review them with your client before you can determine whether a guilty plea will be entered at a later date.

D. Meeting the Client

> *I've learned that people will forget what you said, they will forget what you did, but people will never forget how you made them feel.*
>
> —Maya Angelou

Your relationship with your client is paramount. Your entire case rests on your ability to effectively tell your client's story. You must approach your client from the standpoint that he is not just someone you represent; he is the person you are fighting for. He does not need a lawyer; he needs a gladiator—a warrior as big and as powerful as he can get. Therefore, the better you understand your client and his case, the better and more effective warrior you are going to be.

As a general rule, the more time you spend with your client the better. This is especially true if he is not a likeable person or if his story is going to be a particularly hard sell. Your most important task in that instance is to find something in your client to love and concentrate on that. If you do not find a way to love him—really *love* him—you cannot authentically believe in him or his story, much less sell it to a jury. No matter how ruined, every human being has a quality about him that is worthy of your love. You must find it.[4]

It is easy to find reasons not to visit with your clients, especially when they're in jail. But put yourself in their shoes. They often have few friends, no family support, no resources, no faith in themselves and very little in you. The last thing in the world your client needs is proof that his last hope on this planet—you—have abandoned him, too.

As soon as you possibly can after taking the case, meet with your client. DO NOT DELAY. At the first meeting, do not begin by jumping immediately into the facts and details of the charges. There will be plenty of time for that later. Your client is no doubt frightened, knows no one, and may have never been incarcerated before. Jail is a terrifying experience. Everyone and everything is a threat. Your client has no idea what is going to happen to him, but all he can

---

[4] Gerry Spence imagines his client as a young child, full of innocence, hope, and promise. Before the world turned on him.

think about is the worst-case scenario. He sees no hope. He desperately needs someone whom he can trust to be his friend and give him something to hang on to. You must be that person.[5]

Therefore, the most important thing you can present to your client at the first meeting is a smile, a calm demeanor, and a confident sense of hope. There's always hope. Things are rarely as bad as they seem. Give your client a reason to calm down and an opportunity to relax and think rationally.

Later, when time allows, spend time listening to your clients' story. Don't act as if you are pressed for time, even if you are. They've been rejected by "important" people their entire lives. Show them that you are different, that you care about them, that you believe in them, and that you are there to fight for them. After all, that's all they've really ever wanted—someone who will stand up for them and make their voices heard. Quite often, whether you ultimately win or lose the case matters little to your client. What they will forever remember is how you treated them and how you made them feel when the chips were down. This lies at the very heart of the reputation that you will earn in the community.

Try to give your client choices. He has so few. The realization that he has no choice but to plead guilty or go to trial and lose is traumatizing to say the least. The more choices your client has, the more power and control he will feel he has over his case, as well as his life. It will empower him. More importantly, it creates hope—the possibility that there is a way out of the mess he's found himself in.

One of the most important discussions you can have with your clients is to clarify what it is they want you to do for them. For the private attorney, it may appear obvious that if they've hired you, they must want you to represent them and to win if it goes to court. But sometimes appearances can be misleading. Sometimes our assumptions can be wrong. They may be seeking something from you that you are not able to provide. Don't fall into the trap of assuming that you know what it is the clients want you to do for them. Simply ask them directly. Take a moment, and ask, "What would you like me to do for you in this case?" Be prepared for them to be taken somewhat aback by this question. This may be the first time in their lives

---

[5] Now you really begin to see why we are referred to as "counselors."

that anyone has ever thought enough about them to ask them what they really want.

It is a critically important question. Their answer might surprise you. Whatever they ask of you, be as honest as you can in your response. Do not overpromise; chances are you will underdeliver. If you are certain you can provide what they seek, then tell them that. If you are certain you cannot, then tell them that, too. "Why?" you might say. "Why tell them bad news right out of the box?" Ask yourself this question: When do you want them to hear the bad news? Now, when you can discuss it and deal with it openly and honestly, or when the verdict is announced in open court? Be honest and realistic, even perhaps a bit conservative in your assessment of their situation. It is far better to underpromise and overdeliver than the alternative.

Many of your clients may be angry and unwilling to participate in reasonable and meaningful conversation. Remember that anger is a secondary emotion. It is a response to something else. Almost always it is grounded in *fear*. Many of our clients have endured traumatic childhoods, including verbal, physical, and sexual abuse, sometimes at the hands of their own parents. They trust no one, for everyone they've ever trusted and believed in has betrayed them and let them down. It is therefore no surprise that when our clients express anger, they are really reacting to the chronic and overarching fear they have endured for much of their lives. Look beyond your clients' anger, not only as a way of understanding and communicating with them, but as a device by which you can also help the jury understand and connect with them.

When you meet with your clients, be as positive and reassuring as you can. They know that things are bad, and you don't need to pile it on. Be hopeful and upbeat if possible; give them the feeling that even though they're in a tough spot, you are there with them and you will never, ever, abandon them, betray them, or sell them down the river. You will always be honest and truthful with them. Look them in the eye and tell them that. You are their champion. Promise them that you will see them as often as your schedule permits. If they're in jail, at least once a week, if possible. And it doesn't have to be for long. Sometimes you may not have any news to report or anything of substance to discuss. It doesn't matter. They need to see a friendly face once in a while, if only for a few minutes.

If you see your client in jail on a fairly regular basis, even if only to spend a few minutes shooting the breeze and seeing how he's doing, the most amazing thing will happen. Your client will begin to feel that you are there because you really do care about him, and not simply because you're being paid to do it. He will look forward to seeing you. It will be the absolute highlight of his week. He will be excited to share things with you. He will be proud that you represent him. He will brag to other inmates what a good job you are doing for him, even if you're not actually doing all that much. He may even start to believe that if someone like you cares about him, his life is worth living.

It will have collateral ripple effects as well. Other inmates will notice that you care about your client and that you take time to visit him. They will soon ask their own attorneys why they aren't doing the same for them. You will be approached in the jail by other inmates who want to fire their attorneys and hire you. This will, of course, translate outside the walls to the local community at large. You will even be noticed by the jail guards as someone who cares. They will begin to show you extra (or at least *some*) respect. They may allow you to fudge a little bit on the time limits set for visitation. They will like to talk to you. They will even refer other new inmates to you who have yet to hire an attorney. Most amazing of all, you might even receive a call one day from a law enforcement officer who saw the way you treated your client and wants to hire you to represent him in his own legal matter. And to think all you ever did was to show some kindness to someone you didn't know and to whom you owed nothing other than legal advice.

As you meet and get to know your client and his story, keep in mind the following guidelines for improving and enhancing your relationship with him:

Five Universal Truths

1. People feel the need to be *respected*.
2. People would rather be *asked* than be *told*.
3. People have a desire to know *why*.
4. People prefer to have *options* over *threats*.
5. People want to have a *second chance*.

Good Listening Skills

- Eye Contact
- Avoid Distractions
- Body Language
- Gestures
- Silence
- Acknowledge the Story ("I hear you")
- Validate ("What you say is important to me")
- Empathize

E. Investigation

Victorious warriors win first then go to war, while defeated warriors go to war first, then hope to win.

—Sun Tzu

He who knows only his own side of the case knows little of that.

—John Stuart Mill

Perhaps more than any other factor, a thorough investigation is the key to success in the courtroom. The great trial lawyers investigate their cases far more exhaustively than their opponents, for it is in the details that the key to a successful case lives. That being said, no matter how strong you believe your case to be, trial is always a risk. As will be repeated throughout this manual, it is always better to settle a case if you can than to go to trial. Therefore, the goal in case preparation is to win the battle without resorting to fighting. In other words, prepare your case so well that your opponent is afraid to step into the courtroom with you.

Innovation and creativity are the hallmarks of a good investigator. Thinking "outside the box" yields great rewards in this business. A general rule of thumb regarding investigation is that "more is better." If you want to get a good feel for what your client was experiencing at the time of the incident, visit the scene personally with your investigator. Take numerous photographs—more than you think you'll ever need. View the scene from every angle. Ideally, visit the scene at the same time of day or night the incident occurred. Sometimes the presence or absence of light makes all the difference. Due to the placement of certain objects, sometimes witnesses are not able to see what they claim to have seen.[6] Also, visiting the scene will likely prompt you to think of questions the jury may have regarding the evidence. Your ability to anticipate those questions will enable you to provide answers during the trial that will be to your advantage.

Another area of investigation concerns conducting thorough interviews of the witnesses. If possible, interview the state's witnesses, including the "victim" and any experts. The prosecutor doesn't represent them, so there is no ethical issue regarding your making contact with them. Therefore, he is not permitted to prevent you from interviewing them. While some witnesses may elect not to be interviewed, you should at least make the effort. You would be surprised how often the prosecutor fails to interview his own witnesses.

Many attorneys interview witnesses by themselves. This avoids having to take the time to prepare your investigator or other third person to do it. While there is nothing wrong with that, it makes you a witness if the persons you're interviewing change their story later at trial. Therefore, whenever possible, have your investigator interview witnesses rather than doing the interviews yourself. Or, if you prefer to conduct your own interviews, then bring along a third party, such as your investigator or your paralegal, so that you can call them to testify at trial if the witness changes her story.

While it may seem counterintuitive to talk about the importance of jury instructions in the early phases of case preparation, the importance of designing your investigation around the jury instructions you anticipate submitting to the court at the end of trial cannot be overstated. Having a solid handle on what elements of the charged offenses the prosecutor must prove at trial will drive your investigation and help guide you in preparing your defenses. As soon as possible after taking the case, study the charges and related jury instructions in order to start planning where your investigation should go.

---

6 Case in point: An attorney was representing a defendant charged with delivery of a controlled substance to an undercover officer in a bar. The transaction was allegedly witnessed by another officer who testified that he was looking through the window of the front door of the bar at the time. Upon visiting the bar, the attorney discovered that while the front door did have a window, it had been boarded up and painted over for several years. The case was dismissed.

1. Private Attorneys

As with virtually anything in life, the quality of the result you obtain depends on the amount of effort you put into it. Garbage in, garbage out. This is certainly the case with investigation. There is no substitute for thorough investigation. Most private attorneys engage in small-business operations and thus may not employ full-time investigators. That is a luxury that only bigger firms can usually afford. A good investigator is worth every penny. Great cases have been won or lost on the strength of the pretrial investigation. This is often the case in criminal prosecutions.

With all due respect to law enforcement investigators, they are often unable, due to time constraints, to invest the kind of time and effort into a case that it really requires in order to accomplish a first-class job. As a result, stones are left "unturned," thus allowing the defense attorney to take advantage of numerous opportunities. If you undertake the defense of a criminal case, be sure to determine as early as possible whether you might need the services of an investigator. Discuss that with your client, for you will need to have an understanding early on as to the amount such services will cost and whether you or your client will front the expense.

2. Public Defenders

Most public defender offices employ investigators. This is a wonderful resource that is often underutilized. You will know early on in your case whether you will need to use the services of your investigator. Don't hesitate to do so.

Since your investigator will no doubt be busy with assignments in other cases, try to engage him as early in the case as possible, so that he will have the time to do what you need him to do. Take the time to brainstorm ideas with your investigator in order to maximize the effect of his efforts. Think outside of the box. Put yourself in the jury box. Ask yourself what evidence you would like to see if you were there and how you would like it presented. Crawl inside your client's "hide" and see the case from his eyes. Why did he do what he did? Consider how you wish to present the evidence to the jury to ensure they see it the way he did. In this business, you are limited only by your imagination. The more creative you are, the better your chances are of winning.

3

Arraignment in the Lower Court (Misdemeanors Only)

For states that utilize the prosecutor-charging method (filing an "Information" or a "citation"), the arraignment in the lower court is the first formal opportunity for the defendant to enter a plea to a misdemeanor charge. The plea options are "Guilty," "Not Guilty," "Not Guilty by Reason of Mental Illness (NGMI)," or with permission of the court, "No Contest" (*nolo contendere*). At any stage of the proceeding, the defendant or any proper person acting on his behalf may enter a plea of "Not triable by reason of mental illness" (otherwise known as "incompetent to proceed").[1]

Upon the entry of a plea of "Not Guilty," the matter may automatically be set for trial, or it might instead be set for a scheduling conference. The heavy volume of cases at the lower court level likely does not permit the court to initially schedule that number of cases for trial. The vast majority of cases result in negotiated guilty pleas, thus making the scheduling of trials difficult. The scheduling conference eliminates much of that confusion.

Scheduling conferences can be informal and may be held either in the court's chambers or perhaps in the courtroom on a regularly scheduled basis. In some states, they are mass settings involving a large number of cases, and many attorneys (both defense and

[1] For a detailed discussion of the procedures involving such mental illness pleas, see Chapter 9.

prosecutors) are present. It affords counsel the opportunity to review the discovery and discuss the matter with their clients and the prosecuting attorney beforehand, to determine whether to settle the case or try it. The judge will go down the list and inquire of the status of each case, and decide whether it is likely to be tried or whether a guilty plea is imminent.

If a case appears likely to settle in a guilty plea, the judge may either set the matter for a rearraignment date to enter the plea or another scheduling conference. If the case appears headed for trial, the judge will set either a trial date or another scheduling conference. A number of scheduling conferences may be scheduled in a trial in order to allow sufficient time to determine its ultimate resolution. However, the court is also mindful of the speedy trial clock and will ordinarily not permit counsel to put the case off for much more than ninety days after the initial arraignment.

A. Initial Appearance (Felony)

If your client is charged with a felony, he will initially be seen in the lower court. Be mindful of the date and time of his arrest. In many states, if arrested without a warrant the defendant must be seen by the court within a certain time (often seventy-two hours) after arrest. If the defendant is held longer than the allotted time without a hearing, the matter is subject to immediate dismissal.

At the initial appearance, the defendant will be advised of the charges against him, the maximum possible penalties, and his constitutional rights. Bond will also be set (unless it is a first-degree murder case), and the matter will be scheduled for a preliminary hearing. A detailed analysis of what is involved with preliminary hearings is contained in Chapter 5.

B. Preparing the Client for a Guilty Plea (Misdemeanor)

The process of entering a guilty plea in the lower court may be considerably different than in District Court. Since a guilty plea at this level is limited to misdemeanors, there tends to be much less formality, and often the plea negotiations and agreements reached there are much more abbreviated. However, the substance and the process are similar.

Plea agreements may be reduced to writing in the lower court. However, they are always entered on the record before the court. Therefore, all material terms and conditions of the agreement should be articulated on the record so as to avoid any ambiguity and misunderstandings later.

With these two exceptions noted above for the lower court, the preparation of your client for entry of a plea of guilty in either the lower court or District Court should be followed as set forth in Chapter 7.

C. Re-Arraignment

If a case has been resolved in the lower court through a plea agreement, the court shall set the matter for a change of plea hearing or re-arraignment. At that hearing, the defendant and the prosecuting attorney shall appear and enter into the agreement, and recite the specific terms and conditions to the court, on the record. Once the defendant's plea is entered on the record, and the court has adjudicated the guilt of the defendant, the court may proceed to imposition of the sentence.

In many cases, however, the court may instead set a separate date for a sentencing hearing, and order that certain information be made available to the court and parties prior to that date. Information such as criminal history, a mental evaluation to determine whether the defendant requires counseling for drug or alcohol abuse or domestic violence, victim impact statements, restitution figures, and other related information is typically requested. If the required information is not completed by the sentencing date, the court may continue the hearing until all of the information has been obtained and provided to the court and the parties.

4
Trial in the Lower Court (Misdemeanors Only)

If efforts to resolve the case prior to trial have failed, then you must proceed to trial. If it is a jury trial, please refer to the felony jury trial materials found in Chapters 10 through 17, as the guidelines are the same regardless of whether the charged offense is a misdemeanor or a felony.

A. Bench Trial

If the matter is set for a bench trial, the fundamental preparation is the same as if it were a jury trial, with the obvious exception that you don't have to worry about involving a jury. Thus, there is no preparation for voir dire or for exercising juror challenges. However, you must prepare to be just as persuasive in your presentation to the court as if you were before a jury. Magistrates are human beings, too.[1] They are just as persuadable as any juror. And as you will learn in this manual, since we are all "jurors," we must focus our persuasive efforts on those parts of our case that are appealing.

Many attorneys believe it is easier to try a case before a judge rather than a jury for several reasons, the most obvious one being that it involves less anxiety and preparation than a trial with a jury.

[1] So I've heard.

Since you most likely are very familiar and therefore comfortable with the judge, as opposed to a roomful of jurors whom you don't know, there might be a slight reduction in these factors, but for all intents and purposes there should be no reduction. You must be just as prepared for the judge in your witnesses and materials, and in your presentation. It is still theater after all.

Judges see a great deal of bad lawyering. Therefore, they are interested and excited when they see an attorney who stands out from the rest. Someone who is alert, prepared, confident, dramatic, in control of her case, and knows what she is doing. At the end of the day, a bench trial is a trial, and you are telling your client's story to an audience of one rather than twelve. Other than that, there should be no difference in your approach.

A final word on bench trials is necessary. If you have a case with very bad facts or a client who is difficult and not easy to care about, you might think it is to your advantage to waive the jury and try the case to the court instead. After all, you might say to yourself, the court might understand his defense (especially if it is "legal" or "technical"), whereas a jury might not. Thus, you believe your client might stand a better chance of acquittal with a trial to the bench.[2]

While there may be the occasional case that fits that category, such thinking is usually flawed. If you have such a case, that may be all the more reason to opt for a jury trial. As you will also learn in this manual, being a criminal defense lawyer is not for the timid. The odds are overwhelmingly against you. You have very little to work with. It seems that were it not for bad luck, you'd have none at all. That is precisely the moment that you should remember that, while all of that may be true—all things being equal—all things are *not* equal.

The great equalizer in such cases is that the prosecutor still has to prove the case. If the facts are particularly bad, the prosecutor can

[2] In reality, this is not what you're thinking; you are merely rationalizing your fear. In truth, you are frightened of trying your case to a jury because you don't know how in the world you can convince twelve people who are total strangers to acquit your client. You don't have a good defense, and you fear that they will reject you and that you will have lost your client's case and along with it a little more confidence in yourself, not only as a professional, but perhaps even as a person. As a result, you want to avoid a jury trial altogether. But all this is just fear. Keep reading.

be lulled into a sense of false security, thinking there is no way he can lose. In those instances, he may not realize that he can't prove what he thinks he can. He may have ignored certain flaws, assumed the presence of witnesses who won't appear or the introduction of evidence he doesn't have. That kind of hubris changes everything, especially with a jury.

As a defense attorney, you possess the one weapon in your hopelessly depleted arsenal that is still the most powerful force ever unleashed in a courtroom in this country—the right to a trial by jury. If you are (still) reading this manual, then there is something inside of you that keeps whispering to you that there must be something more that you can do; something more you can be; other skills you can learn; something to make you more powerful in the courtroom. In short, something you can do to transform yourself from a garden variety, face-in-the-crowd "litigator," into a true steely-eyed warrior for your client.[3]

Fasten your seatbelt, Buckaroo, and hang on. If you continue reading this manual and undertake to put into practice what you learn, you will never again consider waiving a jury.

B. Jury Trial

Preparing for a jury trial in the lower court is for all intents and purposes the same as if you were trying a felony jury trial in District Court. Due to the volume of cases and time constraints, however, few jury trials are conducted at this level. (For a detailed review of preparing for a jury trial, please refer to Chapters 10 through 17.)

Sometimes the mere threat of trying a jury trial in the lower court is enough to shake loose a reasonable plea offer from the prosecutor. Like you, the prosecutor doesn't have the time to work on his cases either. The last thing he needs is to prepare for a jury trial in a misdemeanor case. The only caveat to using this tactic is that if it fails, you had better be able to put your money where your mouth is and be prepared to try the case.

---

[3] I have no idea what a "litigator" is. I have a pretty good idea of what a "trial lawyer" is though.

5
Preliminary Hearing

When you don't know where you're going, any road will lead you there.

—George Harrison

The preliminary hearing (or "probable cause hearing") is one of the most important stages of a criminal case. It is the first "failsafe" stage of the case and presents a tremendous opportunity for the defense attorney. It is the first opportunity for the defense to publicly test the strength of the state's case.

The preliminary hearing is held in the lower court and is typically scheduled within ten days of the defendant's initial appearance after his arrest, if the defendant is in jail. That date may be extended, however, if the defendant agrees to waive the time limit in writing. If the defendant is released on bond, that date may be extended for an additional specified period, unless a waiver of that limit is obtained.

There are two types of waivers: a waiver of the time limit and a waiver of the entire hearing itself. Either one must be in writing and obtained with your client's consent. The lower court may have preprinted forms for those purposes.

You may wish to consider waiving the **time limit** for several reasons. You may need more time to review the charging documents and meet with your client or the prosecutor in order to determine the nature of the case, and whether you will need to proceed with the preliminary hearing or resolve the case in some other way. Waiving the time limit is often acceptable because it allows more time for you to work on the case without giving up anything in return. You still have the option of proceeding with the preliminary hearing at a future date if necessary.

Waiving the preliminary hearing entirely is another matter, however. The preliminary hearing is one of the most, if not THE most valuable hearing in the criminal defense arsenal. You should weigh the decision to waive it very carefully, for the following reasons:

- It is the first (and only) "free" opportunity for you to glimpse a preview of the state's case prior to trial. It is an adversarial proceeding, on the record. This means that you will have the opportunity to cross-examine the witnesses (usually law enforcement officers) and commit them to their testimony on the record, which will then set them up for possible impeachment later at trial if their testimony or the evidence changes.
- Quite often, the prosecutor has not studied his case closely or carefully enough at that stage to accurately assess its "long term" strengths and weaknesses. Therefore, it presents a wonderful opportunity for the defense to dig around and uncover weaknesses that can be exploited later at trial, before the prosecutor realizes he has any problems.
- Even if you believe that the case is unlikely to be tried, and that you and the prosecutor are likely to negotiate a resolution of the case with a guilty plea in District Court, it is strongly recommended that you never waive a preliminary hearing. There is too much you don't know at this point in the case. Circumstances can change. You may suddenly find yourself heading for trial, and if you waived the preliminary hearing, you've deprived yourself of a chance to gain an advantage over your opponent.

The standard of proof at a preliminary hearing is "probable cause" (essentially "more probable than not," i.e., 51% likelihood or better). The state has the burden of proving by a preponderance of the evidence:

- Whether there is probable cause to believe the charged offense has been committed; and
- Whether there is probable cause to believe the defendant committed it.

The state must produce witnesses and evidence in order to establish their burden. The evidentiary rules are greatly relaxed, and hearsay testimony is generally admissible.

If, after the hearing, the court determines that the state has carried its burden as to both criteria, the case is transferred, or bound over, to District Court for all other proceedings, including trial. If, however, the court determines that the state has failed to prove either or both criteria, the charges (or at least the affected charge) will be dismissed and the defendant's bond released. The case may be re-filed any time thereafter, however, since jeopardy has not yet attached.

The chances of a case being dismissed at the preliminary hearing are extremely remote. Therefore, it must be kept in mind that even though it is possible to convince the lower court to dismiss the case, that rarely happens. The state nearly always has sufficient evidence at the preliminary hearing to successfully bind the case over to District Court. You should therefore assume that it will be bound over. If you do get the case dismissed, that's icing on the cake. However, dismissal of the charge is not your most important goal at this point.

Your overall goal at the preliminary hearing is not dismissal—it is discovery. You go to the prelim in order to test the state's case by cross-examining witnesses on the record as far as the court will allow. That should provide you with enormously valuable information for use later at trial.

In almost every instance the state will call the arresting or investigating officer as its sole witness, who then testifies under oath about not only what he may have personally observed, but since hearsay is admissible, also to what all other witnesses, including the defendant, did and said. The defense should exploit this opportunity to every degree possible. That includes issuing subpoenas for other police officers who were involved in the investigation and arrest, as well as any other fact or eye witnesses. The prosecutor may likely move to quash such efforts, but part of being a trial lawyer includes sending a message to the prosecutor that you're in it to win it, and that you will not be intimidated by anything he does to stop you.

The primary reason that the state does not ordinarily call more witnesses is twofold: 1) There is no need since hearsay is admissible, and thus a great deal of time and effort is saved; and 2) The additional witnesses are not exposed to cross—examination by the defense, and thus "tied down" to their testimony under oath that would be presented later at trial. While not nearly as complex as a jury trial, the preliminary hearing is nevertheless a critical stage of a felony case, and requires no less the same manner of preparation.

A. Preparation

In order to properly prepare for a preliminary hearing, you must fully understand the dynamics at play. While there is no jury present, and the guilt or innocence of the defendant is not in issue, the credibility and veracity of the witnesses, as well as the substantive plausibility of the evidence, are just as much under scrutiny as if the jury were seated. The cross-examination of the witness and evidence should therefore be prepared with the same careful consideration.

Prior to the hearing, meet with your client and review the case in detail. Go over each charged offense and the elements required to prove each one, so that you clearly understand your client's position. Put a great deal of thought into analyzing where to attack the state's witness. As stated earlier, the prosecutor and the investigating officer likely do not know nearly as much about the facts and details (and thus the truth) of the case as they think they do. That is to say, this early in the case they may have made certain assumptions about what they believe the evidence will show and have discounted or ignored other evidence to the contrary. By thinking about these things, you will begin to develop some ideas as to where you can probe effectively.

Overall, the very best approach the defense can take on cross-examination at a preliminary hearing is twofold: First, do not worry about the fact that you don't know anything about the case. Simply wade into it and ask as many questions as you can. Second, identify and concentrate on all of the areas that the investigating officer did *not* investigate.[1]

Due to time constraints and fatigue, officers don't always uncover all of the "rocks" in a case. They tend to shortcut the investigation process by stopping their investigation once they've turned over only enough rocks to establish probable cause. As a result, many times they leave behind a field littered with undisturbed rocks. While there may be nothing under those rocks of any evidentiary value, the fact that the officer did not turn them over to verify that is crucial, for with every rock they admit they didn't turn over, it allows you to argue what they *could* have found had they done so. (How do they know they wouldn't have? They never looked.) This is the basis of reasonable doubt. And that is where the defense case lives and breathes at trial. The more you can get the officer to admit under oath at the preliminary hearing what he did *not* do in his investigation, the more holes you can punch in the state's case at trial, and you can portray him as a lazy cop who missed important evidence of your client's innocence.

Concentrate on the questions he *didn't* ask your client or other witnesses, the locations or places he did *not* examine or search, the evidence he did *not* seize, the notes he did *not* make (or keep), and so on. And never argue with the witness as to the importance or significance of such failures, or what he would have learned had he done those things. That is an argument you cannot win with him, at least at this point. Seek only his admissions as to his failures.[2] They will form the basis of the argument you will make to the jury at trial. Remember: The defendant does not have to prove that his theory of the case is right; he merely has to convince at least one juror that the prosecutor's theory is wrong.

Although it should go without saying, ***do not overlook testing the state's establishment of identity and jurisdiction.*** It is so elementary, and prosecutors are often so focused on presenting the evidence of the underlying offense, that they sometimes miss it entirely.

---

[1] Even though you are cross-examining the witnesses, remember your goal here is discovery. Feel free to use open-ended questions at this stage. Things will be much different at trial.

[2] See the materials on the cross-examination of police officers at Chapter 14(I).

Along with proving the defendant probably committed the crime, the state must also prove with each charge:

1. That the defendant has been identified in open court as the person who probably committed the offense.

and

2. That all of the events about which the witness has testified occurred within ________ County (in your state).

They are elements of each case and must be proven by the state. Listen carefully. Sometimes the court even tunes out these questions because they're tired or because they assume the prosecutor asked them. If they weren't asked, and there is no testimony as to these elements, the state's case has failed and the charges must be dismissed. You would be amazed how often this happens, even to seasoned veterans. If you find yourself in this delightful position, move to dismiss the case at the conclusion of the state's evidence.[3]

B. Motions

Motions are typically not filed at the preliminary hearing stage, primarily because most motions are not necessary or relevant. Since the defendant's guilt or innocence is not at issue, hearsay evidence is admissible, and if there is no jury present, there is usually little need for the defense to file a motion *in limine* or a motion to suppress evidence, or other such dispositive pleadings to limit testimony or evidence. Occasionally, defense counsel may attempt to subpoena other fact witnesses, including the victim, to appear at the hearing. A prosecutor must then file a response, which takes the form of a motion to quash the subpoena. The courts almost always grant those motions.

While there is no rule prohibiting either party from filing motions at a preliminary hearing, courts have generally held that defense counsel does not have a right to unfettered discovery at that stage, nor does defense counsel have the latitude to broadly probe the circumstances

[3] Even though the state can refile the charges since jeopardy has not attached at that stage, you have still taught the prosecutor a valuable lesson: He should never underestimate you. You are teaching him to respect you. That will pay off later.

under which evidence was seized, as the issues before the court are so narrowly defined.[4] Substantive and dispositive defense motions seeking suppression of evidence, as well as all other pretrial motions, are typically filed after the case has been bound over to District Court.

An exception is made if you feel that your client is not competent to proceed with the case due to mental illness. You may file a motion for a mental examination with the lower court at any time seeking suspension of proceedings pending a mental examination. Once that examination is completed, the court will determine what direction the case will take from there.[5]

C. Dismissal of Charges

An oral motion to dismiss the charges is the one motion the defense typically makes at the conclusion of the preliminary hearing. If the magistrate determines that either or both criteria of probable cause constituting the offense have not been proved, the charge will be dismissed. This means that if the defendant is in custody, the bond will be discharged, and he will be released as soon as possible. Jeopardy has not attached at this stage of the case, however, and the charges can be refiled at any time.

If the charges are to be refiled, it will likely be sooner rather than later. Sometimes it is possible for the charges to be refiled within a matter of an hour or two, and thus the defendant will be rearrested and detained before he is released onto the street. This is particularly the case in situations where the offense is serious, and the state is concerned for the safety of the victim or the general public. The prosecutor will simply call the jail after the hearing and tell the deputy to take his time processing the defendant so that the new paperwork can be prepared and served at the jail.

---

[4] In response to such efforts, the prosecutor will likely object, and the court will often admonish defense counsel by saying something like "*Counsel is not permitted to undertake a fishing expedition. You will confine your questions to the matters the witness testified to on direct examination. Objection sustained.*" This does not mean, however, that you should not attempt to catch a few fish. Just don't make it an "expedition."

[5] For further details on such a motion, see Chapter 9.

The decision to recharge the case will be determined largely by the reasons it was dismissed. If the error was procedural (i.e., no evidence of jurisdiction or identity was presented, or some other element of the charge was inadvertently omitted), then the case can easily be refiled. If, however, the state presented all evidence and the court determined that it was insufficient on its merits, then the prosecutor will likely discuss with the officer and a supervising attorney whether or not it would be worthwhile to refile the case. The evidence the state lacks may be unavailable either now or indefinitely.

D. Should the Defense Present Evidence?

Even though, as in a trial, the defense has the right to call witnesses and introduce evidence at the preliminary hearing, it is almost never done. Since you know virtually nothing about the case at that point, why risk exposing your witnesses, or worse—your own client—to cross-examination on the record by the prosecutor months ahead of trial for no reason? Remember, one of the defense's greatest strengths is the advantage you retain by not having to reveal or prove anything to anyone prior to trial. Presenting a defense at the preliminary hearing is never a good idea, for several reasons.

First of all, the issue of your client's guilt is not before the court. The only issue the court must consider is whether your client *probably* committed the alleged offense. By introducing evidence to rebut that, all you accomplish is to show the court that you have a defense that may or may not be useful at trial. Moreover, the court is likely to shrug off your evidence to the contrary by claiming that it presents nothing more than a question of fact for the jury to determine at trial. The question at this stage is not whether you have evidence to rebut the state's case; it is whether the state has sufficient evidence to bind the case over to District Court for trial. Your evidence therefore means nothing at the preliminary hearing.

By introducing evidence, you also present your defense strategy to the prosecutor well in advance of trial, enabling him to thoroughly prepare for it. Why would you do that? Since the defense is not required to introduce any evidence at trial, why would you do it at the preliminary hearing?

If your client testifies at the preliminary hearing, not only does the prosecutor glean the details of your anticipated trial defense, but your client's testimony is under oath and becomes a permanent record of the case. He is then bound to whatever he said if he chooses to testify later at trial. And since he will be cross-examined, God knows what the prosecutor will get him to say.

If the defendant's trial testimony differs materially from that given at the preliminary hearing, he may be also impeached by the prosecuting attorney on the inconsistency. For these reasons, it is never a good idea to present evidence at the preliminary hearing, and it is a terrible idea to put your client on the stand. Don't do it.

E. Adjusting Bond

As long as the case is still in the lower court and has not yet been bound over to the District Court following the preliminary hearing, the lower court retains jurisdiction over the case for all purposes, including bond modification.

It is quite common for bond to be modified at this stage of the case for a variety of reasons. Usually, it is because the defendant does not present a significant flight risk or risk of harm to the community. The prosecutor may offer to reduce the bond if the defendant agrees to waive the preliminary hearing. Although quite tempting, and your incarcerated client may wish to jump at that opportunity, you should hesitate to accept that offer. Your client will be giving up a huge opportunity to test the State's case in exchange for his freedom. Remind your client that bond can be addressed any time, in any court. Moreover, if the prosecutor is willing to release your client at this stage of the case, you can certainly advise the District Court of that fact at the arraignment when you request a bond review hearing.

A more sinister variation of this game is also played by some prosecutors from time to time. An attractive settlement offer may be extended to your client, on the condition that he waives the prelim. However, if your client elects to go to the prelim, he is then informed that the offer shall be withdrawn and no further plea offers will be made, and that if he is convicted at trial, the prosecutor shall seek incarceration. This tactic punishes your client for exercising his constitutional rights. It is unethical for a prosecutor to do this.[6]

If the prosecutor behaves in this fashion, you should absolutely call him on it. Remind him of his ethical duty and obligation under the law, and that if he does not straighten up you will be obliged to contact the state bar and file a grievance against him. The prosecution gets away with behavior like this because we are intimidated and afraid to stand our ground. Remember who you are, what your role is, and that your client is counting on you. The only way the defense ever gains any respect is if we demand it and fight for it. Make the prosecutor sorry he ever filed the case against your client.

Sometimes the court will agree to reduce bond at the conclusion of a preliminary hearing, even though there is sufficient evidence to bind the case over to the District Court, if the court feels that the evidence is thin and chances for conviction at trial unlikely. However, once the lower court has bound the case over to the District Court, it is generally reluctant to modify the bond. Some courts claim that once the case is bound over, they have automatically lost the jurisdiction to consider such a modification. Other courts simply defer the motion to the District Court, since that tribunal may also address the issue of bond at any time thereafter.

F. Closed Hearings

On rare occasions, the state or defense may request that a preliminary hearing be closed to the public. Almost always this involves a sexual assault case, particularly involving a child. The court typically has a

[6] In a criminal case, the government is responsible for safeguarding the substantive and procedural due process rights of the accused. That is because the government retains all of the power in the criminal justice process and the defendant none. Prosecutors are not only advocates, they are also charged with the ministerial duty to seek justice. This responsibility carries with it specific obligations to see that the defendant is accorded procedural justice and that guilt is decided upon the basis of sufficient evidence, and that special precautions are taken to prevent and to rectify the conviction of innocent persons. *See* Moe v. State, 110 P.3d 1206 (Wyo. 2005), on rehearing 123 P.3d 148 (Wyo. 2005). ("Because the goal of the criminal justice system is the attainment of justice, the role of the prosecuting attorney differs from that of an advocate in a civil case.")

policy in place regarding such hearings and motions, and the court will act on it accordingly without a great deal of input from you.

You should be aware, however, that the press and news media enjoy a good deal of clout with the courts. The extent to which the media is permitted to be present and report judicial proceedings is often addressed in the criminal rules. Generally speaking, it is at the discretion of the court, subject to detailed limitations. (See also Chapter 11(A).) It is not unusual for a lower court to close a preliminary hearing to the public, only to have the decision appealed by the local press on First Amendment grounds.[7] This effort is often successful. You should review with your supervisor what the applicable office policy is regarding how to respond in such situations.

G. Discovery

The release of the state's discovery materials to the defendant is typically governed by state statutes and rules of criminal procedure. The general practice is that the defense is not entitled to receive any discovery from the state in a felony case until after the case has been bound over after the preliminary hearing and the defendant has been formally arraigned in District Court.

The rationale for this would be that it is not until the case has reached that stage that the formal charges are confirmed.[8] Usually, it is in response to the defendant's motion for discovery and subsequent order by the court.[9]

---

[7] "The First Amendment right of access cannot be overcome by the conclusory assertion that publicity might deprive the defendant of the right to a fair trial." Press-Enterprise Co. v. Superior Court ("Press-Enterprise II"), 478 U.S. 1, 13–14 (1986). It is considered too speculative a reason and can properly be addressed in voir dire. *Id.*, at 15. Before a court can close a preliminary hearing or trial, the court must make "specific, on the record findings . . . demonstrating that 'closure is essential to preserve higher values and is narrowly tailored to serve that interest.'" Press-Enterprise II, at 15. Trial courts are required to consider alternatives to closure even when they are not offered by the parties. Presley v. Georgia, 558 U.S. 209, 214 (2010).

[8] The preliminary hearing is essentially the "confirmation" process. It would seem premature to permit discovery until it has been determined what charges are in fact going to proceed to trial.

[9] Absent the entry of a discovery order, the state is under no obligation to permit discovery. While defense motions for discovery are typically filed after the District

This is the primary reason why wide-ranging discovery interrogation at the preliminary hearing by the defense is not ordinarily permitted by the court. Usually, the only information in the hands of the defense at the preliminary hearing is a copy of the formal charging documents.[10] However, that is precisely the reason that the primary goal of the defense at the preliminary hearing is discovery. Since they're not going to hand it to you, you've got to wade in there and take it.

Court arraignment, there is nothing to prevent the defendant from filing a motion for discovery prior to the preliminary hearing, in the hopes of obtaining an order at that stage. Ordinarily, the lower court will deny such motions as premature.

[10] On occasion, depending on the prosecuting attorney's discretion (and mood) and the nature of the case, more extensive discovery may be disclosed. But the defense has no legal right to demand it at that stage. This doesn't mean, however, that you shouldn't ask for it.

6
Representation Before the Grand Jury[1]

The federal government and some states prosecute criminal cases through the use of grand jury indictments. Practice rules and statutes, as well as practice manuals, are widely available and sufficiently detailed, so as to be far beyond the effective scope of this manual. For that reason, the information provided herein is essentially an overview of the federal grand jury system. To the extent that any of the information contained in this chapter may be applicable to any state grand jury system, the reader is strongly advised to research the law of that particular jurisdiction for further information. Aside from the grand jury system of prosecution, the remaining information in this manual is equally applicable to the federal or any state jury trial process.

Generally speaking, the grand jury process takes the place of the preliminary hearing in other courts. The purpose of a grand jury is to investigate alleged criminal behavior, which includes the power to issue subpoenas, take testimony under oath, and determine whether

[1] The framework of this chapter was provided by Thomas B. Jubin, a close friend, colleague, and superb trial lawyer.

sufficient probable cause exists to support the filing of formal charges by issuing an indictment.

Unlike a preliminary hearing, a grand jury is not an adversarial proceeding. Grand jury hearings are not public. Defense counsel is not permitted to attend a grand jury proceeding. The prosecuting attorney is the sole presenter before the panel and totally controls the information presented to the jurors. The testimony presented is not ordinarily subject to public disclosure. There are few limitations on a grand jury's right to investigate. Generally speaking, it may investigate anyone for any criminal offense. As a practical matter, however, the prosecuting attorney directs the scope and focus of the process.

If, on the one hand, the jurors find sufficient probable cause to support formal charges, indictments are prepared and served on those individuals who are formally charged. If, on the other hand, probable cause is not found, no indictment is issued. Instead, a document entitled "No True Bill" is submitted.

While defense counsel may not be present during the giving of testimony, there are ways that you may effectively protect your client. You are either representing a witness before a grand jury who may be a "target" or "subject" of the underlying investigation (and thus subject to indictment) or merely a witness presenting factual information. Regardless, you must meet the client beforehand and thoroughly understand the client's role and position in the case before he testifies. It is of paramount importance that the client understands that any testimony given before the grand jury must be truthful. It is not uncommon for witnesses to be indicted for lying to grand juries, the penalties for which are significant.

If the client is a "target" of the investigation, she may have received a letter from the prosecutor's office advising her of that fact. That means that the grand jury is investigating alleged criminal conduct on the part of the client and that formal indictment is a possibility. In those instances, the "target" client may or may not be subpoenaed to testify. If she is, however, you must help her obtain protection.

A client who is a target may seek protection from criminal culpability in one of two ways: either by seeking immunity from prosecution under applicable statutory authority or by invoking the right not to testify against oneself through invocation of the Fifth Amendment to the Constitution.[2]

Seeking protection from prosecution through the granting of immunity is useful in cases where multiple individuals may be targets. Your client may be seen by the prosecution as a valuable asset to the prosecution of those individuals and therefore might be willing to participate as a witness against them in further hearings, or at trial, in exchange for immunity. Typically, if your client has been advised that no indictment is being sought against her, then counsel should request that the assistant U.S. Attorney contact the Department of Justice and seek authority to grant immunity from further prosecution.[3]

A client who has been subpoenaed as a witness to testify before the grand jury, but who is otherwise not a target, must be protected, particularly if he may have had any involvement in the alleged criminal enterprise under investigation. In addition to the options noted above, counsel should advise the client that while testifying under oath, he has the right to seek advice of counsel before answering any question put to him. Although counsel is not present in the courtroom to give such advice, the witness may be excused from the room to meet with counsel separately and confidentially.[4]

A. Initial Appearance in the Lower Court (Felony)

If your client is indicted for a felony, he may initially be seen in either the U.S. Magistrate Court or the District Court. At the initial appearance, the defendant will be advised of the charges against him, the maximum possible penalties, and his constitutional rights. Bond will also be set and the matter set for formal arraignment in District Court (if initially held in the Lower Court).[5]

If your client is charged with a misdemeanor, he will ordinarily enter a plea of "Not Guilty" before the magistrate judge; the case will

---

[2] It should be noted that invoking the Fifth Amendment is not admissible in any subsequent criminal trial. It is, however, admissible in a civil matter.

[3] *See* 18 U.S.C. §§ 6001 – 6005.

[4] Some attorneys tell their clients to excuse themselves and seek advice of counsel *after every single question*. While that is perhaps possible, it is better practice to simply prepare your client for the types of questions she will likely face.

[5] For further details on the arraignment process, see Chapter 7.

then proceed with exchange of discovery and, if necessary, the filing of dispositive motions. At some point prior to trial, the U.S. Attorney may make a plea offer of some sort. If a plea agreement is accepted, the court will set the matter for a rearraignment or change of plea hearing. If plea negotiations fail, the matter will proceed to trial. If convicted, the client will have an opportunity to appeal any errors of law to the United States District Court and from there on to the appropriate Circuit Court of Appeals.

It should be noted that the federal government does not use grand juries for indictments on misdemeanor offenses. Those are simply charged by information, complaint, or citation by the U.S. Attorney.

7
Arraignment in District Court

In felony cases, the District Court arraignment is the first formal opportunity the defendant will have to enter a plea to the charge. It is therefore a critical stage of the criminal process.

The defendant cannot ordinarily waive her appearance at the arraignment; she must usually appear. The plea options, as noted in Chapter 3, are Guilty, Not Guilty, Not Guilty by Reason of Mental Illness or Deficiency (NGMI) or, with permission of the court, No Contest *(nolo contendere)*. The defendant may also enter a plea of Not Triable by Reason of Mental Illness (NTMI) at any stage of the proceeding from that point forward. Unless the plea is NGMI, the court will also set a tentative trial date, as well as dates and deadlines for the filing of plea agreements, motions, and pretrial memoranda.[1]

The vast majority of pleas initially entered by the defendants at this stage are "Not Guilty," primarily because the parties have not yet had the opportunity to thoroughly review the discovery and negotiate any plea agreement. The defendant needs to review the discovery and meet with you, and you need to meet with the prosecuting attorney to review the case and possible plea options before any change of plea can be considered. Once that process is complete and

[1] If the plea is NGMI, please refer to Chapter 9.

a plea agreement has been negotiated, the defendant then notifies the court that a change of plea hearing (also called a "rearraignment") is requested.

Following the arraignment, the defense typically files its standard postarraignment motions, such as motions for discovery, demand for speedy trial, Rule 404(b) disclosures, and so on. The arraignment is also the date by which the "speedy trial" clock typically begins to run.

A. Preparing the Client for a Guilty Plea

Entry of a guilty plea is one of the most critical decisions your client may ever make. The ramifications of it will echo throughout her lifetime. Accordingly, it is vitally important that you prepare your client very carefully. Whether in the lower court or District Court, the basic guidelines for preparing your client for changing her plea are the same. Accordingly, this section should be considered equally applicable to both forums.

The process of entering a guilty plea in the lower court may be considerably different from that in District Court. There is much less "formality," and often the plea negotiations and agreements reached there are much more abbreviated. Because of the volume and time constraints in the lower court, cases are sometimes negotiated and concluded within minutes.

However, they are always entered on the record before the court. Therefore, all material terms and conditions of the agreement should be articulated on the record so as to avoid any ambiguity and misunderstandings later.

Criminal defendants may wish to enter a plea of guilty for any number of reasons. Usually, it is because they are guilty of the offense charged or of something close to it. The prosecutor may be willing to offer a reduced sentence, or even a suspended one, in exchange for an admission of guilt.

Sometimes a defendant may want to plead guilty in order to merely expedite the court process, permitting her to satisfy a jail sentence and obtain an earlier release. Often the clients are not overly concerned about whether they actually committed the offense charged or whether the state can prove it beyond a reasonable doubt. Their primary concern may be incarceration, and the less of it the better. Care must be taken in these situations to ensure that the client knows and fully understands that there may be a defense to her case, and while it may not appear to be the best defense, it may be a defense nonetheless. Once she enters a guilty plea, she forever waives her right to claim any defenses, whether or not she knows about them.

While the court will review with the defendant in some detail on the record the constitutional rights the defendant waives by entering a plea of guilty, it is your duty as counsel for the defendant to ensure that your client is thoroughly and properly advised of her rights prior to appearing before the court.[2] If the defendant later decides that she doesn't like how her case resolved, and she files a motion to withdraw her guilty plea, claiming that you were ineffective in your representation of her, she will blame you and not the judge. For this reason, it is sound practice to prepare a detailed, exhaustive written advisement of the defendant's constitutional rights, as well as the direct and collateral effects a waiver of those rights will have on her life. After reviewing them with her, have her sign and date the document and keep it in your file. It may become a critically important document when the day arrives—as it inevitably will—that a client claims you did not adequately advise her prior to her guilty plea.

Occasionally, you will have a client who insists on pleading guilty, even though he may deny having committed the underlying offense. As you were taught in law school, these are known as *Alford* pleas.[3] An *Alford* plea is used in those cases where the court will permit a defendant to enter a guilty plea to a criminal charge and consent to the imposition of a prison sentence, while the defendant is either unwilling or unable to admit to his participation in the acts constituting the crime. In those cases, the prosecuting attorney must establish

---

[2] While the vast majority of courts are fairly thorough in this process, not all are. In some cases, defendants enter guilty pleas without being adequately advised by the court on the record of any substantive right whatsoever. This is why you should never assume the court will take care of this critical aspect of the guilty plea process.

[3] North Carolina v. Alford, 400 U.S. 25, 91 S.Ct. 160, 27 L.Ed.2d 162 (1970). Acceptance of an *Alford* plea requires that there be "strong evidence of actual guilt" to negate the claim of innocence and to provide a means by which the trial court can test whether the plea was intelligently entered.

on the record the factual basis underlying the plea.[4] Generally speaking, the factual basis must clearly establish that the weight of the evidence supporting guilt is substantial and that the defendant would likely be convicted of the offense after a trial.

The purpose of an *Alford* plea is to allow the defendant to take advantage of a plea agreement containing recommended sentencing terms that are more favorable than if the defendant were to be convicted after a trial or after the entry of a "cold plea," without the benefit of a recommended reduced sentence. It goes without saying that an *Alford* plea requires that defense counsel be exacting and exhaustive in preparing a client for such a plea.

The client must understand that when pleading guilty to any offense, whether felony or misdemeanor, he must admit to each and every material element of the offense. Moreover, he must not equivocate with the court on any of them. This is particularly important when he is pleading guilty to a specific intent crime. You must prepare your client to be ready to admit that at the time of the offense, he possessed the statutorily required intent to commit not only the act, but in certain cases, the specifically intended result. Courts sometimes have little patience with a defendant who wastes the court's time by going through the hoops of a guilty plea and then balks at the element of intent.

You must also make sure that your client understands what the proposed plea agreement—if there is one—specifically includes and does not include. There must not be any vagueness regarding the definition of terms or conditions, and all material terms must be clearly articulated and understood. There must never be any "unwritten" or "verbal agreements" or "gentleman's agreement" with the prosecuting attorney. Such agreements have a curious habit of disappearing at the most inopportune moments. All terms to any plea agreement should be in writing and signed by all parties. All terms and conditions concerning the charges to which the defendant is pleading guilty, the charges being dismissed, the recommended sentence, and any other material terms and conditions must be expressly set forth

---

[4] In comparison, a "No Contest" plea does not require the prosecutor to establish the factual basis. The court merely finds that the probable cause statement in the charging papers constitutes sufficient factual basis for the charge.

on the record at the change of plea hearing. Generally speaking, any term or condition that is important to the defendant must be in writing or it will be deemed never to have existed.

The defendant must appear for a change of plea and sentencing hearing. However, there are occasions in the lower court when that requirement may be waived, with permission of the court and, of course, your client. Because a number of cases that are resolved in the lower court involve low-level misdemeanors and defendants who reside out of state, the judge may permit you to enter your client's guilty plea in writing and will not require his or her presence.

B. The Conditional Guilty Plea

In addition to the plea options set forth above, there may be an additional plea commonly entered into at both the lower court and District Court levels—the conditional guilty plea. This plea is frequently entered in drug cases, where the defendant has filed a pretrial motion to suppress evidence seized during an arrest or search.

If the defendant was unsuccessful at suppressing the evidence, a defendant is allowed to enter a guilty plea while preserving the right to appeal the court's denial of his motion to suppress. If successful on appeal and the case is remanded back to the trial court, the court will permit the defendant to withdraw his guilty plea. The defendant may then either seek dismissal of the case (if the critical evidence is now suppressed) or proceed to trial.

C. The Non-Resident Client

A guilty plea to a felony has collateral effects if your client is a foreign national or illegal alien. They become subject to deportation from this country if convicted of certain criminal offenses. Typically, a conviction of any offense considered an "aggravated felony" under federal law will trigger deportation proceedings. 8 U.S.C. 1101(a)(43). An aggravated felony has been defined and interpreted to mean *any* offense, *felony or misdemeanor*, which is a "crime of violence," in that it encompasses a threat or use of force, or evidence of fraud or other moral turpitude. *Omar v. INS*, 298 F.3d 710 (8th Cir., 2002). Thus, for example, a conviction for misdemeanor vehicular homicide, check fraud or false pretenses may thus arguably qualify as a crime of violence under applicable federal law. This could subject the client to deportation, and/or seizure of property and other assets. Even if not subject to deportation, it may be that if the client leaves this country to travel abroad, and then returns, she may be subject to official inquiry and held for questioning. Those questions must be researched and the client must be advised thoroughly prior to the entry of a plea of guilty.

Since many practitioners may not know or have immediate access to the answers to those particular questions in any given case, it is recommended that counsel should first contact an immigration attorney in order to obtain the information necessary to properly advise the client prior to the entry of any guilty plea. Failure to do so is considered malpractice, and ineffective assistance of counsel.

8
Discovery

We're gonna need a bigger boat.

—Roy Scheider as Chief Brody, *Jaws*

A. From the State

Discovery can be a somewhat contentious area, although suffice it to say that discovery in a criminal case is ordinarily not nearly as complex or acrimonious as it can be in civil cases. As noted earlier, submission of discovery by the state is typically not even considered until after the defendant has been bound over from the preliminary hearing and has appeared for arraignment in the District Court.

Discovery from the state generally takes the form of written or recorded or oral statements made by the defendant, the defendant's prior criminal record, all police reports, charging documents, physical, mental, laboratory, or other scientific reports, and any and all seized physical evidence, including video and audio recordings, witness statements, tangible objects, photographs, and any other item that the state intends to introduce at trial. The state has an ongoing obligation to produce any additional discovery as it becomes known.

The defense should file a full and formal motion for discovery, as well as other standard pretrial motions immediately following the District Court arraignment. The state won't release any discovery until such a motion is filed and the court signs the accompanying order. Time is of the essence to the defense, and the sooner you file your motion the sooner you can receive the discovery and get cracking on your case preparation.

One area that seems to be the source of much anxiety and concern is the failure by the state to produce discovery and the existence of any particular piece of evidence that has not been produced in discovery, as well as the extent to which the prosecuting attorney personally may be aware of it. There are several variations on this theme.

A typical example would be if you were to see an entry in the police report that indicates a video tape or digital recording of the incident exists and was submitted into evidence by the officer, but the recording was not provided to you in discovery. In relatively small communities, it is usually far easier to resolve the problem with a phone call to the prosecuting attorney than it is to go through the formality and time to draft and file a motion to compel discovery for that item. Given that the officer noted in his report that the recording existed, and it is quite likely that the prosecutor has viewed it (or at least agrees that it may exist), your telephone call should ordinarily be all that is necessary to produce a copy for you.

Another type of problem that can occur is more vexing. You may discover that certain evidence of which the prosecutor is *not* aware exists which has not been produced in discovery by the state. As an example, let's assume that the prosecuting attorney was not aware that a recording of the incident existed. Assume that there was no mention of it anywhere in the report, and the only reason you know of its existence is that you happened to run into the officer on the street and he told you about it. Even if the prosecutor knows nothing about it, she is responsible for producing it in discovery. Again, a simple phone call should resolve that problem. The prosecutor should then contact the particular law enforcement agency responsible for the case and request that it be produced, or at least made available to you for inspection and copying.

The agency will respond by either (1) producing it; (2) denying that the evidence exists (they don't have it); (3) denying that it was seized (they don't have it); or (4) claiming that it was inadvertently lost or destroyed after being seized. At that point, you must follow up with the officer who notified you as to the recording's existence, and see if he can track it down or determine what happened to it. If the recording or item is of evidentiary significance (e.g., a recording of the incident that depicts your client; blood or bodily fluids used for DNA analysis), you should take the precaution of arranging for a detailed interview of the officer, including having him sign an affidavit as a predicate for filing a motion to compel discovery of the evidence or, alternatively, a motion *in limine* to exclude it from being introduced by the state at trial, as well as a motion to dismiss, on the grounds of spoliation, and violation of discovery rules. You may also need to subpoena that officer as a witness at the hearing.

The most troublesome issue arises when you are notified that the state intends to introduce evidence at trial that you were previously informed did not exist or was otherwise not available. This is a clear-cut violation of the discovery rules, especially if you have previously demanded production of just such evidence. This is tantamount to withholding evidence. The defense attorney should certainly file motions seeking to exclude the item from introduction at trial, along with motions to dismiss and, in the appropriate circumstances, possibly motions for sanctions to be imposed by the court, including submitting a grievance to the state bar (if the violation was egregious). Intentional withholding of evidence from the defense is among the most serious acts of misconduct a prosecuting attorney can ever engage in. Since the state has the burden of producing items for discovery and review by the defense prior to trial, the fact that the prosecutor personally may not have known of the item's existence (or may even have been led to believe by the officers that it did not exist) is no excuse.

The question sometimes arises as to whether certain evidence in the possession of the state qualifies as "exculpatory" and thus discoverable by the defense. This evidence can take the form of informal agency reports, probation notes, uncorroborated police reports, personnel files and personal notes of the officers, and any other documents containing information about the defendant or other witnesses in the case which would typically not be publicly filed. If you believe such evidence exists and is relevant, you have an obligation to demand that such evidence be produced for your inspection and copying by the state. A responsible and ethical prosecutor should produce such evidence, although she may not wholly agree with your interpretation of such evidence as being "exculpatory" and may seek the protection of a court order.

Understanding discovery and its limitations would not be complete without discussing what is becoming an increasing problem: prosecutorial misconduct. Since the burden of proof is on the state, the prosecuting attorney is responsible for providing copies of, or at least access to, any and all evidence that the state intends to introduce at trial. More and more prosecutors are failing, either intentionally or through neglect and mismanagement of their offices, to properly comply with this obligation. It should *never* be tolerated by the defense, regardless of the reason.

Prosecutorial misconduct is a serious ethical violation and can result in reversal of convictions and imposition of various sanctions. It is conduct that violates a defendant's rights regardless of whether the prosecutor was unaware of it or whether he never intended such results. Common types of prosecutorial misconduct include the following:

- Plea bargain offenses (failure to perform specifically)
- Failure to disclose exculpatory evidence
- Use of inadmissible evidence
- Vouching / character assassination
- Inflammatory statements
- Mischaracterization of the evidence or the law
- Unacceptable courtroom behavior

Defense counsel must be vigilant in guarding against these and other violations of their clients' rights. We are at all times advocates and must never be afraid to bring to light any violation by the state. We must also seek appropriate relief, including moving for sanctions, dismissal of the case with prejudice, as well as a mistrial. Stand your ground and make your record.

These discovery abuses often occur shortly before trial. Defense counsel may have tried repeatedly—and unsuccessfully—to obtain discovery in time to prepare for trial. Many defense counsel may therefore believe (albeit erroneously) that seeking a continuance of the trial date might be the appropriate resolution because it buys more time.

A continuance of the trial date does NOT solve the problem, however. It merely forces the client to waive his right to a speedy trial, while allowing for the least restrictive sanctions to be imposed upon the state by the court. You can see the obvious inequity in that resolution. That doesn't adequately address the state's responsibility for having failed to follow the rules which resulted in prejudice to your client. *Refusing* to continue the trial date in light of the speedy trial demand will place great pressure on the court to strike the state's evidence and dismiss the case. Finally, it goes without saying that your client must be made aware of the problem and should be willing to press the issue.

B. From the Defense

Whatever evidence the defense seeks to introduce at trial must be released to the state prior to trial. Such discovery is likewise governed by state statute and rules of criminal procedure. Those materials typically include written or recorded statements of any witness (other than the defendant), documents and tangible objects, including photographs, and reports of scientific or medical examinations and tests. That obligation is ongoing.

To what extent you may be obliged to reveal other evidence to the state prior to trial is an area of some debate. Some feel full disclosure is always best, whereas others believe that the less revealed the better. As a general rule, the defense should reveal only what is necessary prior to trial, and the less the better. The major exception to this rule, however, is when you believe that you possess solid evidence of your client's actual innocence.

There is always the possibility (albeit highly unlikely) that the state has made a mistake (i.e., charged the wrong person) or is unaware of exculpatory evidence. It serves no good purpose to conceal such evidence from the state.[1] In fact, it may further ensure that your client will be convicted, particularly if you are somehow prohibited

---

[1] Those attorneys who gleefully rub their hands in keen anticipation of waiting to spring the exculpatory evidence on the prosecutor at trial are foolish, not to mention reckless. They are pandering to their own egos. What if the evidence is not admitted?

from introducing such evidence at trial. If that occurs, the fact that you purposely withheld such evidence from the state may constitute malpractice, for it places your client at terrible risk. In such cases, disclosure of exculpatory evidence to the state early on might result in dismissal of the charges, which is, of course, your ultimate goal. No matter how strong you believe your case is, it is always better to settle it if you are able to rather than try it.

9
Motion for Mental Evaluation

This guy goes to a psychiatrist and says, "Doc, my brother's crazy. He thinks he's a chicken." And the doctor says, "Well, why don't you bring him in?" And the guy says, "I would, but I need the eggs."

—Old Vaudeville Joke

The entry of a plea of Not Guilty by Reason of Mental Illness (NGMI) and/or Not Triable by Reason of Mental Illness (NTMI) presents a unique challenge for the defense attorney. The defendant may enter such pleas upon his appearance at the arraignment in District Court or at any time prior or subsequent thereto. He may then move for a suspension of all proceedings and request a hearing to determine whether he is mentally competent to proceed further. Such pleas are typically governed by state statutes and criminal rules of procedure. The defendant must be held to the legal standard defined by the statute that was in effect at the time of the commission of the offense.

The statutory language may limit the defense of mental illness to such severe diagnoses as schizophrenia or such other significant and severe mental diseases. Additionally, some states do not recognize the defense of diminished capacity or involuntary intoxication. It should be noted, however, that in those states that do recognize it, a defendant may not be permitted to introduce evidence of any mental illness or involuntary intoxication, unless he has first entered a plea of NGMI.[1]

Once your client has entered an NGMI or NTMI plea, all further proceedings are ordinarily suspended pending a review of the defendant's mental state. Once that evaluation is complete, a report is submitted to the court and the parties. The state and the defense may then have the option, upon a showing of good cause, to seek additional evaluation by an examiner of their own choosing. A hearing is then held to consider the findings. If the court determines that the defendant is fit to proceed, the court may first determine whether to commit the defendant to a designated facility, hold him in confinement, or release him on bond. If, however, the court determines that the defendant lacks mental fitness to proceed, all further proceedings shall be suspended and the court shall commit him to a designated facility for a reasonable period of time to determine whether there is any likelihood that he will regain his fitness to proceed at some point in the future.

Once committed, if it is later determined that the defendant has recovered and is fit to proceed, the court ordinarily resumes criminal proceedings. However, if the defendant does not regain fitness to proceed and it does not appear likely that he will recover his fitness within a reasonable amount of time, it is likely that the state will have to dismiss the case. However, the defendant may still be retained pending initiation of civil commitment proceedings.

Experience reveals that, in most cases, once the initial evaluations are complete, the defendant is found to be competent to proceed. The state must then proceed with prosecution of the case. However, even though the defendant may be competent to proceed, there may still be a question as to whether he was mentally ill at the time he committed the offense. Again, in most cases, the defendant is declared to have been mentally competent ("sane") at the time, although there may also exist professional diagnoses describing a variety of mental illnesses

---

[1] The federal statutes dealing with the entry of a plea pursuant to a mental health defense are found at 18 U.S.C. §§ 4241–4248. Additionally, F.R.Cr.P.12.2 requires that the prosecutor and the court be timely notified of the defendant's intent to pursue an insanity defense.

from which the defendant may suffer but that are not sufficient, in and of themselves, to qualify as defenses to the offense charged.[2]

If it is determined that the defendant was sufficiently mentally ill at the time he committed the offense, and thus is not legally responsible for his actions, it is likely that the state will have to dismiss the case. Absent an outright dismissal, however, the court will not be willing to simply take it off the docket and otherwise suspend it indefinitely because it presents an obvious problem with statutory and constitutional speedy trial requirements.

[2] For example, a significant portion of criminal defendants are found to be suffering from "antisocial personality" disorders and "schizo-typal" disorders. While they are mental illnesses, they are not defenses to a crime.

10
Preparing Your Case for Trial

I push my cases as hard as I can and I think it's my duty and my job to do so—to the edge. I don't think I should leave a margin. I think if I leave a margin, I leave the margin for the benefit of these people (opposing counsel).

—Gerry Spence

A. Generally

Preparation of your case for trial does not begin the day you file your pretrial memorandum. You are already out of time. It begins the day that you receive the case and interview the client (and in no case later than when the case is bound over to District Court).

Never assume that any case that you undertake will be resolved through a plea agreement. Just because the facts of a particular case suggest that it is unlikely to be tried or that it should be settled early is not an acceptable reason to avoid preparing for trial at the outset. The first thing that will happen is that the case doesn't settle and you find yourself trapped with no time to prepare your case. You cannot count on the court to save you by granting a motion to continue the trial to a later date.

Assuming the court does agree to continue it, at best all a continuance will accomplish is providing a limited time for you to prepare some personal notes for voir dire, opening, closing, and so on. There will not be sufficient time for you to identify, locate, and interview witnesses, retain necessary experts, and prepare exhibits. At that point, you are left with either "winging" a half-prepared trial (which is malpractice), or desperately offering a plea resolution to the prosecutor containing terms that are likely unacceptable to your client. In addition, your credibility has been seriously damaged. You will be perceived as someone who can be shoved around, in the belief that you will again cave in. Therefore, to avoid these pitfalls, simply treat every case as if it will need to be tried.[1]

When you first take the case, spend some time reading the file and reflecting on what the case is really about. Get a feel for the "big picture." For an example, the defendant might be charged with homicide, but that may not be what the case is really about. It's really about self-defense, or mental illness, or heat of passion, or family honor, or an accident, and the like. The facts and the dynamics of the evidence will dictate what type of case theory you must develop.

Once you get a gut feel for where you sense the case is really grounded, you should prepare your case *backwards*. That is, you must start with determining what instructions you want given to the jury because once the instructions are prepared, they will give you the foundation on which you build your entire case. Once you decide what jury instructions you want, you must then create your closing argument. When you give your closing argument, you may want to show certain instructions to the jury, to help them understand what they should be looking for during their deliberations. Once the closing argument is framed out, then proceed to the cross-examination of your opponent's witnesses. After that, then proceed to the direct

---

1 My father told me on numerous occasions to "treat every case as if it were the *Scopes* trial." Of course, in today's world, he would no doubt substitute "*O. J. Simpson*" for "*Scopes*," that case having surpassed *Scopes* as being commonly considered the "trial of the century." (In 1925, substitute teacher John T. Scopes was charged with violation of Tennessee's Butler Act for teaching human evolution in the public school system. Popularly known as the "Scopes Monkey Trial," it pitted the concepts of religious fundamentalism against scientific modernism. Scopes was represented by famed defense attorney Clarence Darrow, and the prosecution was handled by three-time presidential candidate and nationally recognized orator William Jennings Bryan.)

examination of your witnesses and so forth. Continue to work backwards to construct every stage of your case based on the framework of your case theory and theme. Thus, everything you build in reverse will, when turned around, flow naturally toward that goal.[2]

As soon as possible following the preliminary hearing, meet with your legal assistant and any other member of your anticipated "trial team" (including your investigator), and start brainstorming and planning for the trial. Although you may not have yet received discovery from the state, identify and discuss all potential witnesses and what types of physical evidence you may need.

Consider whether you will need an expert witness to explain particular areas of scientific or technical concern. The earlier you identify them and secure their availability, the better. Experts usually need a good deal of advance notice. Also inquire as to whether your office manager will require notice of the need for an expert, in order to submit any forms and authorizations required to pay their fees. Discuss whether proof of your case will require the creation or utilization of any demonstrative exhibits, such as charts, graphs, models, or enlarged or aerial photographs. These often take a great deal of time and effort to prepare—not to mention expense—but they can make a tremendous impact at trial.

Another useful approach is to ask yourself, *"How can I lose this case?"* and *"If I were the prosecuting attorney, how would I build my case to convict the defendant?"* By "crawling into the hide" of the prosecuting attorney, you will begin to see where your case needs to be strengthened.

B. The Theory of the Case and the Case Theme

> *"Oh, shit!" is not a case theme.*
>
> —Larry Pozner

When the investigation is completed, one of the most important things to do before embarking on a detailed case preparation is to

[2] Many world-class athletes use this technique. Rather than try to determine how they can win, they start with the assumption that they have won, and then they work backwards to determine how they did it.

develop the theory of the case and the case theme. The theme will frame your case, keep you focused, and be the filter through which every phase of your case will be constructed. It will form the cornerstone of your presentation to the jury and will be introduced to the jury for the first time in your voir dire. In many cases, it will be the first words out of your mouth in your opening statement. It will be the focal point of every direct and cross-examination, and it will be hammered home in your closing argument. A theme can be so effective that it can convince the jury to even ignore or nullify the law if that is the only way to reach a just result. Its importance, therefore, cannot be overstated.

In order to develop the theme of your defense, you must first develop your client's story, which is your *theory* of the defense case. All of this begins with becoming thoroughly familiar with not only all of the facts, but the details of your client's story. You will present the theory of your case in the most effective way possible—telling the truth by telling your client's story.

Telling your client's story is more than simply describing to the jury your version of the facts. It is a cohesive narrative that combines fact with persuasive "word pictures," that do more than simply tell a story. It tells the story of your client's *innocence.*

The case theory and theme are not the same thing. The "theory of the case" is your client's version of what, why, and how it occurred. Your theory should have persuasive facts, strong emotions, a legal basis for the jury to find your client innocent, vivid imagery, and concrete language. It should be client-driven, listener-driven, and a compelling and believable story. You must select only one theory. Having more than one will confuse the jury and undermine your credibility with them.

After immersing yourself in the facts, you must then take a step back and take a long look at the entire picture. Think about the defendant and who he is. Think about the victim. Why did the crime happen the way it did? Who were the supporting players? What were the motivations? What was going on behind the scenes? A picture will begin to emerge from the mist. The more you think about it, the more you will clarify it. Discuss it with your trial preparation team. Share ideas. Brainstorm. You will recognize it when it appears, for it will be absolutely pure and true and indestructible.[3]

Once you are certain you have identified the theory, you must then refine it until you can capture the entire theory in *one or two sentences*. This becomes the *theme* of your case. That theme will now drive your entire case and will be the words you will most likely first utter to the jury when you stand to make your opening statement. The "theme" is the distilled "song" of your client's story of innocence. It is the battle cry that knits together and runs through every phase of the trial. It should be powerful and give the jury something they will not forget as they assemble around the table to begin deliberations when the trial is over.[4] The jury will measure the facts as you presented them in your theory to the validity of your theme. If it's a perfect fit—which it should be—you have assembled a persuasive case.

Another effective method for developing your case theme is to create a list of your favorite movie quotes. Hollywood spends millions of dollars paying writers to conjure up clever lines of dialogue and arresting slogans on posters.[5] Many of them can be adapted easily to fit the theme of your case.

Sometimes the jury can help you establish your case theme. Once in a while you may have a situation arise where you simply cannot conjure up a case theme early on. You may be looking for a dramatic or "pithy" introductory sentence in your opening statement. Pay close attention during your voir dire. Keep your ears open. More often than not, one of the jurors will articulate the perfect case theme in a response to a question. Using it as the theme to introduce your

---

[3] An effective technique for thinking about and developing the theme of your case is to watch episodes of the original classic television show, *The Twilight Zone*. Series creator and writer Rod Serling introduced every episode with about a fifteen-second monologue. In those fifteen seconds, he told you everything you needed to know about what you were about to see. He set the stage. He created the mood. He grabbed your attention with his words. Some were unforgettable.

[4] Recall the O. J. Simpson murder trial which perhaps produced one of the most famous case themes ever: "If the gloves don't fit, you must acquit!"

[5] For example: "In Space No One Can Hear You Scream" *(Alien)*; "We Are Not Alone" *(Close Encounters of the Third Kind)*; "The Truth is Out There" *(The X-Files)*; "Just When You Thought it Was Safe to Go Back in the Water" *(Jaws)*.

case will be the perfect way to demonstrate to the jury how in tune you are with each other. For that reason, you should remain flexible and ready to change or adapt your theme if circumstances require it.

C. Jury Instructions

Among the first things you should consider in preparing for trial are the jury instructions. Since the case eventually comes down to the jury being instructed on the law of the case, it follows that every single aspect of the trial should be prepared through the lens of the instructions. They will orient you to the specific defenses you will need to establish, and get you thinking as to how best to present them.

The best time to review jury instructions, and in general to start preparing your case, is after the District Court arraignment. At that point, it will have been determined what specific charges are going to be tried to a jury. Whenever the court sets a trial date, you should consider that date to be set in stone and unchangeable. It will force you to prepare on time. As a general rule, never be the one to request a continuance of the trial date. You should always be prepared on time. Not only will this enable you to be ready for trial, but it will give you the psychological edge of being confident in your preparation. Set deadlines for the completion of various stages, such as witness notification, evidence preparation, and drafting of legal memoranda and motions, and stick to them.

The majority of instructions are typically gleaned from the Criminal Pattern Jury Instructions in your jurisdiction. If you are utilizing the latest edition, chances are the language is correct. However, it should never be assumed that it is. This is particularly true if your case involves frequently changing or evolving areas of law. Never assume that the pattern instructions accurately reflect the latest version of the law. If you are wrong, and the court does not catch it prior to advising the jury, you may have accomplished nothing more than building reversible error into your case.

Occasionally, you may wish to draft and submit an instruction that is not covered by applicable law in your jurisdiction but has been obtained from another jurisdiction. Courts are very reluctant to adopt instructions from outside jurisdictions. If you intend to rely on it, you should have a strong and persuasive argument prepared for the court.

This is also true if you wish to draft your own jury instruction. Sometimes a particular local case may define the law in a way that resonates well when excerpted into a jury instruction. There is nothing wrong with drafting your own instruction as long as you are able to support it convincingly with applicable law and explain why existing instructions are inadequate.

D. Witnesses

Identify and interview all witnesses as early in the case as possible. Do not rely on the opinions or summaries of your investigator to determine which witnesses to call or what the witnesses know. Often, what a witness has told the investigator or the law enforcement officers is only a fraction of the story.

As a trial lawyer, your job is to tell the complete story of your client's case to the jury. You must make it come alive in order to establish your credibility over that of your opponent. In the courtroom, whoever tells the best story wins. That means that the more details you learn, the more you know about your case. The only way for you to obtain those details is to meet with each witness and interview them.

As mentioned earlier, never meet with a witness alone. Have your legal assistant, investigator, or someone else on your trial team with you. This will ensure you have a witness as to what was said, in the event that the witness decides to alter his story prior to or at trial. Do not ignore the opportunity to interview witnesses who may be called by the state, particularly the law enforcement officers. The more you know about your opponent's case, the more you know about yours.

1. Deposing Witnesses

Occasionally, it may be necessary to preserve the testimony of a witness if the witness is expected to be unavailable at trial. The law regarding when a witness may be considered "unavailable" is usually set out in the rules or statutes. The party seeking to depose the witness has the burden to establish the necessity of the deposition. The deposition may be oral (utilizing just a transcript), or it may also include a video deposition (often used in child sexual assault cases).

The defendant has a right to be present at any deposition, although he may waive that right in writing. In addition, the defendant has a right to be present in the same room and to see the witness during the deposition, and this also applies to the victim of alleged sexual assaults, including those involving minor children. Prohibiting the defendant from being present and observing the witness may be a violation of his right to confront the witness under the Confrontation Clause of the Sixth Amendment.

Unlike a discovery deposition in civil cases, a deposition in a criminal case is usually considered a trial deposition. This means that any objections should be made at the appropriate time, on the record. In an effort to streamline the proceedings, some attorneys rely on "continuing objections" rather than stating the same objection every time it is warranted. While it indeed may save time, not to mention wear and tear on the participants, continuing objections can be problematic. Some courts take the position that a party must state any objection separately each time they wish to make it and that simply relying on a "continuing objection" to the same manner of inquiry acts as a waiver of any further similar objections if they are not specifically articulated each time.[6] Therefore, though tedious, it is best to make a separate objection each time it is warranted and not request a continuing objection.

The scope and manner of the examination and cross-examination are such as would be allowed in the trial itself. The deposition may be used for any purpose that live testimony would be, either at trial or any other hearing. It may be read into the record and used as substantive testimony in the event the witness is unavailable at trial or for impeachment purposes if the witness testifies at trial in a manner inconsistent with the deposition testimony.

2. Expert Witnesses

Occasionally, a situation may arise where you need the testimony of an expert in a particular field. Experts can be wonderful and

---

[6] A continuing objection is simply when an attorney objects by saying, "Same objection," when referring to a previously articulated objection. The attorney may also add, "I request a continuing objection on this question." You should then object, and insist that he make a new objection each time he feels it is necessary.

exasperating at the same time. They are usually quite busy and difficult to pin down for interviews, not to mention trial appearances. Yet, in the right case the effort must be made, for the payoff can be significant.

A good rule of thumb is to obtain the very best expert you can afford. This is one area of trial practice where you obtain the justice that you pay for. The better the expert, the more credible—and less impeachable—his testimony. Ideally, the best possible expert is the person who literally "wrote the book" on the particular subject in question.[7] These experts are usually very difficult to secure and quite expensive. But in the right case, it could make all the difference.

If you have determined that you need experts to testify at trial, schedule a time to meet and interview them as early in the case as possible. This will help both of you to determine what facts are crucial to develop in the discovery and subsequent testimony, and which can be disregarded. Bring along any evidence you wish the expert to review (or better yet, provide such evidence to the witness before the meeting), and question him regarding any additional evidence or exhibits that would be more helpful to explain his opinions at trial. Be sure to provide him with all documents and materials relevant to the case, especially those on which the prosecutor intends to rely. Work with the expert on neutralizing any such evidence. Once the expert's opinions are clarified, meet with him again prior to trial once the exhibits are completed in order to finalize his presentation and correct any last-minute errors. Arrange for the expert to examine your demonstrative exhibits or models to ensure their accuracy and become familiar with them, especially if the witness intends to use them during testimony.

One additional thought about experts: Never miss an opportunity to find out early what your opponent's expert is going to say. If the state has designated an expert, you have an obligation, if not a right to seek to investigate what that expert's anticipated testimony is

[7] The great trial lawyers commonly utilize this technique. They will identify the leading treatise in the world on the particular subject and then retain its author as their expert. Many times, your opponent's expert may have studied or relied on that very treatise as the basis for his opinions. Watching the hapless expert writhing in discomfort as he is destroyed by the author of the very work he relied on is a scene to behold. This is the stuff of great courtroom drama.

going to be.[8] Sometimes the prosecutor will simply tell you. If not, a very effective method is to simply call up the expert, identify yourself, and ask if he would agree to arrange a time to meet briefly with you at his convenience and review his testimony. There is nothing unethical about that. The prosecutor does not represent that expert. It is up to the expert whether or not to meet with you.

Occasionally, the expert will not agree to a meeting unless the prosecutor has consented. In that case, call the prosecutor and offer to set up a meeting *with counsel present* to informally interview their expert. Quite often, the prosecutor is startled to learn that the testimony is not as strong as she had hoped, thus paving the way for an opportunity to settle the case prior to trial. You have absolutely nothing to lose. The worst that can happen is that the prosecutor does not consent to the interview, in which case you are in no worse position. Moreover, you can now cross-examine the expert at trial regarding his refusal to meet with you without the prosecutor's approval.[9]

Experts are not necessarily always retained; quite often they are nonretained. These experts include law enforcement officers, doctors and nurses who treated your client or the witnesses at the hospital, ambulance attendants, and first responders. While such witnesses ordinarily testify only as to treatment rendered and conditions and behavior observed, as opposed to offering opinions as to causation, they can be permitted to offer opinion testimony on the ultimate issue of fact as long as the proper foundation is laid for their testimony.

Regardless of whether the expert is retained or nonretained, if she is being called to offer her opinion as to the ultimate question of fact, it is imperative that you cross-examine her as to the *assumptions* she made in forming her opinions. It is not unusual for an expert witness

---

[8] The disclosure of expert witnesses and their anticipated testimony is vastly more extensive in civil cases than in criminal. Contrary to the civil rules, a party in a criminal case enjoys no general federal or state constitutional right to discovery, nor does any statute or court rule entitle him to such. Nevertheless, you should still seek to discover it, if possible.

[9] *See* Chapter 8(A), "From the State." Note, however, that some states may *not* permit the defense to discover reports, memoranda, or other internal state documents made by the attorney for the state or other state agents in connection with the investigation.

to base professional opinions on assumptions that are incorrect or even nonexistent, thus rendering her opinions invalid. Probe thoroughly in your examination. An expert whose opinions are suspect due to the invalidity of his foundations should be made the subject of a *Daubert* pretrial motion to prohibit him from testifying at trial. In some jurisdictions, however, the discovery rules may not require the parties to disclose the expert's opinions, thus making it impossible to determine whether you need to file a *Daubert* motion.[10] When you don't know what the state's expert is going to say, file a demand for disclosure since you have a right to know what it is.

E. Evidence

Again, meeting with your trial team after the District Court arraignment will enable you to start orienting yourself as to what types of evidence you will need to establish your case. As early as possible, arrange to meet your investigator at the law enforcement agency and review the evidence in the locker. Become familiar with it, so that you can form questions and develop answers much in the same way that the jurors will. It will also help you to determine whether you will need to utilize demonstrative exhibits or retain expert witnesses. Arrange to visit the scene of the crime, especially during the same time of day that the incident occurred. Nothing will ever substitute for your having visited the scene. It will enable you to thoroughly understand what occurred, so that you can competently explain it to the jury as you tell the story. It will also help you form the questions you will ask the witnesses when they testify on the stand.

This is also the time to begin focusing on what investigation may be required. Witnesses may need to be located and interviewed, documents may need to be tracked down and copied, and photographs and other evidence may need to be obtained.[11]

---

[10] Daubert v. Merrell Dow Pharmaceuticals, Inc., 509 U.S. 579, 113 S.Ct. 2786, 125 L.Ed.2d 469 (1993).

[11] As stated earlier, in some cases it may be necessary to preserve the testimony of a witness through a deposition. In a child sexual assault case, the prosecution may wish to preserve the trial testimony of the victim through a video deposition that would then be played at trial.

1. DNA Evidence

Juries have become very accustomed to the introduction of DNA evidence in criminal prosecutions.[12] Despite the fact that DNA evidence has been with us in the courtroom for some thirty years or more, it is remarkable that many prosecutors and even crime lab technicians and other so-called experts display little knowledge or understanding of it. It is not unusual to encounter a prosecutor who believes that if DNA evidence has been obtained in a case, it therefore must conclusively implicate your client, regardless of whether it in fact does not. This can be a difficult bias to overcome with both the prosecutor and the jury.

The simple fact is that DNA evidence can be tremendously powerful evidence as long as it is obtained, tested, and understood properly. It has freed many who have languished on Death Row, and it has likewise condemned those who otherwise would have escaped justice. But like any other form of potentially damaging evidence, the well-trained defense attorney can neutralize its effects with the right preparation.[13]

Like a fingerprint, a DNA sample must be introduced through witnesses who are specially trained in its properties, as well as the correct methods of recovering it from a crime scene and later analyzing it. Once a proper foundation is established by the witnesses, the court then determines its admissibility. Conversely, problems with the foundation can scuttle efforts to introduce it. That's where we come in.

---

12 So much so that in cases that do not involve DNA evidence, prosecutors are well advised to deal with its absence in their voir dire.

13 I know next to nothing about DNA. I do know that it is an acronym for deoxyribonucleic acid, which is an amino acid found in human cells. It contains certain chemical properties and characteristics which, when properly analyzed, act as a type of genetic "fingerprint" unique to each one of us. Humans can transfer their DNA into the open environment in a number of ways, which allow it to be discovered and collected as evidence. DNA is located in blood, saliva, sweat, urine, semen, hair, skin, bone, teeth and fingernails, to name a few examples. As a result, DNA can be discovered in most any location where any of these substances may be found. Essentially, anything we touch with our bodies or bodily fluids has the potential of retaining our DNA, thus leaving it for others to discover and collect. There. I've just told you everything I know about DNA.

The good news is that the methods and protocols for properly locating, collecting, transporting, storing, testing, and analyzing DNA are so critical that any variation, no matter how slight, has the potential of skewing, if not completely invalidating, the results. Even better news is that a surprising number of police officers, detectives, and crime lab analysts get it wrong because they are not trained consistently and thoroughly. Unfortunately, the bad news is that many defense lawyers are in the same boat.

But we need not worry, for the key to neutralizing DNA evidence lies not so much in our understanding of it but in our ability to seek out those who do. When you have a case that contains DNA evidence and its presence and/or reliability is contested, you should immediately secure the services of a reputable and credible expert. Ideally, if you have the resources, you should retain the "world" or "national" expert. If not, then a few telephone calls to the nearest metropolitan university or medical school should be able to route you to the person you need.[14]

Avoid the "Plan B" approach: doing it yourself. By reading some journal articles and a treatise or two on the subject, you may be able to gather a rudimentary knowledge of DNA sufficient to sustain you through a passing conversation with a microbiologist at a cocktail party, but that's not good enough. You must make an effort to become a "quasi-expert" on the subject.

Even if all you are able to do is talk with an expert over the phone, ask for advice on how and where to most effectively attack the state's evidence. If you are attacking the state's DNA evidence on the grounds that it wasn't obtained or tested properly, you simply have to know what you're talking about. A hallmark of a great fighter is knowing when not to step into the ring. We should never be reluctant to set our egos aside. We're usually not nearly as smart as we think we are.

---

[14] There are many "experts" who advertise in national magazines, but be careful. They may look good and have a slick, professional-appearing advertisement, but the proof is in the pudding. Ask for references and follow them up. If they balk, hang up. One of the best ways to locate a good expert is by word of mouth. Talk to other lawyers who have used one.

Obtaining *all* of the state's documentation regarding the DNA evidence is critical.[15] The more information you are able to funnel to your expert, the better. Once your expert has all the necessary data, work with her to clearly identify what is wrong with the state's analysis and discuss creative ways to effectively demonstrate it to the jury so that they will get it.

2. Demonstrative Evidence

The art of telling a great story often depends on the quality of the "special effects." Just ask Steven Spielberg or George Lucas. In the appropriate case, a well-thought-out piece of demonstrative evidence can make the difference in the verdict. As early as possible, brainstorm with your team in order to get a feel for what the most effective presentation will require.

A good point of reference is to ask yourself what it is you have to prove and what the best way would be to dramatically demonstrate it for the jury. Once you have chosen the appropriate presentation or model, seek the best professional possible to help create it. Again, this is not an area to skimp on. Spend the money to obtain the best exhibit possible.[16] Make it as accurate and as detailed as possible.

---

[15] This includes the raw analytical data from the technicians and their notes, and the results of all tests performed, regardless of the results. Don't forget that one of the most valuable sources of information is the testimony of the officers(s) at the preliminary hearing, as to how the samples were collected at the crime scene.

[16] One of the mantras of a great trial lawyer is "you are limited only by your imagination." Some truly innovative and effective demonstrative exhibits I have seen include (a) a scale model section of a state highway approximately 5 feet long, including a model car and truck in a wrongful death case; (b) a scale model, approximately 3' x 3', of a Caterpillar-tracked back hoe scraping away rock in a quarry next to a "hanging wall" of rock that collapsed upon it (it actually "collapsed" in the model!); (c) a scale model of a high school gymnasium, approximately 4' x 2', complete with parquet floor and floor markings, including figures representing some 20+ wrestlers present during a practice in which the coach purportedly assaulted one of them; (d) the actual automobile involved in a drug possession case that was cut into sections and then reassembled in front of the jury box in the middle of the courtroom, to demonstrate what the arresting officer could *not* have seen at the time he stopped the defendant; and (e) a full-scale re-creation of a room in which a murder took place.

Sometimes a simple presentation can be just as effective. One of the greatest closing arguments I ever saw was given by the attorney representing a female prison inmate charged with killing a correctional officer after he raped her in her

Generally speaking, bigger is better. Such exhibits often take considerable time to prepare. The earlier you commit to them the better. If you decide to introduce it into evidence, see if you can get the prosecutor to stipulate to its admissibility.

One of the great things about professionally constructed models is that they frequently capture the attention of the court. People love to play with models, and judges are no different. If they become fascinated with a particular exhibit you wish to introduce into evidence, the fact that they are taken with it will contribute greatly toward the likelihood of its admission.

F. Plea Negotiations and Agreements

In the criminal justice system, plea agreements are the grease that keeps the machine rolling. There are far too many cases to actually try. Over 90% are resolved through a plea agreement. Therefore, we must become adept at negotiation.

One must always negotiate from a position of strength. As the defense attorney, you rarely know the strength of your case until well into the case. That is the primary reason that you should avoid engaging in settlement discussions with the prosecutor early on. You need time to work with your client, investigate the facts, interview witnesses, visit the scene, talk to experts (if necessary), and so on. This will prevent you from giving away the farm when you sit down at the bargaining table.

To be sure, there will be times when you may want to approach the prosecutor either immediately after the filing of charges or at the conclusion of the preliminary hearing and propose a plea deal. Be careful of making this move. At this point in the case, you know very little, if anything, about your client's case. While in many instances the state's case may appear formidable, remember that it is assembled with the intent to survive solely upon a finding of probable cause at the preliminary hearing. Quite often the prosecutor knows little more about his case than you do. There may very well be a viable defense lurking within those facts. Unless you are thoroughly familiar with

---

cell. The attorney simply used masking tape to re-create the dimensions of the tiny cell on the floor of the courtroom in front of the jury box and gave her entire closing argument while standing in the square. Her theme was "Who was in control?"

the defendant's criminal history, certain of the facts on both sides of the case, and know what your client seeks as a result of the case, avoid striking a deal too soon.

On the other hand, the prosecutor may approach you early on with a plea proposal. While you still may know very little about your client's case, this is a situation where it may be to your client's advantage to consider a plea agreement, particularly if it is a significant offer. You should still be cautious, however, and review the facts of the case with your client very carefully to determine whether a viable defense exists. If such a defense appears unlikely, and if your client is interested in negotiating a plea agreement, then there certainly is no harm in engaging in such discussions.

Barring these exceptions, however, the general rule is that once you have a clear understanding of the strengths and weaknesses of your case, meet with your client and have a frank discussion about what options exist for her. Be honest with the client about what you believe the state can prove, and what your defense is. Discuss the possibility of her testifying or not testifying, and what the jury's likely reaction will be either way. After reviewing the case, ask your client how she would like to resolve the case. Does she want to go to trial, or is she interested in negotiating a plea agreement? If she wishes to go to trial, and you have been honest with her about all possible results, then you are simply committed to going to trial. You then must switch to "combat mode," get your game face on, and load your guns.

If, however, your client wants you to negotiate a plea agreement, then you must find out the limits she is willing to accept. It is critical that you and your client have a crystal clear understanding of her "bottom line." There can be no ambiguity about it. You can accept no offer from the state on your client's behalf unless and until you first fully advise your client of it and obtain her consent. To consent to or accept a plea offer without your client's consent, or to make offers to the state without your client's authority or consent, is malpractice. It is a serious breach of your fiduciary duty to your client and can result in professional disciplinary action. *Don't do it.*[17]

---

[17] You must convey to your client every plea offer made by the prosecutor, even those you believe your client would never agree to, and you must likewise convey the client's response to the prosecutor. Be sure to preserve in writing what each offer and client response is.

Try and craft a resolution to the case that results in something a bit better than your client's "bottom line." In that context, as stated earlier, try to "underpromise" and "overdeliver." It makes you look like a hero in your client's eyes.

For example, assume your client tells you that his bottom line is "X," and he gives you no authority to go beyond that. In your negotiations, if the prosecutor asks you what your "bottom line" is, respond by saying you have no authority to go beyond "W." The prosecutor does not need to know that is not your client's real bottom line. Thus, if you settle it, you may then return to your client and happily report that you obtained a better result than he hoped for. And if the prosecutor will not accept "W," then you at least know you have the wiggle room to offer "X" if you must.[18]

Once a plea agreement is reached, it should be reduced to writing (at least in District Court). A plea agreement is a contract. All parties must sign it. Make sure that the agreement contains every material element agreed upon. Your office may have forms available, as well as other prior agreements to use as templates. In most cases, however, the prosecuting attorney will draft the agreement. Be aware of what current caselaw requires regarding certain elements and provisions, and how they are to be interpreted.

Never assume that the state has been advised of, or agrees with, any particular provision. There are no "unwritten understandings" or "gentlemen's agreements" in a plea agreement. As far as the court is concerned, if any term or condition is not expressly articulated, it does not exist. Be sure that the version of the agreement that the state has signed and has submitted to you for approval is in fact the plea agreement that you approved and intend to enter. It is not unheard of for a prosecutor to later claim that he was misled as to certain terms and conditions of a plea agreement long after it has been signed and filed with the court. It is therefore a good idea to review the plea agreement carefully after the state has signed it, and before your client signs it and it is filed with the court, to ensure that it is the exact plea agreement that you intended.

---

[18] It goes without saying, obviously, that the prosecutor is almost certainly employing the same tactics.

G. The Proffer and Proffer Letter

The plea negotiation process may also include a "proffer." This is a request by the prosecuting attorney for your client to meet with certain state agents and be interviewed regarding your client's involvement in criminal activity involving other persons. Proffers are frequently used in federal (and in some state) drug investigations as a means of obtaining evidence against co-conspirators, particularly those higher up the ladder. Under the right circumstances, it is not only a tremendously effective tool for the prosecutors, but it can also present an opportunity for your client to significantly improve his or her situation.

A proffer is typically initiated when the prosecuting attorney issues a "proffer letter" to your client, inviting her to meet with government agents in an informal setting and be interviewed regarding her criminal involvement with others.[19] Following is a typical example:

April 20, 2020

Defendant's Attorney

Public Defender's Office

Re: State v. Defendant

PROFFER LETTER

Dear Ms. Attorney:

The State of _________ is interested in pursuing a proffer with your client, __________, regarding his knowledge of drug trafficking and other crimes as a step towards identifying a mutually acceptable resolution of the criminal charges pending against your client. If your client is interested in engaging in such a proffer with the State of _________ and its agents, the following terms and conditions will apply:

First, the purpose of the proffer is to give your client a one-time opportunity to provide to the State of _________ a complete and

[19] A proffer letter should never be confused with a "target letter." A proffer letter simply affords your client an opportunity to better his position through a truthful, informal off-the-record interview. A target letter, on the other hand, notifies your client that she is in the cross-hairs of a grand jury investigation and that she may be indicted on criminal charges as a result.

truthful account of your client's involvement, including the involvement of all others of whom your client has any knowledge whatsoever, in the crimes which are the subject of the State's investigation. The information supplied by your client will be evaluated by the State in connection with its consideration of an appropriate resolution of this case. However, your client understands and agrees that the State has made no promises regarding the nature of an appropriate resolution, and the State is not obligated to enter into any agreement whatsoever with your client concerning a potential plea agreement, future sentencing recommendation, or otherwise.

Second, it is absolutely crucial that your client be completely truthful in every respect, with no material misstatements or omissions of fact. Otherwise, the chances of receiving a favorable plea agreement or favorable future sentencing recommendation from the State will be seriously diminished, if not lost altogether. Further, any plea offer or offer of leniency will be expressly conditioned upon your client having proffered truthful information without material omissions. The determination of what constitutes a "material omission" is within the sole discretion of the State. If it is determined that your client has been untruthful or has omitted information material to the prosecution or investigation of this matter, your client will have breached this agreement.

[NOTE: Every proffer letter will differ by jurisdiction. Some may include language detailing what the ramifications of a breach are. It may entitle the State to make full use of such proffered statement and rescind the protection provided for under this agreement. DO NOT AGREE TO SUCH A CONDITION. The prosecutor cannot unilaterally make full use of your client's statement and rescind the protection originally agreed to.]

Third, for purposes of the proffered information only, the State shall provide your client with direct use immunity subject to the limitations and conditions described below. No statements made by your client during the proffer will be used in the State of ____________'s case-in-chief against your client in a criminal case, except for crimes of violence which may be disclosed by your client during the course of the proffer. The definition of "crime of violence" is left to the sole discretion of the State.

[NOTE: Again, there may be language that threatens to use statements made by your client in any prosecution for making false statements, obstruction of justice, or perjury based on acts committed or statements made during or after the proffer. DO NOT

AGREE TO SUCH A CONDITION. The prosecutor cannot unilaterally make full use of your client's statement and rescind the protection originally agreed to.]

Fourth, if your client testifies under oath as a witness in any proceeding, including a trial, and offers testimony materially different from any statements or other information provided during the proffer, the State of ______________ may cross-examine your client concerning any such statements or information provided during the proffer. In addition, in the event your client were to represent to the court or to the probation office, by means of oral or written representation, cross-examination, or otherwise, facts which are materially different from any statements made or other information provided during the proffer, the State may present as rebuttal evidence any such statements or information from the proffer.

Fifth, the State of ______________ may make derivative use of your client's proffered statements or information. Thus, this proffer agreement does not extend to your client full transactional immunity under the Fifth Amendment in connection with the statements or other information provided during the proffer. You and your client agree that, by giving a proffer under the terms of this agreement, your client is not entitled to a *Kastigar* hearing at which the State would be required to prove that all of the evidence it would introduce at any criminal trial in which your client is a defendant is not in any way directly or derivatively tainted by the statements or information provided by your client during the proffer. See *Kastigar v. United States*, 406 U.S. 441 (1972).

Sixth, this agreement applies only to the statements or information provided by your client during the course of the proffer. This agreement does not limit the State's use of any physical evidence, statements, or other information obtained from your client outside of the proffer.

[NOTE: Finally, there may be language regarding the confidentiality of the agreement included, requiring that your client shall not permit or authorize any person, including attorneys, to disclose the content of the proffer interview to any non-government representative without the express prior written approval of the prosecutor. Further, that any violation of the confidentiality of the proffer interview will make further cooperation with state law enforcement officials impossible; will permit the State, at its discretion, to void the proffer agreement; and will permit the State to use statements made by your client in any prosecution based on

the acts described during the proffer. DO NOT AGREE TO SUCH A CONDITION. This condition is likely unethical.]

Finally, your client understands and agrees that this document constitutes the full and complete agreement between your client and the State of ____________.

If your client wishes to engage in a proffer under these ground rules, you and your client must sign this letter where indicated below. Once signed, please return the original to me and retain a copy for your files.

Sincerely,

Prosecuting Attorney

APPROVED: ___________________________ DATE: ___________

Defendant

___________________________ DATE: ___________

Attorney for Defendant

As can be seen in the example above, the terms and conditions of the proffer are detailed and specific. They are also non-negotiable for the most part. Essentially, the prosecutor retains total control and discretion over whether to offer your client any favorable consideration in a plea agreement, and to what extent. Moreover, the prosecutor will not agree to act upon any disposition unless and until your client has first fully complied in all respects to the agreement. That may mean including agreeing to testify against other defendants if they decide to go to trial. This ensures that the prosecutor gets what he paid for, and your client doesn't "game the system" by agreeing to do something she later refuses to follow through on. Your client also wins by not having anything she tells the agents used against her (conditionally).

The atmosphere of a proffer is relaxed and informal and is usually held in a conference room or other location in the prosecutor's office. The prosecutor is there, along with one or more law enforcement agents who are working on the case. There is no court reporter; the client is not "testifying" under oath. There is no judge. You are there with your client. The prosecutor will present an original copy of the proffer letter to you and your client and will then go through its terms and conditions in detail with you. You and your client will then sign it (if you haven't previously done so). If you need to re-negotiate certain terms and conditions of the proffer, do not wait until the day of the proffer to do it. Have all terms and conditions hammered out and agreed upon ahead of time.

The interview is typically conducted like a discovery deposition in that the prosecutor and/or the agents will question your client. Your client may take a break whenever she wishes for whatever reason; she may consult with you, use the restroom, etc. The only requirement is that she must tell the absolute truth.

Your client may naturally be reluctant to be completely forthcoming. However, the "ace in the hole" that the prosecutor retains is that neither you nor your client fully knows what the state's agents know. They almost always know much more than your client believes they do. In other words, they will know when your client is lying. Therefore, it is in your client's best interest to reveal as much as she can for a couple of reasons: First, the more truthful she is, the more trustworthy (and thus more valuable) her information is; second, the agents will be supportive of the prosecutor's desire to offer a favorable deal; and third, the better the information, the better the deal.

If, during the interview, the agents accuse your client of withholding truthful information, that is usually a good time to take a break. Meet with your client privately and "encourage" her to be honest. She has nothing to lose. If she refuses, or if she has decided she no longer wants to cooperate with the agents, then for all intents and purposes the interview is over and the case proceeds against her. Since proffers are usually a "one-time" deal, that will most likely scuttle any future worthwhile plea negotiations.

For obvious reasons, you should only consider a proffer if it is in the best interests of your client. A proffer will not always be offered, but in the right case, it could make a huge difference in your client's life.

H. The Pretrial Memorandum

Shortly before trial, the court will require that the parties submit their pretrial memoranda. This will help the court determine the length and complexity of trial for docketing purposes. It is also a good way to determine whether the state is willing to stipulate to the introduction of any facts, so as to streamline the presentation of evidence.

It is easy to fall into the trap of waiting until you prepare and file your pretrial memo before reviewing and preparing your case for trial. That is malpractice. If you wait until then to review your case, it is too late to give full consideration to all of the factors in play. You have no time to utilize your imagination—and that of your team—to be creative where it counts. Moreover, you now have no time to solve substantive problems. You should start preparing the elements of your pretrial memorandum no later than following the District Court arraignment. That way, when the filing deadline approaches, all you need to do is plug in all the information.

Be sure to list all witnesses, even those who may not be testifying. The dynamics of a trial can change unexpectedly at a moment's notice, and you may find yourself having to call a witness you did not anticipate. If you have not listed the witness, the court may not allow you to call her to the stand.

You should distinguish between witnesses that are "will call" and "may call." The "will call" witnesses are those whom you are certain will be called to testify, and you are representing to the court and counsel that you will produce them. Those witnesses that are "may call" are those who might testify, but there is a possibility they might not. Therefore, you are putting the parties and the court on notice that you are not guaranteeing their appearance. The purpose for doing this is to provide the court and opposing counsel with a rough idea as to how many witnesses are likely to testify at trial. The state often does the same. That way, if, on the one hand, you need to call witnesses that the state has listed as a "will call," it means that they will appear at trial, and you do not have to subpoena them separately. On the other hand, if such witnesses are listed as a "may call," you would need to serve them with a subpoena to secure their appearance. In the event that the state has not specified which witnesses are "will call" or "may call," assume that they are all "may call," and subpoena those whom you wish to appear.

The same holds true for evidence. List all evidence, even items you may not intend to use, for precisely the same reason. With respect to demonstrative evidence, you should list and identify any such items, with the understanding that you should notify the court as to whether opposing counsel will have any objections prior to trial.

List all jury instructions you wish the court to consider at trial.[20] If there are any instructions which you feel are particularly troublesome, or if you wish to submit instructions that you have tailored specifically for the case that you want the court to consider (other than stock instructions), submit them with sufficient identification so that the court understands what it is you intend to do. Make sure that you also submit tailored instructions regarding your client's defense(s) that he intends to introduce. These are typically the "theory of the defense" instructions, and you have a right to submit them.

Identify a section of the memo to address any miscellaneous issues that may be of interest to the court prior to trial. For example, if you have particular witness issues, intend to file any pretrial motions, or wish to solicit any stipulations from opposing counsel, you should extend the courtesy of notifying the court so that arrangements can be made to schedule such motions for hearing.

Finally, any pretrial motions should be filed simultaneously with the pretrial memo and identified specifically therein. That way the court can review and prepare all of them to be considered at the same hearing rather than be caught unprepared if you file one late.

I. Briefs, Motions, and Deadlines

> *"Whoever knows he is deep, strives for clarity; whoever would like to appear deep to the crowd, strives for obscurity. For the crowd considers anything deep only if it cannot see to the bottom: the crowd is so timid and afraid of going into the water."*
>
> —Friedrich Nietzsche

[20] It is a good idea to submit two sets, one with references and one "clean" set ready for submission to the court at the instruction conference. Include all instructions you believe you might need, including any relating to lesser-included charges. They can simply be discarded if not needed. This will save time when the court prepares the instruction packet for the jury.

> *The difference between the right word and almost the right word is the difference between "lightning" and "lightning bug."*
>
> —Mark Twain

A good deal of your credibility is derived from the quality of your work product—the documents you draft. Considering the time, effort, and money you have invested in your legal education, there is simply no excuse for your written work product to be less than perfect. While it seems to be a symptom of modern culture that proper grammar and spelling skills have gone the way of the steam locomotive and butter churn, you are an officer of the court, and your ability to communicate with others, particularly the court, is your stock in trade.

Everything you file will be read and reviewed by your peers, notably, other counsel, partners, associates, supervisors, judges, appellate judges, perhaps even the Circuit Court of Appeals or the United States Supreme Court. No matter how good you are in the courtroom or how smart you are, your reputation as a professional can be completely unraveled with a badly composed pleading. Judges will talk about it with other judges and with counsel. Your pleadings will be discounted and will not be given the credit and respect they deserve. Your ability to win legal arguments will diminish. Your credibility will suffer.

This does not mean that you should write in complicated or flowery "legalese." Quite the contrary.[21] The hallmark of the greatest writers is their ability to convey their meaning in simple, clear, and concise language. Consider the story about Ernest Hemingway. It is popularly believed (though never proven), that during the height of

---

[21] We've all been guilty of it at one time or another. There are few things courts detest more than reading a pleading that is bloated with repetitive arguments and phrases, pretentious Latin terms, double-spaced footnotes longer than the text on the same page, citations listing ten different cases when one would do (all from far-flung inapplicable jurisdictions), not to mention misspellings and improper grammar, in an effort to make the writer appear "scholarly." Unfortunately, that is not the word that immediately comes to mind for most courts. Courts do not have time to slog through reams of densely packed, self-serving gratuitous argot. It is therefore to your advantage to write clearly, simply, and sparingly. Make your point and move on.

his career, Hemingway decided to enter a national writing contest. The terms of the contest were simple: whoever wrote the most meaningful story using the fewest words would be the winner. Hemingway's entry? "*For Sale: Baby Shoes. Never Worn.*" The entire story consisted of just six words. He won. Consider for a moment the extraordinary thought process that went into that entry, and you will understand how difficult it is to write well.

The point is this: invest the time and effort into your work to make it worthwhile. If you are uncertain about how to spell a word, look it up. Don't rely on the word processor to do it for you. Uncertain about paragraph structure or grammatical composition? Look it up.[22] As often as possible, review every document you and your legal assistant generate. Your assistant may be a world-class grammarian and winner of the National Spelling Bee at age 9, but it's your name on the work product, and you are responsible for its quality. It reflects your professional ability and it is worth the effort.

Be honest and thorough in your legal research. We are all pressed for time, and none of us have the time to draft even the most elementary pleadings, let alone spending hours on Westlaw. However, your reputation is on the line. When citing case authority for your position, take the time to actually read the cases in their entirety. Do not fall into the trap of citing only the headnotes listed in the digests. While they may appear to be supportive on their face, they may be wrong. Remember, those headnotes are drafted by staffers who may or may not have a legal background. Their job is to pore through countless Appellate Court opinions and summarize the relevant points of law. Sometimes they get it right, and sometimes they don't. There are few things more embarrassing for a lawyer than to stand before the court and self-righteously base his entire argument on a particular holding in a case he saw in a headnote (but didn't bother to actually read) and have his opponent quote extensively from the text of the opinion itself which in fact holds against you, while he's handing a copy of the case to the judge.[23]

---

22 One of the best books you will ever use is *Elements of Style* by William Strunk and E. B. White. It is just a little slip of a paperback, and it has been a classic best-seller since 1919.

23 Usually accompanied by the biggest shit-eating grin you ever saw.

In cases that are legally complex or present novel issues requiring extensive research, an effective tactic is to address every significant case cited by your opponent and digest each of them, one at a time, showing the court that the cases do not support the point your opponent believes they do. This tactic can be demoralizing if done well, for it demonstrates that you researched the opponent's cases more carefully than he did; thus, it enhances your credibility, not to mention your chances of winning your argument.

As stated above, pretrial motions and briefs should be filed contemporaneously with the pretrial memo, even if the court has specifically set separate deadlines. You should only file a motion later than the pretrial memo if it pertains to an issue that you did not anticipate earlier. Set aside sufficient time to draft all motions, so that you do not have to slap them together at the last minute and request a continuance of the filing deadline from the court. Courts do not look favorably upon the counsel who is constantly seeking continuances. It sends the court the message that he is not prepared. The great trial lawyer is always prepared.

1. Motions *in Limine*

In preparing your pretrial memo and accompanying motions, consider whether you wish to move to limit any evidence the state will likely seek to submit at trial. There is almost always something that the prosecutor is trying to insert into the case that shouldn't be admitted. Motions *in limine* are typically based on objections that the evidence is being submitted for an improper purpose, such as improper 404(b) evidence, hearsay, relevance, undue prejudice, work product, and attorney–client privilege.

A motion *in limine* is a very useful, powerful tool in the defense arsenal. Consideration for its use should be applied to all of the state's evidence prior to trial. Never assume that it is admissible or that the prosecutor knows how to get it admitted. It is surprising how much of it is often held to be inadmissible.

2. Rule 404(b) Motions and Motions to Suppress Evidence

It is common for the defense to file pretrial motions to suppress evidence based on lack of probable cause for a search, and it is also usual for the state to file motions to admit collateral evidence pursuant to rule 404(b). Such motions are easily anticipated, and the nature of the evidence in your case will inform you as to whether such a motion is likely or needs to be filed. When you receive a motion from the state, address it promptly. Do not delay it to the point where you must ask the court for a continuance. As with any motion you file, prepare it carefully and professionally. Cite relevant caselaw and other legal authority clearly and accurately. Courts appreciate a well-researched and well-written motion and accompanying brief. It is another opportunity for you to "look good."

It is also a good idea to take some time prior to trial and think of any evidentiary issues that might crop up. Prepare a well-researched trial memorandum on each one, and have it ready to hand to the judge if the need arises. Courts appreciate that kind of preparation, and it makes you "look good."

Whether responding to the state's motion or advancing your own, it goes without saying that you must be completely familiar with all of the facts of the case prior to the hearing. It is easy to get into the habit of "winging" an evidentiary hearing. You may be pressed for time, and the judge has set aside a limited time for the hearing and he is irritated that you are late. Or the witness is late and did not appear to review the case with you ahead of time. This is a recipe for disaster.

A motion to suppress evidence based on an illegal search is often filed where there is a search warrant, a warrantless search incident to arrest, or a highway traffic stop (a *Terry*-type stop).[24] In cases where there is a video tape of the search or the traffic stop, the tape will frequently contain audio or visual evidence of the basis of the search (the "totality of the circumstances") upon which the state is relying to support the search and seizure of evidence. These tapes frequently contain evidence that either refutes or mitigates such evidence. They are therefore a gold mine of information to the defense and must be reviewed completely and carefully prior to drafting your motion to suppress. Your failure to demand and review such evidence prior to filing your motion or attending a hearing on the motion (or, God forbid, appearing at trial) is malpractice.

Although you are free to call your client to testify at a suppression hearing, as a practical matter you should not do so unless you

---

[24] Terry v. Ohio, 392 U.S. 1; 88 S.Ct. 1868; 20 L.Ed.2d 889 (1968).

have no choice. Ordinarily, anything the defendant testifies to at the hearing cannot be used against him at a later trial for purposes other than impeachment with his hearing testimony if he testifies at trial differently than he did at the hearing.[25] Moreover, why give the state any opportunity to cross-examine your client under oath before trial? Since there is no issue regarding the defendant's guilt or innocence at the suppression hearing, your client's version of the events is not necessary or relevant at that point. The state's sole burden is to prove that the evidence was seized lawfully, and thus the only version of the events that the court will consider is the evidence produced by the state. You should also obtain a transcript of the testimony in order to prepare your cross-examination of the officers at trial and hold them to their sworn testimony. Order the transcript from the court reporter before leaving the courtroom.

J. Working with the Prosecuting Attorney

Just because you are adversaries in the courtroom does not mean that you and the prosecuting attorney should not get along with each other. Part of your credibility depends on the nature and quality of your relationship with opposing counsel. Your adversaries are not "the enemy," "the bad guys," or "the black hats." To be sure, they are your opponents, but they are also your colleagues, and they are at least as smart and talented as you may believe you are, and in some cases, even more so.

Never give your opponent any opportunity to legitimately criticize you about anything. By that I mean you should always be kind and respectful, willing to listen, reasonable in your responses, and utterly trustworthy in your assurances. Deliver on your promises and admit to your mistakes. Fight hard but fair. Be prepared to extend a helping hand when the situation calls for it. You may need the favor returned someday, perhaps sooner than you expect.

Having said this, there may be times when you are confronted with a prosecuting attorney who plays fast and loose with the rules of ethics, evidence, and criminal procedure. This can present a genuine

---

[25] *See* Simmons v. United States, 390 U.S. 377, 394 (1968); United States v. Hardwell, 80 F.3d 1471 (10th Cir. 1996).

challenge to you, for as the defense attorney you must be on your guard at every moment. You must be able to object in a timely way to any questionable conduct and make your record. More often than not, the area that seems to generate most concern is discovery abuses.

For reasons I have never understood, some prosecutors believe that it is acceptable to withhold exculpatory evidence or to wait until the eve of trial to release a truckload of discovery material to you. If exculpatory material is withheld, you may not know it until after the trial and your client has been convicted. Then you must address the problem in postconviction motions. On the other hand, late submission of discovery can provide an opportunity for you to take advantage of the prosecutor at trial.

Some defense attorneys may panic upon receiving late discovery, realizing that there is no way to properly review and prepare for that evidence in time for trial. Accordingly, they might seek a continuance of the trial in order to buy some time. That is a mistake. The state is required to produce discovery timely and completely prior to trial. Delinquent discovery is a violation of the rules of criminal procedure and is likely a violation of the court's Pretrial Order, if there is one. If you receive a substantial amount of discovery at the last minute or discovery that is significant in its nature, regardless of the volume, it prevents you from adequately preparing for it in time for trial, especially if it will require you to interview additional witnesses, retain other experts, or prepare other evidence to rebut it. It therefore prejudices your client in that it precludes you from acting in your full capacity as effective counsel, thus depriving your client of his Sixth Amendment rights.

While continuing the trial date would certainly relieve the pressure by buying you more time to prepare, it does not properly address the prosecutor's underlying material professional misconduct. It is not insignificant, and appropriate sanctions are available.

The problem you face is not simply carving out enough time for you to prepare your case. You must also punish the state for its misbehavior and prevent it from reoccurring. Merely continuing the trial date does not ensure that the state will comply with its discovery obligations in the future. Instead, it absolves the state of *any* responsibility to timely produce the information and shifts that responsibility to the appellant. Going a step further, in reviewing the adequacy of a sanction order, some Appellate Courts have recognized that a deterrent aspect should be considered. A sanction that imposes only a continuance or orders the state to provide the discovery immediately before trial is insufficient.

Additionally, do not be afraid to move for a mistrial. The court may agree with you, especially if the prosecutor has a history of such behavior. Most of all, know the law. A prosecutor who engages in this type of behavior frequently does not know what the law is or purposely disregards it. If you know the law, you will be able to not only make a suitable record, but the court may very well agree with you if you are seeking to exclude evidence, dismiss the case, or prohibit the prosecutor from otherwise acting improperly. In instances where a prosecutor has a history of this type of behavior, the court may very well have had a belly full of it.

K. Working with the Court

> *Your Honor, with all due respect, if you're going to try my case for me, I wish you wouldn't lose it.*
>
> —Paul Newman
> as attorney Frank Galvan in *The Verdict*

One of the most important areas where your credibility comes into play is in your relationship with the court on the record. Often, being an advocate requires that you disagree with a magistrate on a particular point of law or disposition. It is crucial that you maintain your integrity in the discharge of your professional duties, while at the same time not become so entrenched in your passion that you blur the line between what is personal and improper and what is not.

Like you, most every judge you will encounter will ultimately want to believe that he or she has done the right thing in court. If the decision goes against you, so be it. Be sure to make your record so that if the matter goes up on appeal you will have properly preserved your objection. But always treat the court with the respect it deserves.[26]

[26] For an example of what can happen when things occasionally go dreadfully wrong and what you can do about it, see Chapter 11(B), "Dealing With a Hostile Court."

Judges enjoy and appreciate good lawyering. They don't see it very often. Too often they must endure hour after hour of dreary argument, presented in numbing monotones by dull, unimaginative counsel, and punctuated only by the lunch break or the sound of counsel falling out of his chair. If a judge feels that she can decide the issue in a matter by simply reading the pleadings and briefs, she will. That is why it is so important to develop credibility in the drafting of your pleadings and in your personal interaction with the court. It could subconsciously tip a judge's decision in your favor, if it is a close call. At all times, be the kind of lawyer that a judge looks forward to seeing in the courtroom. When you stand to make an argument, you want the court to think, "This is going to be good."

L. Continuing the Trial

A continuance is not something that you should get into the habit of seeking. Notwithstanding the time constraints, amount of work, number of cases, unavailability of witnesses, and so on, seeking a continuance of a trial date is generally frowned upon. Judges are extremely protective of their dockets, primarily because there is not enough time on their calendars to hear everything that is scheduled. When they do manage to squeeze everything in and schedule trial dates, it is with the understanding that the dates are usually reliable. Nothing in the world aggravates a judge more than reorganizing their calendar months in advance to schedule a week-long trial, only to have the parties seek a continuance at the last minute because one of the parties isn't prepared. This utterly destroys the court docket, and the judge then finds himself with a gaping hole in his calendar that is too late to fill with anything else. Courts are therefore extremely reluctant to grant continuances.

A motion for continuance sends the message that you are not prepared. You should develop the mindset that you are always prepared, no matter what.[27] Having said that, it is inevitable that, once in a while, you may need to seek a continuance for a variety of reasons. Make sure that those situations are as few and far between as possible.

---

[27] The classic joke among trial lawyers—particularly public defenders—is: "We're always ready, never prepared."

Make sure that you notify all witnesses, particularly those who need as much advance notice as possible. And don't forget your client. Make sure that the client is the *first* to be consulted, so that he doesn't have to hear it on the street or on the news. You want to clear such a decision with the client first, so that he understands your reasons for doing so. And *never, ever* assume the court will grant a continuance. The courts sometimes don't. For that reason, do not represent to your client or anyone else that you have obtained a continuance until you confirm it directly with the court.

Trials are stressful, frightening things for your client. And the closer the date looms, the worse it becomes. Your client may "talk tough" early on about insisting on going to trial, only to get cold feet as the date approaches. Your client may want to delay the trial for a variety of reasons, some of which may be valid, while others may simply be the result of nervous anxiety. While your client certainly has the right to decide whether or not to go to trial, he does not necessarily have the right to dictate whether the trial is continued. That is a tactical and strategic decision that is yours alone to make, taking into account the best interests of your client. If your client insists on continuing the trial, it is important for you to meet with him and frankly and openly discuss his reasons for doing so. In many cases, he is simply afraid.

A more difficult situation arises when you feel, for legitimate reasons, that the trial should be continued and your client refuses to consent. As stated earlier, the reasons for continuing a trial can vary, but almost always it is based on your belief that more time is needed to adequately prepare. After meeting with your client and reviewing your situation, your client may not agree. He may or may not be able to articulate a reason, or his reason may be, in your opinion, entirely unreasonable. Since the court typically will not continue a trial without the consent of the defendant, this presents a significant dilemma.

As a practical matter, the defense should routinely file a written demand for speedy trial at the same time that all other standard motions for discovery are filed, after the initial arraignment is held in District Court. That will automatically trigger the requisite trial time limit. The defendant's consent is required for a continuance primarily for the reason that the defendant has a constitutional right to a speedy trial. This is established as a safeguard against unreasonable delays, which would be prejudicial to the defendant. The trial therefore typically cannot be waived without his consent. However, if the court determines that there is a justiciable reason to continue the trial over the objection of the defendant, the trial may be rescheduled for any reasonable period of time thereafter, even if it exceeds the time limit.

When meeting with your client, you must explain to him that even if he objects, the court is likely to grant a continuance unless he is able to prove it would constitute a substantial prejudice to his defense. It is not sufficient to merely argue that it would further aggravate his already heightened pretrial anxiety or extend his pretrial incarceration. It goes without saying that if you and your client find yourselves at opposite sides of this argument, your filing of a motion to continue may likely result in a strained attorney–client relationship. In that situation, you should be sure and clearly indicate to the court in your motion that the defendant objects to a continuance and then set forth his reasons.[28] However, you must make the effort to make your client understand that a continuance would be in his best interests and enhance his chances of acquittal. At the hearing on the motion, the court will likely address your client directly and ask for his input on the record.

---

[28] It would also be a good idea to draft an affidavit for your client to sign, setting forth in detail his objections and the reasons therefore, and attaching it as an exhibit to your motion.

11
Setting the Stage

The true genius in war is the one who can do the average thing when those about him grow hysterical with emotion and fright.

—Napoleon

All battles are won or lost before they are actually fought.

—Unknown

Well, this is another ass whippin' I'm fixin' to take.

—Garvin Isaacs

As stated above, you should start preparing for trial at the outset of your case and in no case later than immediately following the District Court arraignment. The longer you wait, the less time you have to prepare. And time is an asset that is in precious short supply.

As the trial date approaches, it is only natural that you will feel increasingly anxious. Thousands of details will begin swirling in your head, and you will find it difficult to keep everything straight. Therefore, the best thing you can do to help manage your stress is to create a written "battle plan," which is nothing more than an outline of everything that needs to be done, and a date by which each must be completed. Then simply follow the plan and cross each one off as you do it. This will reduce the cacophony of all that noise in your head to a clear, workable outline. It will dramatically reduce your stress, and increase your confidence by reinforcing the fact that you are ready to go.[1]

Study the evidence carefully to determine what the nature of your defense is and which of the elements should be the focus of your attack. Once you have narrowed the focus of your attack, identify which witnesses you will need to call (or cross-examine) in order to present evidence supporting your theory of the case as to each element.

A. Dealing with the Press

In the vast majority of criminal cases, the presence of the news media is not significant. Ordinarily, the only person who must deal with the media to any substantial degree is the prosecuting attorney. However, depending on the nature and public profile of the case, there may be times when the defense attorney may be contacted by the media and asked to comment.

If you are a staff public defender, inquiries by the press can, and must, be referred to others in your office responsible for public comment. Generally speaking, it is not recommended that any defense counsel comment publicly on any case. You should be mindful of your state rules of professional conduct, which addresses public comments by counsel regarding ongoing cases, or matters under investigation. Even if the rules permit counsel to make certain public comments, it is a generally better practice to decline any such comment and thus avoid the possibility of running afoul of the rules.

A true defense lawyer does his talking in the courtroom and doesn't try his cases in the press. At the very least, this will protect you from inadvertently revealing confidential client communications,

[1] One of the instructors on the faculty of the Western Trial Advocacy Institute (WTAI), Steve Rench, developed *The Rench Book*. For every trial, he prepared a small three-ring binder that was divided into numerous tabs, from "Preparing the Winning Case" to "Closing Argument." As preparation continued, he would enter ideas and notes into each section of the notebook as they occurred to him. It proved invaluable as trial neared.

promising something you won't be able to deliver at trial, or otherwise violating the rules.

B. Dealing with a Hostile Court

One of the most difficult things to address at trial, especially for younger or less experienced counsel, is how to handle a judge who appears to be dead-set on preventing you from trying your case. Although fairly rare, it can happen. Examples run the gamut from a judge who is simply not current on the latest Appellate Court decisions to judges who display open hostility to you or your client and take aggressive acts to thwart your efforts.[2]

You must first and foremost always act respectfully and professionally when addressing the court. It is part of your ethical obligation as an attorney and officer of the court. This is true even if the judge acts disrespectfully to you. Always keep your cool and maintain

---

[2] Here is an actual example: An attorney was aggressively cross-examining a witness in a sexual assault trial and was scoring substantial points in the process. Angry at (or jealous of?) the attorney's success, the judge interrupted at one point and barked: "Counsel will cease this line of inquiry immediately. The witness is doing the very best she can to answer the questions truthfully and honestly." Realizing the judge had grossly interfered with his case by interrupting him and improperly commenting on the credibility of the witness, the attorney replied: "Your Honor, that was an improper comment by the court, and I request that I be permitted to voir dire the jurors to determine which, if any, heard the court's comments." The judge turned to the jury and asked for a show of hands of those who heard the comment. All of the jurors raised their hands, to which the judge then replied, "Let the record reflect that none of the jurors raised their hands."

Undaunted, the attorney dug in: "Your Honor, I move for a mistrial. This court has purposely and intentionally misrepresented the record, when in fact all of the jurors raised their hands, and has thus demonstrated a clear bias and prejudice against the defendant in this case and an inability to preside over this trial fairly and impartially. Furthermore, the court has precluded me from cross-examining an adverse witness which I have a constitutional right to do and has therefore made it impossible for me to discharge my duties under the Sixth Amendment as effective and competent counsel for my client." "Motion denied," the judge snapped back, adding, "Counsel, I am going to hold you in contempt of court." The attorney responded, "Go ahead and hold me in contempt. I have done nothing wrong. I will not only take this up on appeal, but I will also file a grievance with the State Bar and Judicial Ethics Panel and we'll see what they think about this." The two glared at each other silently for a moment, then the judge spoke. "Apology accepted," he replied. "You may continue."

your composure, especially in front of the jury. Your instincts as an advocate may demand that you lash out at the judge but resist the temptation to do so. Nothing good will come of it.

The terror of confronting a hostile court arises from our uncertainty as to what we can do about it. Always remember: *If it doesn't appear on the record, it didn't happen.* Make certain that the court's comments or behavior are completely and accurately reflected on the official reported transcript of the proceedings. Have the courage to stand your ground and state your objections clearly in accordance with applicable law. The judge knows that if his misbehavior appears on the record, he's in trouble (or at the very least it cannot be claimed it didn't happen). Move for a mistrial if necessary. It doesn't matter if it is denied. Make it impossible for an Appellate Court to ignore the event. In essence, call the court's bluff. More often than not, you may win. It also sends the right message to the court and to your opponent: You are there to take care of business and will not be intimidated.

Part of being a true advocate and warrior for your client is to be willing to risk being reprimanded in front of the jury, or even held in contempt, for acting properly and ethically on behalf of your client. If you are right and you make your record, any discomfort you suffer will be temporary. When the chips are down, never, ever back down. Stand your ground. Remember, it is alright to be afraid, but *we will not be intimidated.*

C. Using Computers and Audio/Video Equipment

Modern technology has unquestionably revolutionized the practice of law, particularly the presentation of evidence in the courtroom. Jurors today are more conditioned than ever to watching video and other computer-generated images during a trial. The problem, however, is that such technology can be both a blessing and a curse. Jurors are much less receptive to long presentations than they were in the past. Their attention spans have been considerably shortened. They want things delivered quickly, like their food. They don't want to have to think too much. Subtle nuances are lost: They want things spelled out for them. They also want to be entertained. They don't want to be bored. Form is elevated over substance. This places a tremendous responsibility on the trial lawyers. Instead of being advocates, we increasingly find ourselves becoming producers, emcees, and game show hosts. As stated repeatedly throughout this manual, a jury trial is all theater.

If your case requires presentation of an audio or video tape or a computer-generated image or reconstruction, make sure that you obtain as good and professional quality as possible. Many such videos are surveillance tapes. Their quality is mediocre at best and often poor. Unfortunately, there is not much you can do to enhance their quality without risking being accused of altering the original image. The best you can do is to make sure that the equipment used for playback in the courtroom is in good working condition, that it is placed so that it is easily seen and heard by the jury, and that a person trained in its operation is tasked with running it. Before trial, seek the court's permission to set it up and conduct a number of rehearsals, so that at the critical point in the trial everything works as desired. It is almost assured that if you don't, it won't work at the appointed time, no matter how carefully you have prepared it. Therefore, always have a "Plan B."

If you are creating a new original video presentation, utilize whatever resources are available to you to obtain the most professional result possible. Nothing impresses like good quality. It sends the message that you are serious and that this case is important enough to warrant that kind of attention to detail and excellence. It is almost always worth the money, and it shows respect for the jury. In a nutshell, it makes you look good.

12
Voir Dire

"Would you tell me, please, which way I ought to go from here?"

"That depends a good deal on where you want to get to," said the Cheshire Cat.

—Lewis Carroll, *Alice in Wonderland*

What I like and what I need's two different things.

—J. D. Jordan, *Calamity: Being an Account of Calamity Jane and Her Gunslinging Green Man*

Nothing about preparing and trying a jury trial is easy, and the most difficult and most challenging part of a trial is, without question, voir dire. No other aspect of trial is more terrifying, misunderstood, or shrouded in mystery, and no other aspect of trial is more critical to conduct properly. It is the moment when you establish your credibility with the jury. It is that credibility that will largely determine whether you win or lose the case. It is also the only moment when you communicate directly with the jurors, and they with you, in order to find out how the jurors feel about you, your client, and your case. Therefore, it is the part of the trial preparation process that requires the most time, thought, focus, and insight.

Yet, few attorneys understand how to do it, let alone do it well. Mistakes made during the presentation of evidence during the course of a trial can often be remedied. But mistakes made during voir dire are often fatal, for we do not get a second chance to make a first impression.[1] However, a well-conducted voir dire can help win the case for you. The good news is that once you learn to do it properly, voir dire is the simplest, most uncomplicated thing in the world.[2]

A. Voir Dire in Federal Court

In federal court, voir dire is conducted primarily by the court. It is perfunctory, and it deals only with the qualifications of the venirepersons to serve on that particular panel. While this information satisfies the requirements of the rules, it reveals nothing of importance with respect to how the jurors feel about your case. And how they feel about your case is the most important inquiry that must be made.

Every federal court is different. Some judges are aware of the attorneys' need for that insight, and thus tend to allow some time for counsel to address the panel directly in order to obtain it. Other courts, however, do not. In those latter jurisdictions, it is recommended that counsel submit proposed voir dire questions to the court prior to trial which are tailored to uncover that information. While having the court handle such inquiry is a poor substitute for counsel, it is better than nothing.

It is for these reasons that some of you who practice mostly in federal court may be inclined to skip this section. DON'T DO IT! To the extent that you are permitted to engage in voir dire, or to at least influence how the court does it, this section is the most important part of this entire manual.

B. Overview

How many times have we returned to our offices after losing a hard-fought jury trial and voiced this lament to anyone within earshot: *"How could the jury find against me? I had all the facts*

---

1 As Mom always reminded us.

2 Just like golf. All you have to do is get the little ball into the cup. How hard can that be?

on my side!" Well, you may have had all the facts, but the jury had a set of beliefs that viewed your "facts" unfavorably. Your inability to effectively ferret out and deal honestly with those beliefs and feelings in your voir dire doomed any chance you ever had of winning and instead turned your "Victory Gala Bash" into a "Major Disaster Drag."

Essential to understanding voir dire is the concept that the question is not how *you* view the facts and issues of your case but how the *jury* sees and interprets them. And it only begins there. You must also understand how the jurors feel about your client, about the charges he faces, about how he looks and acts in the courtroom, about his story (theory of the case), and about myriad other factors and details. A great trial lawyer understands the psychology of human behavior. And the key to that understanding is realizing that it all begins with you.

As we work our way through this chapter, you will begin to understand that the great trial lawyers are able to communicate so well with the jurors because they have learned to suppress their egos. They have developed the critical skill of making the jurors—and through them the client—the center of attention. Developing this technique is perhaps the most difficult part of voir dire. But it is crucial that we learn to do it, for it addresses what it is that terrifies us most about voir dire—talking to strangers who may not like us, about topics that frighten us.

There is a reason voir dire is so terrifying. The No. 1 fear in the human species is fear of public speaking.[3] Perhaps it is because when we as a species were living in caves and huddled around campfires, we were—and to a degree still are—a tribal species. We depended on the integrity and strength of the group, as well as our role in it, in order to survive. Whenever a member of the tribe behaved in such a way that was unacceptable, the member was singled out and identified to the others as having done something wrong. The member was then punished. Of course, this was a truly traumatizing ordeal, for punishment often meant banishment from the tribe, or even death.

---

[3] Fear of our own death ranks somewhere in the top five. Interestingly, we fear speaking in front of others more than we fear our own death. We would literally rather die than do it.

But banishment also meant almost certain death. So the stakes could not be higher. If the accused member was unable to convince the others of the acceptability of his behavior, he could die. So by being rejected, it meant, quite literally, death.

The same mindset exists to this day, eons later, buried deep within our ancient brains. When asked why we fear speaking before others, we reply that it's because we are afraid of making a fool of ourselves or that we are afraid of failing or of appearing insincere or phony, or untrustworthy, or unsure of ourselves, or ashamed because we don't like who we are, or the way we look or sound, or any one of countless emotions, all of which symbolize and characterize one fundamental—and ancient—emotion: *fear of rejection.*

Here in the twenty-first century, we are still a tribe. We still rely entirely on the tribe for our survival, and we fear rejection from it more than anything else. In voir dire, we strike those jurors whom we do not wish to include on our jury. We literally identify them as having expressed an opinion we find unacceptable or dangerous. And our reaction to that is to eliminate them, to physically order them out of the room, out of the jury panel. Out of the building. Out of the case. Out of our lives. Forever. So after countless eons, rejection still means death.

The jurors know that some in their group will be rejected. A few find the notion of jury service detestable and may intentionally seek to "sabotage" their responses in order to be eliminated. But most jurors are honest and wish to do their best. It is those jurors whom we must learn to communicate with honestly, so that they trust us enough to tell us the truth about how they feel. Part of our learning process includes accepting and thanking the jurors when they tell us they don't like us.

Voir dire is not so much an "art" as it is a science, although there is certainly an artistic element to it. If it were simply an "art," only those few gifted from birth could do it. Voir dire is learned, not inherited. Hear me: Any trial lawyer can learn to do a good voir dire. What makes certain attorneys "artists" at the craft, however, is not simply their knowledge and ability to do it. It is *how* they do it. It is their unique expression of their knowledge and understanding of the science and mastery of the technique that sets them apart. Put another way, they know the method and techniques so well that they are able to free themselves to be artistic with it. The methods and techniques taught in this manual are the very same ones that the greatest trial lawyers learned. Believe it or not, you can do it, too.

A good lawyer should never "wing" a voir dire. It would be tantamount to "winging" an Apollo moon landing. Since the voir dire is essentially the first opportunity for you to present yourself and your case to the jury, it must be painstakingly crafted and delivered. It therefore requires a great deal of thought and exhaustive preparation, more so than any other part of the case. We start the process by understanding ourselves.

Before we can stand before a panel of prospective jurors and delve into their biases and prejudices, we must first stand before ourselves and delve into ours. We must have a firm grasp on knowing who we are as human beings and as persons—what we fear and what we need to survive as members of this tribe we call "humanity." We must strip ourselves of the many outer layers of our psychological walls behind which we hide, and we must honestly face our real selves—but more importantly *accept our real selves*—exactly as we are. By doing so, we discover that we are human beings with the same shared fundamental life experiences as those who are on the jury panel. Because at the end of the day, we realize *we are all jurors*. We must therefore develop and achieve a fundamental understanding and awareness of the common denominators that bind us all together. That is the language of voir dire. It is the universal language of humanity.

Here are some important things to understand about jurors:

- Jurors deliberate and reach verdicts emotionally and justify them logically by focusing on facts that support them.
- Jurors don't believe what they see; they see what they believe. They will selectively sort it out and keep what elements match their belief system. This is "confirmation bias."
- There is a huge difference between "legal" proof and "juror" proof. This difference must be explored in voir dire.
- Jurors believe that if it's in a written record, it's true.
- If there is a hole in your case, the jurors will fill it with whatever seems to fit based on their life experiences. This is why you must anticipate all "holes" in your case and provide the jurors with answers you have already prepared.
- Jurors believe their behavior is normal and perfect, which then becomes the norm (i.e., "reasonable persons").

The concepts of "confirmation bias" and "cognitive dissonance" are present and intricately involved in voir dire.[4] That is why any argument or presentation of evidence to the jury must be done in such a way as to take into account not only *how you intend* for the jury to see it, but also *how they are likely to receive it*. Therefore, you cannot know how a jury will receive your client's story (and, axiomatically, you will not know how to tell it) if you don't know how they feel about certain aspects of it—aspects that are potential problem areas that concern you.

C. The Rules

There are three basic rules of voir dire:

1. Know the law.
2. Know the philosophy.
3. Know the technique.

Learn them, practice them, and study them so that they become second nature to you.

1. The First Rule of Voir Dire: *Know the Law*

We cannot understand—and therefore we cannot get the judge in our case to understand—what we are trying to accomplish in our voir dire if we are not clear on the law. It is our instinct and habit as trial lawyers to focus on how restrictive the law is regarding voir dire. In other words, we tend to dwell on what we believe we are *prohibited* from doing rather than on what we are *permitted* to do. We convince ourselves that because the rules set forth those things we must not do in our effort to communicate, we therefore cannot communicate at all. Judges seem to echo this constriction in their reticence in allowing any kind of substantive voir dire. But a careful reading of the

---

[4] On the one hand, "confirmation bias" is the tendency to search for, process, and interpret information in a way that confirms a person's own preexisting beliefs. On the other hand, "cognitive dissonance" is the mental discomfort or psychological stress that is experienced when a person's beliefs or assumptions are contradicted by new information.

applicable rules and caselaw reveals that the good trial lawyer can rely on them to support a full and fruitful voir dire.

Imagine you are in chambers at the pretrial conference and the judge wishes to make clear his views on voir dire. The judge admonishes you that you shall not, under any circumstance, discuss the facts of the case in voir dire. Nor shall you try to argue your case. The law is clear: No "preconditioning" the jury is allowed! The judge is concerned only with selecting a jury that is "fair and impartial" and will tolerate no deviations from that. In fact, as far as the judge is concerned, the only question that need be asked during voir dire is whether the prospective juror can set aside his or her personal feelings and be "fair and impartial." If the juror says "Yes," that's all the judge needs to know. No other inquiry is necessary.[5]

Sound familiar? Well, the judge is just following the law . . . right? Actually, no. A careful reading of the rules of criminal procedure in state jurisdictions generally provides as follows:

First, we are told what we *cannot* do. A typical procedural rule says:

a. The only purpose of the examination is to select a panel of jurors who will *fairly and impartially* hear the evidence and render a just verdict. The court *shall not permit* counsel to attempt *to precondition prospective jurors* to a particular result, comment on the personal lives and families of the parties or their attorneys, nor question jurors concerning the pleadings, the law, the meaning of words, or the comfort of the jurors.

---

[5] As a young inexperienced trial lawyer, I was just starting my voir dire in a District Court jury trial when the judge interrupted me and barked, "Counsel, approach the bench." Timidly, I complied. I was shaking so badly I rattled. I looked like the Tin Woodsman standing before the Wizard of Oz. He leaned over to me, grasping the edge of his bench with both hands, his face red, and in a voice that could clearly be heard throughout the courtroom, hissed through clenched teeth, "I know what you're doing, counsel. I'm not going to have any of that Gerry Spence crap in MY courtroom. Now GET ON WITH IT!" I was terrified. I thought my knees were going to buckle. The room swam before my eyes, and I could feel my heart hammering against my rib cage. Not having the experience or ability at that time in my career to stand my ground and make my record, I caved. I mumbled something to the jury thanking them for their time and sat down.

b. Counsel *shall not*:
- Ask questions of an individual juror that can be asked of the panel of a group of jurors collectively.
- Ask questions answered in a juror questionnaire except to explain an answer.
- Repeat a question asked and answered.
- Instruct the jury on the law or argue the case.
- Ask a juror what the juror's verdict might be under any hypothetical circumstance.[6]

That does sound quite restrictive. But wait! It says nothing about limiting the discussion of the *facts*. Notwithstanding the restrictions set forth in the rules, counsel is usually permitted during voir dire examination **to preview portions of the evidence from the case in a nonargumentative manner, when a preview of the evidence would help prospective jurors better understand the context of reasons for certain lines of voir dire questioning.**[7] Therefore, it is vitally important that you review the rules and caselaw of your jurisdiction to determine if, and to what extent, you are permitted to do this. Contrary to popular belief that counsel is prohibited from discussing the facts of the case with the jurors, *there may be no such prohibition anywhere in the rules or caselaw other than the limitation noted above.*

Although it is one of the stated goals of the rules that the purpose of voir dire is to uncover bias and prejudice on the part of the panel, why is it that courts almost universally interpret the rules as not permitting any form of inquiry that accomplishes it?

One must keep in mind that bias and prejudice are not attitudes that jurors immediately recognize, can freely articulate, or willingly acknowledge, let alone even admit exist. Courts that restrict voir dire examination seem to accept the curious notion that once a citizen is sworn in as a venireperson, that citizen is somehow suddenly and magically imbued with hyperinsightful self-awareness, which enables him to perceive in a Zen-like state of multidimensional cosmic clarity what biases and prejudices he has, such that he may then remove

---

[6] *See* Rule 24(c), Wyoming Rules of Criminal Procedure.

[7] *Id.*

them and hand them to the bailiff as nonchalantly as if he were removing his jacket. We must therefore convince the courts that a properly conducted voir dire is an active, dynamic process, which is about as "full contact" a sport as jury trials get.

Even though the law is actually in favor of voir dire, it is still an uphill battle to convince the courts to permit any form of substantive voir dire even in the off chance they've actually read the rules themselves. Courts are keen to say that it is because it accomplishes little and takes so much time. I suspect another reason is that lawyers are not very good at it (thus rendering the results meaningless), and a bad voir dire is excruciating to sit through. Also, most judges don't know how to do it either. Notwithstanding this, the process must not be abandoned.

The responsibility for protecting and preserving the voir dire process is shared by both judges and lawyers. As my father, Justice Robert R. Rose Jr., pointed out in his specially concurring opinion in *Patterson v. State*, 691 P.2d 253, 260 (Wyo. 1984):

> I abhor the tendency of trial courts—both state and federal—to refuse to furnish lawyers the opportunity to inquire of venirepersons in such a meaningful way as will permit intelligent decisions to be made about bias and prejudice. The litigants' right to be heard by fair and impartial jurors is a guaranteed right—guaranteed by constitution, rule and decision—yet the tendency . . . is for judges to pretend that a question addressed to the venireperson which asks:
>
> "Do you believe you can serve as a fair and impartial juror in this case?" is sufficient to discharge the fair-and-impartial-jury requirements of the law. This really is judicial sophistry.[8] An answer to this question reveals absolutely nothing about the bias and prejudice which the potential juror may or may not harbor with respect to those matters with which the trial will be concerned.
>
> [I]t is necessary that a litigant, his attorney and the court be allowed to develop such facts and disclose such legal principles

8 "Sophistry" means reasoning or argument that sounds correct but is actually false; an argument that sounds plausible but is intended to deceive.

as are necessary to permit the reaching of an informed conclusion with respect to a prospective juror's bias and prejudice and, thus, his or her ability to serve. This is necessary not only so that an intelligent challenge for cause may be lodged, but also for the purpose of permitting the informed exercise of a preemptive challenge. It is only through exploring the venireperson's "nuances of conscience," through the development of such informed communication as will permit the disclosure of the deeper realities of the intended juror's inner self—that the 'impartial' jury contemplated by the constitutions, the rules, the statutes, and the court decisions will have been made available to the judicial process.

The search for the fair and impartial juror will not be rewarded where inquiry is . . . restricted. The channels of human communication must be encouraged to remain open in order that all concerned may enjoy such an exchange of thought and feeling as will in fact reveal whether or not there exists in the "stream of tendency" of the potential juror such bias or prejudice concerning the subject matter and law of the case as will either permit or prevent the rendering of the fair and just verdict which the law contemplates.

a. *Challenges for Cause*

Challenges for cause are set forth in the statutes or rules and generally provide that such challenges may be taken on one or more of the following grounds:

1. A lack of any of the qualifications prescribed by statute which render a person competent as a juror.
2. Relationship by consanguinity or affinity within the third degree to either party.
3. Standing in the relation of debtor or creditor, guardian or ward, master or servant, principal or agent to either party, or being a partner united in business with either party, or being security on any bond or obligation for either party.
4. Having served as a juror or witness in a previous trial between the same parties for the same cause of action or being then a witness therein.

5. Interest on the part of the juror in the event or question involved in the action, but not an interest of the juror as a member or citizen of a municipal corporation.
6. Having formed or expressed an unqualified opinion or belief as to the action. The reading of newspaper accounts of the subject matter before the court shall not disqualify the juror for either bias or opinion.
7. The existence of a state of mind in the juror evincing enmity or bias for either party.[9]

It is under subsection 7 that the vast majority of important information from the jurors will be gleaned. Knowing the grounds for a challenge for cause is the easy part. The difficulty lies in asking the questions that produce the information upon which the challenge may be advanced and successfully achieved. That technique will be covered in Rule No. 3, below.

2. The Second Rule of Voir Dire: *Know the Philosophy*

Trial is a form of combat. In combat, the goal is to win. You win by controlling the battlefield. You control the battlefield through the strategic and tactical use of power. Since the jury decides who wins at trial, all power in the case is retained by the jury, but they convey it to whomever they trust the most. Your power is thus derived from your credibility with the jury. Thus, credibility = power = control.

Learning voir dire is more than just developing a skill set. You must understand *why* you are doing it this way. Understanding why certain questions must be asked in certain ways and why certain topics must be addressed is the key to this method.

Your greatest adversary in voir dire is lack of time. You must establish your credibility with the jury by winning their trust within the time you are allotted. Therein lies the "art" of voir dire. You must therefore concentrate on *quality* of information rather than *quantity*. You must eliminate anything not designed to produce relevant information. Preparation is therefore critical. It forces you to distill the inquiry and examination process into a simple formula designed for one purpose: "*What do I need to know?*"

---

[9] *See* W.S. §§ 7-11-101, and 1-11-203.

a. Voir Dire and the Defense Attorney

Voir dire for a defense attorney is entirely different from that for a prosecuting attorney. For one thing, in a criminal case juror bias is largely "built in" in favor of the state, since most jurors are good, conservative, law-abiding citizens. A prosecutor generally does not have to work as hard as does the defense attorney, who must overcome significant juror bias against the defendant in order to level the playing field. This bias must be identified, articulated, and effectively neutralized if the defendant is to have a realistic opportunity to receive a verdict of acquittal. That being said, a prosecutor can just as easily lose a case in voir dire where juror bias has not been properly taken into account.

Overall, the primary thrust of the defense voir dire is the same as it is for any trial lawyer, criminal or civil: *You must identify those jurors who are opposed to you and your case so that you can remove them.* To do this, you must focus primarily on those aspects of your case that are troublesome and concern you. You must discover which jurors on the panel are open and receptive to your theory of the case and those who are not. In order to do this effectively, you start with totally and completely accepting the jurors' feelings about your case. In other words, accepting the jurors *as they are.*

b. Accepting the Jurors as They Are

Many of you may have grown up watching *Mr. Rogers' Neighborhood* on television. In every episode, Fred Rogers would clearly state the overall theme of his philosophy: "I like you *just the way you are.*" It is the same for voir dire. We must learn to adopt this philosophy if we are to obtain the information we need.

In voir dire, there is a huge difference between what you *want* to know or *would like* to know, and what you *need* to know. In order to conduct a proper and useful voir dire, you must be able to understand what it is you need to know and how to get it. This is difficult because it is so counterintuitive and requires a tremendous amount of analysis and insight into how not only *you* think and feel, but how the jury thinks and feels, and the clock is ticking. Done properly, this effort will result in you not only understanding your case and being able to communicate with others about it (and in the process, understanding who you really are as a person, and the nature of the relationships you have with your spouse, your friends, your family, your children, your colleagues, and anyone else involved in your life), but in learning what it is you need to know from the jurors. To some who have studied this method intensely and carefully, it is a cathartic experience, literally altering their entire lives.

You must know your case so well that you can identify areas that are weak and present problems for you. This is critical. You must be able to know and understand what parts of your case cause you great concern because this will enable you to identify adverse jurors and eliminate them from the panel.

You also have to understand human psychology so that you can have the jurors help you argue your case. In order to truly know and understand how to talk to the jury, you must be able to "crawl into their hide" and see your case from their point of view. To do that, you must first be able to be comfortable in your *own* hide. In other words, you must have a good grasp on who you are as a person. Being honest with the jury is a cornerstone of this process, and before you can be honest with others, you must be able to be honest with yourself. In a properly conducted voir dire, you will be dealing with others in a more open and profound manner than you have ever before related to other human beings in your life. You must therefore be on solid grounds in your own head. We start understanding who we really are by acknowledging our deepest fear—rejection.

As stated earlier, we are all afraid of rejection. As attorneys we are not exempt from the emotions, biases and prejudices that make us human. We can no more ask a juror to set aside how he or she truly feels about something in our case any more than we can ask ourselves to do so. We fear being rejected by others for expressing what we honestly feel, just as jurors do. We are also afraid of our inability to share those fears with others. A refusal or fear to share ourselves honestly with these strangers means they will not share themselves with us—and we will remain forever strangers throughout the trial.

Gerry Spence maintains that many lawyers get into trouble because they believe that by acting or pretending to be friendly or interested, the juror will trust them. By pretending, however, they are in reality being phony, and their smile is seen by the juror as an attempt to find something negative, or bad, about the juror; some indelible stain that cannot be cleaned. The juror senses that the smile, the voice, the inflection, are hiding something, are masking the lawyer's true purpose: to uncover something that will give him a reason to kick the juror off the panel. In other words, Spence says, to be rejected. Nobody likes to be rejected. Rejection is humiliating and painful. To be rejected is to be discarded, discounted, devalued, thrown away, like a piece of garbage.

Part of trusting the jurors lies in the belief that *whatever they tell you cannot harm you, no matter how blunt or harsh it might be, as long as it is honest.* Not only can it not harm you, but it is a gift to be cherished. It is vital information cloaked in hostile energy. You must accept the energy being directed at you, much in the same way as a martial artist accepts his opponent's energy being directed at him. Rather than meeting it head on and colliding violently with it, the martial artist simply adjusts his stance to accept the energy, totally and completely, and controls it so that it does not throw him off balance. In the process, he enables it to work for him.

Trusting the jury and enabling them to trust you require that you learn who you are, so that you can master your fear and make it work for you. Always remember that reality is never as fearful as the fear of reality. By learning who we are, we come to realize and accept that for all of our accomplishments each of us is just as flawed—and thus just as unique and real and human—as each juror on our panel. We each share fear of failure and rejection. So right off the bat, that realization gives you a point of reference with the jurors. We share a common denominator. We thus have something to talk about. *If you accept yourself for who you really are, flaws and all, you will be able to accept the jurors for who they really are.*

The commonly stated purpose of voir dire is to select a "fair and impartial" jury. But an effective voir dire has nothing to do with picking twelve jurors who can be "fair and impartial." There is no such thing as a "fair and impartial" jury. That's because a jury is composed of people, and people are not "fair and impartial." An unbiased panel is a legal fiction. People are filled with emotion, irrationality, hatred, fear, prejudice, insecurity, anger, distrust, skepticism, and any other emotion or mindset that you can imagine. The only juror who is ever "fair and impartial" is in a grave. Therefore, you must approach voir dire from the standpoint that you know that everyone sitting on the panel has biases and prejudices that you are going to have to discuss and come to grips with.

Hopefully, you are now beginning to understand why you must first be completely comfortable and secure with who you are, which includes acknowledging that you, too, have all of the same biases and prejudices and that you are no more "fair and impartial" than any other member of the panel. The key is to share that fact with the jurors. The humanistic psychologist Carl Rogers termed this the CUE approach:

Congruence
Relating the juror's experience with your own.
Unconditional Positive Regard
Accepting the juror's feelings without conditions or qualifications.
Empathy
Genuinely caring for the value of the juror's experience.

You must create an open and trusting atmosphere in which the juror feels that she can offer her innermost honest feelings, trusting that you will receive them for the precious gifts they are. This is much akin to a therapeutic setting. In the same way that a psychotherapist creates an environment with his patient of safety, security, acceptance, and caring, so must the attorney with the juror. For the goal is the same: creation of a *trust relationship*. Nothing the juror says is rejected—it is accepted as being how they honestly feel. You must build a bridge between the juror's experience and your theory of the case. The more you connect, the better. There are no "wrong" answers. The message you want to send is: *"You are all my friends. I want you to be part of my group,"* not: *"Who can I strike?"* We want to communicate more than we want to isolate. The focus, then, is on making the jurors feel *included*, not *excluded*. This, then, is the basis of the paradox. For it is in the spirit of inclusion that jurors will feel confident and trusting enough to respond honestly to us, thus revealing who we must exclude from the panel.

In almost every voir dire, the attorney at some point encounters a juror who expresses an opinion that is adverse to the interest of the attorney and his client. This is what makes voir dire so terrifying for many attorneys. We are frightened of those who disagree with us, who feel differently than we do, and we perceive them as a threat. Thus, the attorney's instinctive—and very human—reaction is to (1) "run away" from the juror or (2) try and change the juror's mind. After all, don't we want to convince every juror on the panel that our side of the case is the "correct" side? That we represent the "reasonable" side, while our opponent is the "unreasonable" side? When faced with a juror who expresses his or her rejection of our case, we want to do whatever we can to change the juror's mind.

The attorney will then undertake a Herculean, and usually catastrophic, effort to change the juror's mind through a series of increasingly argumentative and hostile questions designed to convince the juror that her honestly expressed opinion is, in fact, wrong. It is tantamount to pounding a square peg into a round hole. The end result is that the juror ends up feeling belittled and bullied, and made to look foolish. Worse, the attorney has learned absolutely nothing about that juror or about how she is likely to vote during deliberations. She certainly has not changed her original opinion and in fact is now resolved to be more intractable than ever. This is because the principle of cognitive dissonance has engaged.

The price of this futile effort is high: Rather than accepting the juror's honest feelings and successfully challenging her for cause, you will likely now have to expend a peremptory challenge to remove her. Moreover, that exchange has had a chilling effect on the other members of the jury, who now fear that if they offer an opinion that is unacceptable to the attorney, they will suffer the same fate as that hapless juror who had the gall to tell the attorney the truth.

We must never, ever argue or disagree with a juror. We must at all times be genuine and honest in our dialogue. We cannot be phony or insincere. Just as we want to be accepted for who we really are, we must therefore accept others for the same reason. It is the only way we can ever honestly communicate with one another. The key to effective communication in the courtroom is to stop thinking and acting and sounding like a lawyer and start becoming a real human being.[10]

---

[10] You know, like we were before we went to law school.

As Charles Abourezk has written in his excellent article, "Demystifying Jury Selection: Group Psychology, Group Formation, and Motivating Jurors through Conversation":[11]

> We have to be prepared to take down our own psychological defenses, our suits of armor, our survival mechanism of judgmentalness—which is all there, in evolutionary terms, for a good reason—so that there is nothing between us and the jury. I must be able to communicate honestly with them both verbally and nonverbally that I accept them as they are, as I hope they will accept me, and that I am ready to merge with and become part of this group.

He further notes:

> Jury panels are a frightening place for jurors, despite their seeming ease, and the more we can do to help them in the process of merging with and being accepted by ourselves and the group, the better chance we have of being branded as a part of that group and having at least some persuasiveness if not outright leadership in the group. Individual jurors want, first and foremost (as do we attorneys) to feel safe in the group, to feel wanted and valued and listened to, and to make sure that we are not being lured in just to eventually be rejected. Under the immediate surface of the group formation that occurs in jury examination there lies true fear and horror of the unknowns of group life. Our first task is to decrease those fears and pull these folks together and make them feel safe, rather than on the short list for social elimination.

Most lawyers conduct a voir dire as if they were cross-examining a juror under a heat lamp. Rather than ask insightful questions, carefully considering the answers and accepting the juror's true feelings without judgment, most lawyers engage in a type of aggressive verbal

[11] Charles Abourezk is an outstanding trial lawyer who practices in Rapid City, South Dakota. A former faculty member of the Western Trial Advocacy Institute and Trial Lawyers College, he specializes in teaching the technique of "psychodrama." (Used here with kind permission of Mr. Abourezk.)

assault, wherein they grapple with the juror over whether the juror is feeling and saying what the lawyer believes the juror *should* be feeling or saying.

None of us likes to be cross-examined, especially about our feelings. Gerry Spence points out that when a lawyer engages in a cross-examination style of voir dire questioning, the juror intuitively knows the end game—that the juror will be judged and found to be wanting in some way and then summarily rejected. None of us like to be judged unless the judgment is positive and supportive. Each of us wants to be acceptable, to be liked or loved or honored in judgment. A lawyer who does not understand these simple truths will often blame the loss of his trial on "stupid, ignorant jurors." There are no stupid, ignorant jurors. There are, however, plenty of stupid, ignorant attorneys.

c. How Jurors Feel

We all tend to like or dislike someone based solely on how we "feel" about them—our observations of their behavior; how they look, how they carry themselves, how they walk, how they talk, stand, how they hold their arms, how they interact with others, and so forth. By the time we walk to the podium to begin our voir dire, and before we ever open our mouths, the jurors have already sized us up. They already know how they feel about us. They've been studying us from the moment we walked into the courtroom.

Despite what the rules, courts and law schools teach us, jurors deliberate and reach verdicts *emotionally*—based on how they *feel*, not how they *think*. Thinking and feeling involve two completely separate areas of the brain. Jurors will then justify the verdict logically through confirmation bias, selecting particular facts that support their feelings. Therefore, the most important questions we ask in voir dire begin with: *"How do you feel . . . "*

d. Voir Dire Is Theater

> *I think good lawyers are good actors. But good acting is telling the truth. It is revealing to the audience the truth about the person whose role the actor is playing.*
>
> —Gerry Spence

Make no mistake about it: A jury trial is another form of entertainment; it is theater. The attorneys, clients, witnesses, court reporter, judge, bailiffs, and clerk are all actors playing various parts, and the jury is the audience. Not surprisingly, certain truths about theater also apply in jury trials, and the trial lawyer who recognizes this possesses a distinct advantage. Much in the same way John F. Kennedy realized what Richard Nixon did not during the first-ever televised debates during the 1960 presidential campaign: *Perception is reality.*

Studies have shown that when we speak to a group of people whom we do not know, they are not listening to what we are saying. Instead, they are evaluating us with the ancient part of the human brain, which subconsciously determines whether we are trustworthy persons. In other words, the group is processing subliminal information we are broadcasting and not our words. Our voice inflections, our eye contact, and our body language are all being processed with one goal in mind: to assess whether or not we can be *trusted.*

It is the process that has protected our species from extinction since time immemorial. It has nothing whatsoever to do with how we think. If we relied on our intellect to safeguard our existence on this planet, it is safe to say that we would have ceased to exist as a species eons ago. It is also a process that, by necessity, operates almost instantaneously. That's why first impressions are so important and why they are almost impossible to change.

We must never act insincerely or pretend that we are being anything other than genuinely ourselves. We can't ever be phony about anything with a jury. They are collectively the most intelligent entity we will ever meet. If we assume that the age of a typical juror is probably somewhere between 25 and 70, give or take, that means that we are dealing with an organism that has a combined human life experience of between 300 and 840 years. They can smell bullshit a mile away. Never promise a jury something that we can't deliver. That is always fatal. Not only will we lose our credibility in an instant, but our opponent may very well stand up at her closing argument and remind the jury about all the things we promised that we didn't deliver.

From the moment we enter the courtroom, all eyes turn to us. The jury anticipates our performance; they expect to be entertained. They hope it will be just like it is in movies and on television: high drama and suspense, and if they're really lucky, a "Perry Mason moment."[12] Of course, those of us who are trial lawyers know that *ordinarily* this couldn't be farther from the truth.

But it doesn't have to be. And it shouldn't be. Why not make our presentations dramatic and interesting? Why not entertain the jury? What does entertainment have to do with voir dire? Just this: If we cannot transform that theatrical mentality and that skill set into something interesting and fun for the jury to watch, we shouldn't be in this business.

In order for us to be trustworthy, we must be credible. We must be perceived as professionals who deliver what we promise. We are never surprised. We calculate and plan everything. We anticipate the unexpected. There is no hesitation. We must present a type of persona that even the judge defers to when he isn't sure of what to do. We must always know what to do (or at least act like it), even when we don't.

From the moment the trial begins, we put on our "game face," and we are consummate professionals.[13] We must cultivate the attitude

---

[12] *Perry Mason* was a television program popular in the late 1950s and early 1960s. Perry Mason was a brilliant criminal defense attorney who had the uncanny ability to win his cases through devastating cross examination of the prosecution witnesses. More often than not they involved murder cases, and each episode was solved by the key witness coming completely apart under Mason's withering interrogation, resulting in the exoneration of his client. The poor district attorney never won a single case. The problem with this approach is, of course, twofold: One, Perry Mason was a terrible cross-examiner, and two: the unrealistic reliance on the success of the case hinging solely on the disintegration of the key witness under cross-examination. In real life, it hardly ever happens.

[13] Because trials are hugely stressful situations, counsel often seeks to ease the tension in the courtroom by sharing jokes, amusing comments, or otherwise pleasantly socializing with opposing counsel. While this conduct may certainly be acceptable in hearings other than a jury trial, such fraternization should be discouraged at trial, and most especially in the presence of the jury. A criminal jury trial is among the most serious endeavors one can ever undertake. The proper frame of mind is therefore critical. It is not a cocktail party. People's lives and freedom are at stake. Moreover, a jury does not understand that type of banter between supposed adversaries. They believe that it is improper and offensive, and it is. It trivializes and cheapens the gravity of the proceedings. It is undignified and disrespectful to the jury. You are there to represent a human being. It is a serious thing. Take care of business.

that tells the jury, "*Whenever I stand up, something exciting is going to happen, and it's going to happen right now!*"

e. *Revealing Our Fear*

In our preparation for voir dire, when we ask ourselves what we *need* to know from the jurors, the answer is quite simple: We need to know how each juror feels about the *weaknesses* of our case. We are not concerned about how the jurors feel about the strengths of our case, for the strengths will take care of themselves. Knowing how the jurors feel about the weaknesses of our case will tell us which jurors are a threat to us when it comes time to deliberate. Once identified, they can hopefully be eliminated or at least neutralized.

Determining how the jurors honestly feel about the weaknesses of our case is the essence of voir dire. It also presents the paradox that makes this approach to voir dire so counterintuitive. It has to do with being honest and trusting enough to reveal what we are afraid of.

Like all human beings, jurors are naturally drawn to persons who radiate power. Powerful persons tend to be trustworthy because power implies competence and safety. They are also the default leaders, for others will follow such persons in order to remain safe. Since jurors are looking for a leader to guide them to the "right" decision, you must become that person.

How do we convey to jurors that we are powerful and trustworthy? We honestly reveal the truth about how we feel about our case, our story, and, more specifically, about what we feel regarding the parts of our case that concern us—that give us anxiety—and that we perceive as being bad or harmful to our case. In other words, we expose our ***vulnerability***—what we fear. By telling the truth, we convey honesty not only with our words, but also our body language. We cannot fake it. The jury can sense it.

We always have fears about our cases; there is no perfect case. If we have a perfect case, we settle it, and we don't try it. But why reveal right off the bat the weaknesses in our case? Isn't that counterintuitive? Doesn't that send a signal to the jury that we are not strong and ready to go to battle? Doesn't that give our opponent the advantage of knowing where to attack our case, that is, where we are most vulnerable? In a word, no. We must do it because it is honest, because it is the truth, and we can never develop a meaningful trust relationship with the jury if we don't do it. Here is why we must do this:

If there is something in our case that worries and concerns us, the jury will discover it and talk about it in their deliberations.

It is a guarantee. That is why we must structure our voir dire around what it is in our case that scares us. This single principle, above all others, is the cornerstone of a successful voir dire. It can be reduced to a simple equation:

$$V + T = C$$

(Vulnerability + Trust = Credibility)

This equation is based on a simple principle that forms the heart of your voir dire:

- Identify what you are most afraid of in your case.
- Talk to the jurors about it.

Here is how it works: Voir dire is all about credibility. And credibility is built on vulnerability, honesty, and trust. Power is derived from credibility. In this chapter, you will learn:

- how to *identify* your case vulnerability,
- how to *reveal it*, and
- how to *share it* with the jury, in a way that allows them to share their feelings about it with us.

Our human instinct is to avoid at all costs revealing to our adversary where we are most vulnerable. But that is the paradox of a great voir dire. By revealing our weakness, we transform it into our greatest strength by creating the trust relationship. And therein lies the secret.

Our instinctive fear is that if we do that, the jury might hurt us with that information. And that is true; they might, but only if we try to hide it from them. After all, our instinct is to hide our weaknesses, to pretend that we have no vulnerability, that it doesn't exist. We then believe we will appear to be strong. The problem, of course, is that the appearance is an illusion. We cannot hide it because we cannot hide the truth. The more we try and hide it, the bigger it will appear, and the more frightened of it we will become. The jurors will know that we are running from it, and they will not respect us.

If we hide it from the jurors, they will still know it exists because they will be told. Not by us but by our adversary. He will reveal it to them at a time when it will do the most damage to us. When we cannot protect ourselves. We therefore must protect ourselves by revealing it to the jurors first.

We are all afraid of facing our fear. Doing so takes great courage. But in facing that fear and revealing what can hurt us, we are showing the jurors that we like and respect them as honest persons and that we trust them not to hurt us.

They will not hurt us because *they gain nothing if they do*. By showing them that we are not a threat to them and that we like and respect them, they will have no reason to fear us. They will then have no reason to hurt us. And since we honestly faced our fear in doing it, the jurors will also see our courage. They will respect us and trust us to tell them the truth. We thus gain credibility in their eyes. Jurors who trust and respect us will protect us from our adversary. They will do it with their verdict.

f. The "Bad News" Juror

Gaining credibility with the jurors will allow the jurors to reveal their honest responses to our questions about how they feel about the weak parts of our case—in other words, the "bad news."

Voir dire is a quest for information, and the type of information we seek most is "bad news." Bad news is the opinion of jurors who are against what we stand for. They don't like us, or our client, or our theory of our case. That revelation is nectar of the gods. It is prized above all others. Why? Because they are in essence revealing to us that they are our "enemy," it is the only type of information that is worth finding. We are trying to identify those jurors whom we want to eliminate. That means we want to find jurors who are a threat to our case. We are not interested in spending much time with those who like us and who agree with our theory of the case. Instead, we want the jurors who don't agree with us or who do not agree with our theory of the case. The only way to do it is to uncover what biases and prejudices they possess regarding our case.

When confronted by bad news, our instinct is to retreat and put as much distance as we can between us and the jurors as quickly as possible; in this way, we can neutralize their ability to hurt our case. We are, in effect, trying to get "out of range." This is a very human reaction born of ancient survival, but it must be overcome. Instead, we must train ourselves to react in just the opposite way—*to approach them as close as possible.* Why? So that we can neutralize them. When do we want to discover the "bad juror"? Now, when we can deal with him safely and remove him—or when he is foreperson of our jury?

That being said, how do we deal with a "bad news" juror? The same way as with any other juror—by totally and genuinely accepting his feelings, no matter what they are. We need to "mine" and "drill down" for enough information to confirm that is how the juror really feels so that we can assess how much of a threat he is. We must *thank* the juror for his honesty and willingness to reveal how he truly feels. Then we use that juror to educate the other jurors and to inquire how many other jurors feel the same way. Because we know that there are others who feel the same way but were too timid to admit it, thinking they would be rejected. Such a juror can help smoke out the others. But we must be very careful not to embarrass him or mock him. We accept his opinions and thank him just like we would anyone else for being honest. Again, what he has given us is a priceless gift.

Another reason we are afraid of the "bad news" juror is that we believe that such a juror will somehow convince other jurors to agree with him, and suddenly we are facing an entire panel of hostile jurors. On the contrary, however, a juror like that won't "contaminate" anyone on the panel. Once we smoke out those "bad" jurors, we nail them down tight so that they can't be rehabilitated by either our opponent or the judge. It's easier to get them excused for cause. Also, finding the "bad" juror will enable us to find the "good" jurors who will actually argue our case for us.

Remember it this way: A great voir dire is like a ceremony in which we exchange precious gifts with each other. Our gift to the jurors is our total acceptance of their honest opinions. Their gift to us in return is their trust and belief in us in telling us how they really feel and, hopefully, their affirmative verdict.

g. The "Good News" Juror

Many attorneys believe that when you come across a "good news" juror, that is, one who clearly likes you and your case, you should make every effort to hide her so that your opponent will somehow not recognize her favorable bias and strike her from the panel, thus depriving you of one of your favorable votes.

First of all, it is impossible to hide such a juror. Your opponent is going to realize instantly that he or she must likely strike that juror. The important thing to realize, however, is that *you need not fear the loss.*

Once you realize that you have uncovered a friendly juror who is likely to be eliminated by your opponent, you must make every effort to wring as much positive benefit from that juror as possible before he is excused. Ask questions designed to flesh out his thought process and the basis for his beliefs. Often, this juror is able to articulate rationales that other jurors had not considered. *Those rationales form the basis of your theory of the case. Essentially, have the juror educate the others on the panel as to why they, too, should be agreeing with you and be your friends.* Although you will likely end up losing that juror, the positive benefit from having the juror publicly express to the other jurors his support for your cause could very well pay huge dividends at the end of the trial. That juror could change a lot of minds. And after all, the prosecutor can't strike everybody.

h. Understanding Jury Dynamics

A jury panel is a complex social group that has its own unique dynamics. Every person is different—some are open, others not. Some are bold, others timid. Some are leaders (or fantasize they are), others followers. But we must be aware of certain fundamental truths about these newly formed groups: they need a leader, and they require a "call to action."[14]

---

[14] Joshua Karton, a professional actor, writer, director, and faculty member of the Western Trial Advocacy Institute (WTAI) and the Trial Lawyers College (TLC), among many others, and one of the best known and most revered trial advocacy experts in the nation, points out that forming a group and becoming its leader is not enough. The jurors must be "called to action" by the leader in order to identify a goal and act on it; otherwise they're merely spectators at a social event. The "goal" of course, is the acquittal of your client.

Charlie Abourezk writes:

> A group in its early stages is puzzled, testing, hesitant, but also dependent. They are looking to the leader for structure and answers, as well as approval and acceptance. You must be that person. You must be the group's leader.
>
> As leader, if you model or demonstrate that frank discussion is of great value, the jury will likewise *adopt that behavior*, and it will help them form a group that will discuss, fight for what is right, and work hard to come to a good decision. More often than not, it will be yours.
>
> All members of the group have anxiety about their role in the group to one degree or another. Whether they feel included, influential, and accepted. If so, they will join the group and the formation will be accomplished. This is important, for you want the jury to be a "closed" group. A group that you alone, as leader, have formed.
>
> If a group member feels unsafe or powerless, they are likely to stay disengaged. That is a problem, for a group that has not fully formed is inhibited, they will look around frantically for a leader or a guide to pull them together and help them figure out what happens next. The jury then becomes more vulnerable to the authority of others in the courtroom, such as the judge or our opponent, and we have lost our leadership or persuasive advantages.[15]

We must probe quickly with penetrating, relevant questions, much like a therapist, and then listen very carefully to the answers. We must understand what the juror feels and use that knowledge to guide the juror into being receptive to our leadership. By doing so, we achieve what is most important—we enable the jurors to see our client's story *through our client's eyes.*

They must be able to do this in order to understand why our client did what he did. If they understand him, they can develop empathy for him. Empathy begets emotional attachment. This is ultimately

---

[15] Used with the kind permission of Mr. Abourezk.

where you need the jurors to be. They need to have some "skin in the game" so that they care about what happens to our client. The challenge is to determine how to get them there.

i. Juror Profiling

Many lawyers believe in tailoring their voir dire to "profile" jurors based on the kind of case they have. You know—certain types of cases call for certain types of jurors. Those lawyers comb through the juror questionnaires trying to glean every nuanced tidbit of information about each one, in the interest of whittling down the list of those whom they believe they want. They pore over data such as what religion and political party the jurors espouse, what bumper stickers they display on their vehicles, and what television programs they watch. They then take that data and distill it into a composite of the "perfect" juror for the case.

Some of that information might be useful, but for the most part all that does is stereotype jurors, with little regard for their individual life experiences, and it completely ignores how they really feel about our case. In fact, it creates tunnel vision and restricts us to seeing only those jurors who appear to fit our predetermined idea of who we believe we want. It also blinds us to everyone else and, more importantly, *to what they are telling us.* Juror profiling tends to stifle the most important aspect of voir dire—communication! After all, why bother talking to a juror if he or she does not appear to fit the mold of the ideal juror you have already created for yourself?[16]

You are not looking for any "type" of juror. This is not to say, however, that jurors with certain backgrounds should be ignored. Depending on the facts of each case, jurors with certain backgrounds may be better suited to serve on cases other than yours. Much of the information you need in this regard can ordinarily be found in

---

[16] What if you exhaustively prepared a list of all the characteristics of the "ideal" juror in your case, only to discover at the start of your voir dire that none of the jurors sitting in the courtroom fit that profile? What would you do? Object? Panic? Request that the judge call another panel of venirepersons? This is why you must learn to communicate effectively with the jurors who are present. You don't get to handpick them from the community. On the battlefield, a warrior must know how to fight on the terrain that is before him.

the juror questionnaires issued by the court prior to trial. Questions should therefore be prepared for those specific jurors in order to solicit responses from them that will tend to reveal certain biases. The point, however, is that you should not automatically eliminate all jurors who do not fit a preconceived model. Talk to them. Be yourself. What you seek is their trust, and as long as you are credible you are likely to get it.

j. Use of Hypotheticals

Many attorneys use some form of hypothetical fact question to ferret out the information they need from the jurors. While some attorneys are successful in using this technique, it really doesn't work well in the long run.

For one thing, you're not being honest with the juror. Rather than simply and honestly asking them how they feel about your case, you engage in a type of quiz-show game that I call, "Can You Guess What I'm Really Talking About?" It is a game that the jurors can never win, and they know it, for they rarely know what point you're trying to make. Nor do you, if the truth be known.[17]

Hypotheticals hardly ever work because you are not being real. Like the ancient Druids dancing around a campfire at Stonehenge, you dance cryptically around the point you are trying to make, daring the jurors to interpret the meaning. You are engaging in a baffling game whose rules only you know, which results in the jurors feeling manipulated, humiliated, and confused.[18] You do this, of course, because you are afraid you cannot do it effectively, and as a result the court is going to shut you down and embarrass you in front of the panel.

---

[17] I have heard attorneys use hypotheticals involving chocolate chip cookies, Neopolitan ice cream, Goldilocks and the Three Bears, black holes, shopping at Wal-Mart, and the Theory of Relativity.

[18] In the movie *Bang the Drum Slowly*, a running joke throughout the film is a card game the characters call "TEGWAR" (the Exciting Game Without Any Rules). A hapless victim is invited to join the game and is dealt a hand. The other players, all of whom are in on the joke, kindly offer "help" by explaining that with each new hand, the values of the cards, as well as the rules of the game, change from what they were moments before. Naturally, the victim never holds cards of any value, regardless of their face value, and the other players always win. In no time he is broke.

Another reason that hypothetical questions are not really effective is that even assuming that you obtain some useful information from a hypothetical, you must still refine it down and translate it into the pivotal question you are still needing to answer. This necessitates engaging in a tedious back-and-forth colloquy with the juror in order to get to that point. In the meantime, the clock is ticking. Better to simply ask the critical question from the outset.

k. *Thanking the Jury*

No matter what the jurors tell us, we must thank them. Their honesty is a precious gift to us. After all, what do we say when someone gives us a precious gift? Our thanks, however, must be sincere and genuine. We must truly feel thankful for the juror's comments. If we don't, they will sense our insincerity and we will lose credibility.

On the other hand, do not thank the jurors for appearing in court. They had no choice. They are there because they were issued summonses by the court. They would rather stick needles in their eyes than sit there answering questions. And when you are finished, thank them for their attention and their honesty.

3. The Third Rule of Voir Dire: *Know the Technique*

> *You can sway a thousand men by appealing to their prejudices quicker than you can convince one man by logic.*
>
> —Robert Heinlein

> *A single belief can defeat a thousand facts.*
>
> —Gary Shockey

Now that you know that you are legally permitted to engage in a reasonably substantive and meaningful voir dire and why you must do it a certain way, how do you do it?

First, as explained above, you must identify what you need to know. You must then draw a line directly to it. You don't want to waste any time getting there. The prosecutor has already bored the jury stiff with his voir dire. You must wake them up and get them involved as quickly as possible. You must now determine *how* to ask the questions that will tell you what you need to know. Those are the questions that will allow the jurors to begin to see the client through the client's eyes, and plant the seeds of empathy and caring for your client.

The best way to understand how to do a proper voir dire is to first observe how *not* to do it.

DO NOT:

1. Refer to your client as "the defendant." (He has a name. Use it. Personalize him. He is a human being with value.)
2. Isolate your client at the end of the table. (There is no greater visual indication that you have rejected him.)
3. Ask any questions that do not relate directly to what you need to know. (For example, ask no questions regarding "who knows who" in the courtroom or on the witness list, and do not draw their attention to how long the process is going to take or has already taken. The prosecutor has likely already done all of that and in the process has completely alienated the panel.)
4. Thank the jurors for their attendance. (They had no choice—they were summoned by court order. Show your respect by simply thanking them for their attention and getting down to business.)
5. Try to explain to the jurors what you are doing or why. (Just do it. *Tick . . . Tick . . . Tick.*)

How many times have we heard a voir dire begin something like this:

> Ladies and gentlemen, thank you so much for taking the time out of your busy schedules to be here today. I know that you were summoned here, so you really had no other choice. Ha! Ha! *(Nobody on the jury is laughing. Or even smiling. They're just staring at you.)*
>
> This is the part of the trial we call "voir dire." It is pronounced "vore deer," or sometimes, "vwar dyre." It comes from the French words meaning, literally, "see and say." However, in the legal context it has been commonly interpreted to mean "to

> speak directly." In this part of the trial, the attorney asks the jury questions so that they can say a little bit about themselves and so that the attorney can determine which of them are qualified to be selected for service in this case. The point is not to try to make them uncomfortable or put them on the spot or embarrass them or anything like that. But these questions can sometimes be pretty personal and awkward. Ha! Ha! *(Hostile stares. A couple of jurors glance at their watch. You can hear a pin drop.)*
>
> I hope that it won't take very long, but we would ask that you bear with us, and we'll all get through it as quickly as we can. Let me start by asking how many of you remember the story about Goldilocks and the Three Bears? *(Quizzical looks. One juror rolls his eyes.)*

Well... that went well, didn't it? The jurors now feel they're in for an experience not unlike having a root canal with no anesthesia while naked during the Spanish Inquisition.[19] Judging from that introduction, the jurors would be better off if the procedure was instead being performed by the Abominable Dr. Phibes.

The jury is not the least bit interested in what the procedure is or what it is called. You are wasting their time as well as your own. The clock is ticking. The judge is grinding his teeth and popping Advils like they're M&Ms and is wishing that you had requested a bench trial.

a. *Incorporating the Theory of the Case*

It is critically important that you tie your case theory to your anticipated instructions and voir dire. For it is in voir dire that you introduce your theory of the case to the jury. In so doing, it forms the foundation on which your examination of the jurors is based, as well as for your opening statement, your examination of the witnesses, and your closing argument.

As the "guru" of jury selection experts, Cathy Bennett, said:

> Voir dire should have a theme like any other effective communication. It should be coherent and tied to the rest of your

[19] *"NOBODY expects the Spanish Inquisition!"*

> case. It must divulge your case theory and diffuse the theory of the other side. In the course of voir dire, you should identify your good jurors, and through them, educate the rest of the panel, while ferreting out those who should be struck. Use this opportunity to humanize yourself, your client and your case strategy, to capture the jurors' interest. Above all, listen to what the jurors have to say and always follow their lead.[20]

The concept of a proper voir dire is based not on finding those jurors who are unbiased, impartial, and fair (because, as I have said, there aren't any), but rather in developing a *trust relationship* between the lawyer and each prospective juror by accepting their biases. This is where the true challenge lies; this is the "hard part" of voir dire. This is what will separate you from the majority of other trial lawyers who flail away in frustration at voir dire and cannot understand why they cannot connect with the panel. In other words, this is where you start earning your fee.

b. How to Start

Before you can begin your voir dire, you must undertake a tremendous amount of work. Remember, voir dire is all about building your credibility with the jury. You must determine what it is you are most afraid of, and then determine how to present your fear to the jury. You then have to determine what the "emotional hook" is you wish the jury to tap into so that it will drive their deliberations. They must trust you completely when you are done.

The best and most effective way to start a voir dire is to simply introduce yourself, your assistant (if any), and your client. Speak calmly in a strong, clear voice, from your diaphragm. Look the jury in the eyes. Take charge of the courtroom. Don't rush.

Have your client sit as close to you as you can. When introducing him, stand behind him and place your hands on his shoulders. Show the jury you are not afraid of him, and that you are comfortable enough with your relationship with him that you can touch him in

---

[20] C. E. Bennett and Robert B. Hirschhorn, *Bennett's Guide to Jury Selection and Trial Dynamics in Civil and Criminal Litigation* 162 (1993). (Used with the kind permission of Mr. Hirschhorn.)

that manner and not have it appear phony. It also demonstrates that you believe in him, care for him, and that he has value in your eyes. In introducing your client, also convey the message that it is something that you are proud of.

Here are three examples:

Example No. 1

Your client, Charlie Williams, is a 50-year-old African American homeless veteran who is a chronic drug user. He has a criminal record (felony and misdemeanor) stretching back nearly thirty years. He lives primarily on the streets, and he's been in and out of numerous jails and penitentiaries. Immediately upon his latest release from the penitentiary, he began using methamphetamine. He used so much that he was awake for eight straight days. He was delusional and hallucinating. One night he broke into a parked vehicle by smashing the passenger window, believing he was looking for his mother. He entered the vehicle and removed a couple of items from the front seat and placed them on the pavement. He then walked away, leaving the items next to the vehicle where he had placed them. Minutes later he was confronted by police, and when asked if he had broken the car window, he readily admitted it. He was then charged with misdemeanor destruction of property and burglary (the state asserting he had the intent to steal the property).

In your interviews with him, you learn that he has always pleaded guilty to every crime for which he has been convicted. In the past thirty years, he has amassed a considerable rap sheet of convictions, including numerous felonies, but he has only gone to trial once, for a petty drinking offense in a public park. When you asked him why he didn't plead guilty to that charge, particularly when he already had a multiple felony record (what harm could it have done, right?), he replied, "*Because I wasn't guilty. I wasn't going to plead guilty to something I didn't do.*"

What is your theory of the case? What is your theme? To be effective, it must honestly portray what happened, articulate your defense and clearly identify what the issue of the case is all about. In your analysis, you would want to consider a number of impressions that come to mind, *e.g.*, your client is a drug addict, he is a multiple convicted felon, he is unemployed, he is not articulate, and he admitted breaking into a vehicle. But what other dynamics are at work here? Your client insists on going to trial. Why? What is your defense? More importantly, what are you going to say to the jury? What are you going to ask them?

First of all, you must articulate what your greatest fear is. Your fear is that you will not be able to motivate the jurors to care about Charlie. You are afraid they will see him as a black man who is not worth caring about. A man who is a life-long criminal and drug addict, who is nothing more than a parasite on society. A homeless loser who has the gall to waste their time after being caught red-handed, and beseech them for a "break." You are afraid they will discard him like a used tissue. And they will if this is how you feel about him too.

The case *theory* is simple: Charlie's been overcharged. He admits he removed the property from the truck, but he didn't take it away or hide it. He's going to trial not because he didn't commit a *crime (he did—he broke the car window),* but because he didn't commit *burglary*. He didn't have the intent to steal the property. Congratulations. You are now the proud owner of a defense based upon a "technicality."[21]

But his answer to your question also reveals something deeper about Charlie. Something much more fundamental, visceral, and emotional.[22] Despite his criminal history, drug addiction, and desperate life circumstances, he is a man of *principle*. He still has self-respect and believes in his soul that he should not be stripped of that. Thus begets the case theme: "*Charlie Williams may be a lot of things, but on that night he was no thief.*"

You now have identified a case theory and theme on which your entire voir dire rests. Your cornerstone of that inquiry thus becomes: "*How do you feel about someone being accused of something he didn't do?*" And as the theme and theory of your case, it is the banner you wave throughout the trial, to the closing argument.

---

21 Some attorneys may scoff at this theory, thinking that the jury couldn't care less about the difference. It's a weak defense, and it smacks of "getting off on a technicality." But here's the thing—*the purpose of this manual is to teach how to create magic with a jury where few others can.* It's not about the facts, it's about the story and how you deliver it.

22 Which is precisely what the jurors are going to tune into. This is where you make the magic.

Now take some time and think about the problem areas—those facts that concern you and present problems for you to overcome. In other words, the "bad news" you're going to have to reveal to the jury. There's a lot of it here. However, ask yourself how much of it is really something you have to deal with. Depending on your case dynamic, you might not have to "explain" any of it to the jury. It would be impossible to, anyway.[23]

Honesty is always the best policy with a jury, so consider the following: Tell the jury that your client will be happy to request that they find him guilty of what he actually did—misdemeanor criminal entry. Your defense now consists of not only insisting that your client not be convicted of something he *didn't* do, but instead be convicted of what he *did* do. The key to your case is that you're not going to hide anything.

This honest approach strikes the jury as one of complete fairness and reasonableness. You are not asking for some unattainable, unrealistic pie-in-the-sky miracle verdict that infuriates the jury. You have also changed the "polarity" of the case, in that the focus is no longer on Charlie. It's now on the prosecutor for having overcharged him, thus putting the prosecutor on the defensive. Moreover, Charlie's horrible criminal history now becomes irrelevant and essentially harmless.[24] Your client is transformed from being an unlikeable criminal loser into a sympathetic fellow who is being pushed around by a powerful government, when all he wants is to be treated fairly. That is precisely how each person on the jury panel would like to be treated. They now begin to identify with Charlie and see him not as a pathetic loser, but as a *hapless and powerless target who is easy to blame—just like they could be.* You've now tapped into that emotional "hook" that allows the jurors to "crawl into the hide" of your

---

[23] In a case like this, it would be "like trying to put lipstick on a pig," as they say. Revealing bad news is one thing; explaining it is quite another. In this business, if you're explaining, you're losing. Explaining implies that you've been caught with your hand in the cookie jar.

[24] In fact, if your client has an admissible criminal record and chooses to testify, it would be essential that you have him affirmatively testify to his entire criminal conviction history during your direct examination of him. Leave nothing for the prosecutor to impeach him with.

client. In other words, they begin to *care* about him, and their instinct will be to *protect* him.

After introducing yourselves and your client, settle yourself calmly and look the jurors straight in the eyes. Take a deep breath. The jury is ready. Then dive right in. The best way to do that is to state something bold—usually the theory of your case, since it is what you want them to remember. In this case, it would look something like this:

> *Good afternoon. Has anyone here ever done something you knew was wrong, but you ended up being accused of something much worse that you didn't do?* (Pause.)
>
> *How do you feel about someone who freely admits that what he did was wrong, but was later accused of something much more serious that he did not do?* (Pause.)
>
> *Has anyone here ever had an experience like that?*

You've established your case theory—the story of your client's innocence. More importantly, you did it in a way that is similar to the opening statement but will almost never trigger an objection that you are being "argumentative."

You may get some hands raised, and you can then follow up on the jurors' feelings and experiences in that regard. If no hands go up, a good way to stimulate discussion is to tell them about a personal anecdote from your own life, or the life of a close friend which illustrates the point. It must be authentic, however.

Assume no hands are raised. You might then say: "*Well, let me tell you what happened to me once*" *(or my brother, cousin, etc.—whichever is true)*. The story must be brief and must clearly illustrate precisely the point you are trying to make. When done, pause and look at the jury and ask again if anyone has ever had an experience like that. Chances are some hands will go up.

You will then base your voir dire on the following questions:

- How does it feel to be accused of something worse than what you actually did? Is that fair?
- How do you feel when no one will listen to your explanation? Even when you admit to having done something?

- How do you feel about people who own up to what they did, and honestly accept the consequences?
- How do you feel about people who admit that they've made mistakes and stumbled along the road in their life, and didn't try to hide it or blame someone else for it?
- How do you feel about a government that targets those people in society who are easy to accuse and abuse, because they have no power and no voice to be heard?
- How do we feel about people who protest that kind of treatment and refuse to be bullied by the government?

You begin to see where this is going. You are fanning the flame of unfairness. And if there is one thing that Americans despise, it is a government that acts like a bully to its own citizens. That is the emotion which will drive the verdict in this case.

Example No. 2

You represent Kyle Miller, an 18-year-old high school senior. Kyle and his girlfriend, Stacey, have been dating for over a year. One afternoon, Kyle sees Stacey holding hands with and kissing another boy. Enraged, Kyle gets on the internet and fires off a series of threatening e-mails to the boy, several of which are disturbingly graphic. The boy shows them to his parents, who in turn go to the police. Kyle ends up being charged with felony assault via social media.

The police confiscate Kyle's computer and recover the offending e-mails. They also interview Kyle, who confesses to sending them. The prosecutor is not offering any deals, and intends to "make an example" of Kyle for other students.

Kyle appears doomed. The state has all the evidence and his confession. It's all coming in. On the cusp of adulthood, young Kyle is poised for certain ruin.

Your fear in this case is that the jurors will see him and judge him through adult eyes. They will filter his juvenile and immature behavior through their years of life experience and maturity, and Kyle will come up wanting. They will set a standard for behavior that Kyle can never reach. How can you make the jury see the case through Kyle's eyes? How will they ever understand—much less forgive—why he did what he did?

You begin your voir dire preparation with determining the emotional "hook" that will resonate with the jurors. A careful analysis of the problem reveals the one word upon which you will build your theory and theme, voir dire, opening statement and the rest of your case: "Betrayal."

It is a powerful emotion. At some point in our lives we've all experienced it. And it hurts, especially when we're teenagers. Take the jury there. Your entire voir dire can now be based on the following four questions:

- Does anyone here know what "betrayal" means?
- Has anyone here ever been betrayed? (Would you mind telling us about it?)
- How did it make you feel?
- How do you wish you had been treated by the adults?[25]

Example No. 3

You represent Tina Smith, a 22-year-old woman who has recently given birth to her first child. She is charged with child endangering for using methamphetamine during her pregnancy. The child tested positive for the drug at birth. When interviewed by the police, Tina admitted to having used methamphetamine several times during her pregnancy. She feels tremendous guilt and remorse. The child has been taken from her and placed in state custody.

While there are certain due process and constitutional issues present, assume that the court has denied your motions to dismiss and suppress. You're heading to trial and all the evidence is coming in.

Again, your challenge is to get the jurors to see the case through Tina's eyes—not theirs. Consider what it is that you are most afraid of confronting with the jury in the case:

> *How in the world could a mother do that to her own innocent child? What she did was inexcusable. What is wrong with her?*

---

[25] The jury immediately had their hands in the air, wanting to respond. The life stories and experiences they related were heartbreaking. Within 15 minutes they were back in high school. They saw and felt what Kyle did. Several wept, remembering emotions which came flooding back instantly, even after 40 or more years. The entire voir dire lasted less than an hour. He was acquitted.

She is the most horrible person alive, and should be convicted instantly and punished severely. There is nothing you can say that would make us care about her as a human being. She's a monster. How could you represent someone that despicable?

Your analysis of what this case is really about focuses on what drove your client to use the drug: *Addiction*. It is the scourge of today's society. Addiction to opiates, methamphetamine, sugar, cigarettes, food, etc. dominates television and popular culture. Addiction in some form has touched almost everyone, and it wreaks havoc in people's lives. Thus it becomes the emotional hook of the case.

Your fear becomes the very first question you ask:

Ladies and gentlemen, why would a pregnant woman use methamphetamine?

Wait for an answer. If no one responds, ask it again. Someone will respond. It is a serious question and you will receive a serious response. It may be an angry one. That's even better, for it opens the door to honestly discussing how we feel about people who are addicts, which is precisely where you want to go.

Now you're on your way. You then direct the discussion to the following additional topics by telling the jury that they are going to see evidence that your client used the drug. Ask questions regarding:

- How do you feel about women who do this?
- Let's talk about addiction and methamphetamine. Who here knows someone who has been addicted to methamphetamine, or someone whose life has been affected by the drug?
- How dangerous is it?
- How strong is its grip on those who are addicted to it?
- How far will someone go to use it? What will they risk?
- How do you feel about that person?
- How should we treat someone who is addicted to it? Should we prosecute them or treat them?

You will quite likely discover jurors who have friends or family members whose lives have been affected or perhaps even shattered by the drug. Now it becomes personal. Now there's a face and a name attached to the devastation. Someone they know and care deeply about. They have experienced and understand the despair, the hopelessness, the anguish, the anger and fear. Most importantly, *they acknowledge the inability to stop using it, no matter what the devastating consequences are.* Take them there. Have the jurors describe it.[26] The more you ask the jurors to tell you how they feel, the more they own the problem. Then they'll give you the solution.

Eventually bring the discussion back around to where you started: "So, why would a pregnant woman use methamphetamine?" Someone on the jury is now likely to say, "Because she couldn't help it." There is your theory and your theme. You will conclude by asking, "How should we treat someone like that—with compassion and treatment, or criminal prosecution?" Wait for it. Someone will save you.

The point is this: Always tell the jury what you fear most, and let them help you solve the problem. People want to help others; it is human instinct. All you have to do is have the courage to ask. Articulating your greatest fear will become your greatest strength, and the foundation of your case. You have allowed the jury to see your clients through the clients' eyes, and not the jury's. They will not condemn. They will now begin to understand. They will also trust you for having been honest, and for accepting their honest answers. You have achieved credibility with the jury. And in the process, you may have just won the case.

c. *Have a Partner*

It should be clear at this point that a tremendous amount of information, both verbal and nonverbal, is flowing and swirling around you while you conduct a voir dire. All of it is valuable. You must collect and process it as quickly and as thoroughly as you can in order for it to be of any use to you. This is why it is important for you to have a "spotter" at your counsel table with you. The "spotter" is assigned the job of taking very detailed and accurate notes during your voir dire as to which jurors are saying what in response to your questions

[26] You will also later cross-examine the State's expert witnesses on these issues, which they will have to agree with. In the process, you will make them your experts.

because you won't be able to. You are busy communicating with the jury, listening carefully to their responses, and thinking about what they're telling you.

That includes making solid eye contact and not looking at your notes all the time. You don't want to miss what is happening with the other jurors while you're concentrating on just one of them. You then consult with your spotter during the jury elimination phase in order to determine who to strike.

d. Don't Embarrass the Jurors

Another problem area that many trial lawyers encounter is not knowing how to find out if jurors have any personal experience with the specific types of criminal act involved in the case. Assuming that the question is important in your voir dire (it might not be), the best way is to simply ask them straight out and not waste time with hypotheticals. However, the manner and method of asking the question depend entirely on the nature of the case. You don't ever want to embarrass the jurors.

For example, assume your client is charged with sexually assaulting a child, but the child didn't report it for a long period of time. You want to know how the jurors feel about your case.[27] In so doing, you might believe that it is necessary to find out how many of the jurors themselves had been victims of such abuse as children. At first blush, you may feel that appears to be a good question to ask that would lead to valuable insights as to how such a juror feels about your case. In fact, however, it has little if any value and could prove very destructive if asked in the wrong way.

First of all, never couch any inquiry in terms that put the jurors on the defensive; expose them to embarrassment or humiliation in any way; or eliminate any chance they will openly and honestly answer the question. By asking, "Has anyone here ever been sexually assaulted as a child?" you might get one or two brave souls to hesitantly—and

[27] It is important to understand why this information is necessary. You may assume that jurors do not like either sexual assault cases or the defendants. But that's not what you need to know. *What you need to know is how they feel about the child's delay in reporting it.* Because that will place the seed of reasonable doubt in their minds.

ashamedly—raise their hands. Chances are, however, you won't get responses from anyone. It is a highly personal and sensitive question, asked clumsily and inartfully in a way that would shock and offend many jurors. Their resentment will be translated into loss of trust in you and, ultimately, in refusing to reveal that information to you.

Instead, ask yourself in your preparation why you would even ask such a question and why you would ask it that way. What possible information of any value could it provide for you? "*Well*," you might say,

> *It will tell me how they feel about that type of crime. They will understand how the victim in my case must have felt, and therefore sympathize with her. That will, in turn, make them more receptive to the state's theory of the case and not mine. I will then want to strike them from my jury.*

That is a huge number of assumptions based on precious little information. Based on those assumptions, why bother listening to their answer, assuming they even give you one? Following that line of inquiry, assume that you turn to that shamed juror for follow-up. What do you ask her now, this gem? "*Tell me more. How did it feel to be sexually assaulted?*"

In preparing for your voir dire, you must be painstakingly careful about the questions you ask and how you ask them. Test each question by asking yourself,

> *Why am I asking that? What would a juror's likely response be? Does that really help reveal the information I need to know? Is there a better, simpler, more direct, more honest way to ask it?*

Again, this is another example of why preparing for voir dire is so exhausting. It requires so much insight and analysis.

No matter what the juror's response to the original question above is, it will reveal nothing about how the juror feels about *your client.* You should be asking the jurors how they feel about the facts of *your case.* That is really the information you need, whereas the question of how many of the jurors were actually victims themselves is not that relevant. Think about it: A certain number of them may very well be victims, but their being victims is not information that is important. After all, you can pretty much assume how they feel about it.

What you are really needing to know is how they feel about someone being accused of sexually assaulting a child and why such a victim would not report the assault immediately. Ask it just that clearly. It may be that during their answers to you some of the jurors voluntarily tell you that they themselves were victims. That is golden. It is far better to learn that fact by letting them reveal it to you in their own way rather than you putting them on the spot in front of others.[28] The fact that other jurors who may also be victims choose not to share that information with you when responding has nothing to do with the validity of their response to the question you've asked them about your case. Their answers are still valid, for it is based on and informed by their own experience as victims.

A much more effective way to find out how they feel about your case is to ask:

> *Ladies and gentlemen, my client, Johnny Jones, has been accused of sexually assaulting a child. How do you feel about someone being accused of that type of crime?*

Wait for a response; you'll certainly get one. Then wade into it and find out how they feel. Identify those who have a knee-jerk reaction against it and who else agrees with them.

You then follow up with:

> *You will hear evidence that the child did not report it immediately. How do you feel about that?*

> (Discuss responses.)

> *Can anyone here think of reasons why a child would not report such an assault immediately?*

---

[28] The question is valid, because you need to know if any of the jurors have been victims of sexual assault. You will need to delve into their feelings about your client and the case, but you will do it in a way that does not put them on the spot by identifying them as victims themselves. This is where a voir dire questionnaire becomes necessary. That question would be asked of the entire panel in a list of other proposed questions submitted to the court prior to trial. The answers would be known only to counsel, so that they may use the information discreetly.

This question is one of the most important to ask, for it accomplishes several things: First, it suggests to the jury that the child might have had a reason not to report it immediately, and not because she was afraid of the defendant. Someone on the panel will suggest that maybe she invented the story for her own reasons or because another family member put her up to it. If one of those reasons is actually what your theory of the case is, you've struck pay dirt. Now find out how many other jurors either agree with that, or at least make room for the possibility that could be the case.

Second, since they articulated it, they now own that theory of the case, which you will elevate into your defense. Their ownership of it invests it with great credibility (as opposed to their having to struggle to find a way to believe it if you had simply told them it was a possibility), and they will make it the centerpiece of their deliberations.

e. Let the Jurors "Own" Your Theory of the Case

As the above examples should demonstrate, the technique being taught is for you to lead the discussion with the jurors to the point where they tell you whether or not they are likely to vote for you (by that I mean your theory of the case). The key is to arrive at various milestones along the way. These milestones emphasize critical aspects of your theory of the case.

You are igniting their emotional fuses by carefully leading the jurors into meaningful discussions about the presumption of innocence, reasonable doubt, the importance of critically examining the state's evidence, and the questionable reliability of confessions. And you are doing it without lecturing them or acting in any way as if you are telling them what to think or believe about your case.

All of these lessons begin to sink in and make a difference in the way the jurors are viewing your case because of the dynamic that is at work. Rather than telling them how they should view your case and your client (which never works), you are leading them to those same conclusions *by allowing them to arrive at them themselves.* By having the jurors themselves articulate those concepts, they begin to view them as their creations. They therefore own them. And by owning them, they ascribe a gravity and level of believability and truth to them that they would otherwise not possess.

Of course, the inevitable result of this process is that you eventually lead them, though a series of increasingly narrow hypothetical fact scenarios, to articulate your theory of the case.[29] At that point, all that remains is identifying those jurors who agree with it and those who don't.

This is what you are ultimately aiming for—your theory of the case articulated—and thus owned by—the jurors themselves. They will be advocating for you.

This process will also reveal which jurors on the panel are bearers of "bad news": the ones likely to believe that a child could never make up a story like that, and so therefore your client must be guilty. Again, that is precisely the response you are looking for because it is honest and clearly reveals the juror's bias and prejudice. It is their gift to you. You can now go to work on mining that similar bias with others on the panel, in preparation for challenging them for cause.

f. Breaking the Ice—Going First

If you want someone to be honest with you, you have to be honest with them. But *you must go first.* Spence calls it: "If I show you mine, will you show me yours?" It kickstarts the credibility-building process.

Why do this? Because the issues you will discuss concern the problem areas in your case. Those are the issues that the jury will discuss during deliberations. And you want to be able to have addressed these very topics up front when you can deal with them—and, most importantly, provide your own answers to them—before the jury begins to deliberate.

This technique is usually necessary when the jurors are reluctant to volunteer information themselves. In the example above of Charlie Williams, assume that your initial question to the jury about how they feel about someone charged with something he didn't do (burglary) did not result in any hands being raised. At that point, it is an excellent opportunity for you to give a personal example of how *you* feel about it.[30]

---

[29] This is how you get the jurors to consider what their verdict might be under a hypothetical circumstance without actually asking them. It's a subtle process, and if done properly, the prosecutor never sees it coming.

[30] This is the personal anecdote referred to earlier.

You will, of course, have already prepared for just this situation. Think of a real event in your life that fits the problem in the scenario. Then tell the jury about it. Since you lived it, you don't have to worry about memorizing anything. You can tell it from the heart. Tell the jury what happened and how it made you feel. When you have finished, look at the jurors and ask, *"I wonder if any of you have ever had a similar experience?"* Hands will go up. Now you have something to talk about. Ask how many tried to explain what had happened, but that no one would listen. Then follow it with the most important question of all: *"How did that make you feel?"* You have now tapped directly into the mindset of your client and developed a direct connection with the jurors.

Even if you don't have a personal anecdote that fits the occasion, you can still include your personal opinions about certain aspects of your voir dire that are important. It all starts with honesty.

Here is an example: Assume that you want to discuss the concept of "presumption of innocence" with the jurors. Your fear is that when the jurors see your client sitting next to you at counsel table, they will assume that he's guilty. If you begin talking to them about their "duty" to presume he's innocent, you will appear to be desperately trying to hide the fact that your client is in fact guilty and that you are trying to change their minds about how they feel about it. Instead of addressing the topic academically, address your fear of it directly and honestly (remember, you must honestly appeal to the jury's emotions—for that is how they will decide the case):

YOU: Ladies and gentlemen, Billy has been charged with a very serious crime. I am concerned that as you sit here in the courtroom today, and you see him sitting next to me here at the defense table, you will assume that he is guilty of everything the prosecutor says he did. How do you feel about that?

(No hands go up. That is not surprising, for no one wants to admit openly that they presume anyone to be guilty. Or, a few will respond by saying, "I think he's innocent until proved guilty." *They say it because they believe that's what you want them to say. But they*

don't believe it. You have not yet arrived where you need to be. Don't panic. Keep going.)

Well, let me tell you how *I* feel about that. I'm here in the courthouse almost every day. Every time I walk down the hallway past this courtroom, I glance through the doors to see if there's anything going on. Occasionally I'll see that a trial is being held. If I see someone sitting next to his lawyer at the defense table, I'll know that it is probably a criminal trial. And you know what goes through my head at that moment? Not, "*Gee, there sits an innocent man being accused of a criminal violation.*" No. The first thing that I feel is, "*I wonder what* he *did?*"

I felt that the first time I picked up Billy's file. I wonder if anyone here feels the same way that I do?

(Here you go. Hands now go up. By telling the jurors the truth about how you feel about your own client, they now begin to trust you with telling you the truth about how they feel about him.)

JUROR: Well, I feel that he wouldn't be sitting there if he hadn't done something wrong.

YOU: Thank you. Thank you for being honest about that. Who else here feels the same way?

(Almost every hand now goes up.)

Thank you. I think we can all agree that's how we really feel about that, isn't it? Billy wouldn't be here if he was innocent, right?

(All heads nod in agreement.)

So, I wonder what we're going to do about that? How can we give Billy a fair trial, and listen openly and objectively to the evidence, if we already assume he's guilty?

(Now the jurors don't know what to do. They've now been exposed as not being fair and unbiased. You must now lead them out of the wilderness by giving them an opportunity to cleanse their guilt and in the process shift over to your side.)

Maybe we should just skip the trial and convict him now. What do you say? Should we do that? Is that alright? Who here feels that would be the right thing to do?

(No hands go up.)

Anybody here feel differently?

(A hand goes up.)

JUROR: Well, I'd like to see the evidence.

(This is a bold position to take. He or she is a leader and may end up being the foreperson of the jury.)

YOU: You would? Why? Why would that matter?

JUROR: Because maybe he's innocent.

YOU: How could he be innocent, if we've already decided he's guilty?

JUROR: Well, we shouldn't do that. We can't think of him as guilty. We must look at the evidence before deciding if he's really guilty.

YOU: Thank you. Who else here feels that way? That maybe Billy is innocent of what they say he did, and we should look at the evidence carefully first?

(All hands now go up.)

Who here wants to see the evidence before deciding if Billy actually did anything wrong?

(All hands go up.)

Thank you. So can we all make room for the possibility that Billy may in fact be an innocent man?

(All hands go up.)

Thank you.

(Now look where you are. You've turned the entire panel around to your point of view by simply acknowledging your fear and thus giving the jurors the permission to admit theirs. They trust you now to always tell them the truth, and they will be more inclined to agree with you each time you do it. And you never once uttered the words "presumption of innocence" or lectured the jury on what they should be feeling.)

Here's another example. Assume that your client is not going to testify. Your fear is that the moment you announce that to the jury, they are going to assume that he's guilty. Once again, you address the problem by not giving an abstract, nervous, and unconvincing lecture on the constitutional right not to testify, but by revealing your honest fear:

YOU: Johnny has not decided yet whether he will testify.[31] The judge will instruct you that he is certainly not required to, and if he chooses not to, you must not consider his decision as evidence of his guilt. How do you feel about that?

JUROR: I don't know. That may be the law, but I'd still want to hear his story.

YOU: I agree with you. I'd want to hear his story, too. Some of you might feel that if he chooses not to testify, that he must be guilty. How do you feel about that? *(Several hands are raised. You select a juror.)*

JUROR: I believe that that's true. I feel that if a person charged with a crime doesn't testify, he must be hiding something. He's probably guilty.

YOU: Yes, I understand how you feel. Thank you. Tell me more.

JUROR: Well, I feel that if a person's really innocent, that they shouldn't be afraid of testifying. I mean, what are they afraid of? If they didn't do it, they didn't do it. They shouldn't fear telling the truth.

YOU: Thank you. Who here feels the same way? *(Discuss.)*

I can tell you one thing: If I were charged with a crime and I was innocent, I would insist on taking the stand and testifying. How many of you agree with that? *(Discuss.)*

YOU: Can you think of any reason why an *innocent person* who is charged with a serious crime, like sexual assault, would choose not to testify? [32]

---

[31] Even if your client has already decided not to testify, don't reveal that to the jurors yet. You need to prepare them for that news. They have to accept that decision before they become aware of it. Otherwise you will find yourself having to explain to the jury why your client didn't testify. As noted earlier—if you're explaining, you're losing.

[32] Subliminal message that your client is innocent.

JUROR: Well . . . I don't know. Maybe he's afraid.

YOU: What would he need to be afraid of? If, as you say, he is innocent, then what does he have to fear?[33]

JUROR: Yeah, I know, but . . . maybe he's afraid that nobody will believe him.

YOU: That could certainly be a possibility. Can you think of a reason why someone charged with a crime *they didn't commit* would feel that if they testified they wouldn't be believed?

JUROR: Maybe it was a terrible crime, like this one is. Rape. Maybe he feels that it would be pointless. That nobody would listen to him.

YOU: Thank you. Anything else?

JUROR: Maybe he doesn't come across like a believable person. I mean, what if he's real nervous or something, or can't talk real well. He would act guilty.

YOU: So, what I hear you saying is that if he isn't calm and collected, but instead is nervous, scared, and doesn't believe anyone would believe him no matter what he said, he might appear guilty even though he really isn't?

JUROR: Yeah. Exactly.

YOU: And you know, the prosecuting attorney is a skilled trial lawyer who knows how to make witnesses look guilty on the stand, even if they're innocent.[34]

Has anyone here ever been accused of something you didn't do, and the more you argued against it the more guilty you looked?

(Discuss.)

YOU: Anyone here ever hear the old Shakespeare saying: "Me thinks he protests too much," meaning that if he wasn't guilty he wouldn't be protesting so much?

(Discuss.)

---

[33] Subliminal message to this juror and to the rest of the panel that this juror believes he is innocent.

[34] You might get an objection here, but ignore it. You've put the point before the jury.

If you were innocent, would you protest a lot?
(Discuss.)
Would you be angry?
(Discuss.)
Do you believe it's possible for innocent people to appear guilty because they protest a lot and are angry?
(Discuss.)

YOU: I sometimes feel that way. I feel that people like that can be irritating and make me dislike them. And if I don't like them, I tend not to care about them and to disbelieve them. Who here feels the same way?
Anyone here feel that the Founding Fathers who drafted the Constitution also believed that to be true? That innocent people can be found guilty simply because of the way they react and come off to other people?

YOU: Thank you very much for sharing your true feelings about that. So, can you make room for the possibility that Johnny might decide not to testify for those exact reasons? *That he is innocent* but is afraid that if he testifies that you will think he's guilty because he might "act" guilty?

JUROR: Yeah, I think I can understand that.

YOU: So, if Johnny, on my advice, decides not to testify for those reasons, how do you feel about that?

JUROR: I feel that would be alright. I understand now why he might not want to. I wouldn't hold it against him.

YOU: Thank you very much.
(To the rest of the panel). Who else here feels the same way as Mr. __(juror)__?
(Repeat with other jurors.)

This is an example of a juror who has initially expressed a contrary opinion but who can be used to educate the entire jury panel to accept your client as a human being with a name who is frightened, rather than a guilty "defendant," while at the same time potentially keeping him as a juror (if need be) who may very well vote to acquit your client.

But what if the juror cannot make room for that alternative point of view? How do you handle a "bad news" juror who is clearly entrenched in his beliefs and is unwilling to consider yours? Rejoice! This is the juror you are looking for. He is a danger to your case, and you must eliminate him from the panel. You do it by "setting the hook" and committing him to his belief so strongly that the court cannot talk him out of it and thus has no alternative but to strike him. You must challenge the juror for cause.

g. *Challenging a Juror for Cause*

One of the aspects of voir dire that many attorneys have difficulty with, regardless of experience, is challenging a juror for cause. As stated earlier, jurors know that not everyone will be selected to hear the case, and some will actively seek to avoid it. Knowing how to strike a juror for cause is critical to the success of your voir dire. Studies have shown that 32% of jurors who should have been struck end up having a significant impact on the verdict.

There are two types of juror challenges: peremptory and for cause. Each party is allowed only a limited number of peremptory challenges. They are essentially "freebies." You are permitted to exercise such a challenge against a juror for any reason or for no reason.[35]

On the other hand, there is an unlimited number of challenges for cause. The challenge must be based upon some aspect of the juror's responses to voir dire questions that indicate he or she has expressed a bias or prejudice such that it cannot be disregarded and set aside. Thus, the juror cannot be "fair and impartial," and therefore must be excused from further consideration as a juror for that case.

---

[35] An important exception to this is if by exercising such challenges, you exhibit a pattern which indicates that you are improperly excluding certain jurors based upon race, or some other impermissible criteria. *See* Batson v. Kentucky, 476 U.S. 79, 106 S.Ct. 1712, 90 L.Ed.2d. 669 (1986). A party may not use a peremptory challenge to strike any juror solely on the basis of race. The *Batson* challenge has also been expanded to include peremptory challenges based solely on gender. J.E.B. v. Alabama *ex rel. T.B.*, 511 U.S. 127, 114 S.Ct. 1419, 128 L.Ed.2d. 89 (1994).

The primary problems that attorneys grapple with in this area are the following:

- How to extract enough information from the juror to establish a cause to strike him.
- How to avoid having the judge completely undo your challenge for cause by "rehabilitating" the juror into changing his mind.

The latter of these two is the more critical element to the success of your efforts. It is difficult to describe the frustration one feels when, you having painstakingly committed the juror to his biased (but honest) beliefs and asking the court to excuse the juror for cause, the judge undoes it all by looking directly at the juror, and nodding his head affirmatively in a stern voice says, "Mr. Smith, you can set aside those personal beliefs and decide this case fairly and impartially, *can't you?*" Unless you have carefully crafted your voir dire to anticipate the court's attack, and prepared the juror for it, the juror will cave-in, the court will deny your challenge and you will end up with this juror on your panel.

In order to shore up the juror to withstand this assault by the judge, you must fortify the juror by convincing him that nobody in the world—especially this judge—can make him change his mind.

Assume that you initiated the same discussion with the jurors, as set forth immediately above, regarding your client's decision not to take the stand to testify, except it takes a different turn:

YOU: Johnny has not decided yet whether he will testify. The judge will instruct you that he is certainly not required to, and if he chooses not to you must not consider his decision as evidence of his guilt. How do you feel about that?

JUROR: I don't know. That may be the law, but I'd still want to hear his story.

YOU: *I agree with you. I'd want to hear his story, too.* Some of you might feel that if he chooses not to testify, that he must be guilty. How do you feel about that? *(Several hands are raised. You select a juror.)*

JUROR: I believe that that's true. I feel that if a person charged with a crime doesn't testify, that he must be hiding something. He's probably guilty.

YOU: Thank you. Tell me more.

JUROR: Well, I feel that if a person's really innocent, that they shouldn't be afraid of testifying. I mean, what are they afraid of? If they didn't do it, they didn't do it. They shouldn't fear telling the truth.

YOU: Why is that?

JUROR: Because the stakes are so high.

YOU: Thank you. So, what I hear you say is that if Johnny chooses not to testify in this case, regardless of his reasons, that you would consider that as evidence of his guilt?

JUROR: I sure would. I really would.

(The juror has now clearly established that he rejects your theory of the case and your client. He is revealed as a "bad" juror. You must now "set the hook"—work to extract sufficient facts to establish cause for his removal, and commit him to it, while simultaneously preparing him to withstand the court's efforts to rehabilitate him and keep him on the panel.)

YOU: And that would be the critical factor for you in this case, wouldn't it, that if he chose not to testify, that's the only factor you would need to know? That no amount of evidence pointing to his innocence would matter?

JUROR: That's right.

YOU: So, no testimony by Johnny, therefore no possibility of acquittal in your mind?

JUROR: Nope.

YOU: Thank you very much. I appreciate your honesty. Now, what if the judge tells you that you must set aside those feelings and beliefs if you are selected as a juror in this case, and be fair and impartial. How do you feel about that?

JUROR: Well, I don't know. I think it'd be pretty difficult. I guess I could try to be fair. Yeah, I suppose I could do it.

(The juror is now essentially challenging you—almost daring you—to strike him for cause. The "battle" is now joined. You must now take control of the situation in a way that not only gives you the information you need to strike the juror, but without alienating the rest of the panel. This is the moment of truth.)

YOU: But it's not that easy though, is it? We may say to the judge that we will be fair, but really we still feel the same way inside, don't we? That hasn't changed, has it? *(Note the use of "we" and not "you." Include yourself, because it's a universal truth. You are tapping into what the juror knows is absolutely true. We can never separate our true feelings about something, even if we deny them outwardly.)*

JUROR: Yeah.

YOU: And you would still have those same feelings that you've described if you were chosen to be on this jury?

JUROR: I'm sure I would.

YOU: And you'd still have them while you listened to the testimony of other witnesses and evidence that Johnny was not guilty?

JUROR: Yeah.

YOU: And you would essentially ignore that evidence, if Johnny does not testify?

JUROR: You bet.

YOU: And you would have a difficult time setting aside your true feelings, because that's the way you *honestly feel*, am I correct? And we're being honest here, right?

JUROR: That's right. That's how I honestly feel.

YOU: Even if the judge told you not to?

JUROR: That's right.

YOU: So, even if the judge were to instruct you to set aside your personal feelings in this case and listen openly and fairly to the evidence as presented, and render a fair and impartial verdict in this matter, if Johnny chooses not to testify, you just can't do that, can you? You simply feel too strongly about it? More importantly, you would not be honest with yourself. You just

couldn't be fair and impartial. To do otherwise would be a betrayal to who you really are as a person.
(You are not being critical. You are confirming his desire to be an honest person. You are forcing him to confront his very personhood. God forbid that he betrays his true self!)

JUROR: That's correct.

YOU: And no one, including the judge, would be able to talk you out of that sincere and honest belief, would they?

JUROR: No.

YOU: *(Kindly.)* Thank you very much for your honesty, Mr. ______. Your Honor, I respectfully request that this juror be excused for cause.

Now, at this point, the Court may or may not grant your request. If it does, then you simply move on to each and every juror you previously identified as feeling the same way, and repeat the process. In the alternative, the Court may try to rehabilitate the juror and inquire directly of the juror whether he would in fact be able to set aside his personal feelings and listen fairly to the evidence. If you have engaged in the above colloquy with the juror, he will likely feel emboldened enough to stand up to the Court's inquiry, thus giving the Court little alternative but to strike him for cause. The effect of this will be significant, for other jurors will likewise feel bold enough to openly state, and stand by, their honest feelings. The panel will have seen how respectfully you treated the juror, and that you did not attack him or belittle him. You accepted him totally and honored his true feelings. You made him your friend. And in the process you demonstrated your trustworthiness to the panel. This is exactly the result you were looking for. If, however, the court succeeds in cowing the juror into submission, and refuses to excuse him, the court will likely not allow you to "re-rehabilitate" the juror. Simply continue on with other jurors. You will have gained tremendous credibility at this point.

If this situation (the failed attempt to strike the juror) occurs, when you have concluded your voir dire, **DO NOT PASS THE PANEL FOR CAUSE.** Instead, renew your request that those jurors whom you sought to be excused for cause be excused. After the court responds to your request by denying it (assuming that it still refuses to excuse at least one of them), simply notify the court that you have nothing further in voir dire, but that you do not pass the panel for cause. You need to make your record on appeal on this point if you lose the case. If you pass the panel for cause after the court has denied your challenge for cause, you may have *waived your objection and your grounds for appeal that the court committed reversible error.* Otherwise, if you have been successful in your efforts to challenge jurors for cause, when you are done with your voir dire examination, pass the panel for cause.

Notice that several "cross-examination" type of questions were used in the example above. As stated previously, you usually never want to cross examine the jurors. However, when building a challenge for cause, it is often necessary to use such questions in order to frame the juror's answers properly and set the hook. In this situation, your "cross examination" of the juror is not offensive, manipulative or threatening. You are helping him express how he truly feels, plus you are shoring him up and giving him the weapons with which to defend himself against the judge's "rehabilitation."

h. The Miracle of Silence

What happens when none of the jurors respond to some questions? Now you are faced with a big empty silence opening like a bottomless chasm beneath your feet, waiting for you to drop in and vanish forever.[36] You can feel the "flop sweat." Our natural instinct is to start talking again simply to fill the silence. Aristotle said, "Nature abhors a vacuum." Silence creates a vacuum that needs to be filled. We continue to talk in front of silent strangers because we are nervous and are afraid of silence. Silence feels awkward. And most of us have just enough insecurity in us to try to avoid it at all costs. Silence suggests that we've run out of things to say and are not smart enough to think of anything else. But the reality is that if you know how to use silence, you can open up whole new vistas of communication.

In voir dire, silence can be very effective. Silence can save you. It creates the vacuum necessary to draw out the jurors' feelings about what you've said. If *you* don't fill it, someone on the jury panel will.

---

[36] "Shark like that, swallow you whole!" From *Jaws.*

All you have to do is wait for it. When your audience realizes that you aren't going to fill it, someone will raise their hand or speak up. Then you can continue. This is very important because it is in silence that the magic happens. By that we mean that not only will the jury save you, but in many cases, as shown in the following example, the jurors will actually argue your case for you.

In the sexual assault example given above, silence can be used in such a situation. Assume that during his interrogation by the police after he was arrested, your client confessed to assaulting the girl. You have asked the panel for their feelings about your fear when they learn that he confessed.[37] You are afraid they will conclude he is guilty and will not consider any other evidence to the contrary. Assume that after expressing your fear to the jury and asking for their feedback, there is no initial response. After waiting in silence for a few long moments, you might say:

YOU: So, I guess that's how everyone here feels. That since he confessed, he must be guilty. Is that how you all feel? Who here feels that way? If someone confesses, they must have done it?
(Ask for a show of hands. Just about everyone raises their hand. If not, then raise your hand and say, "Look! I have my hand up!" It's a true statement because we all feel that way. Now hands will go up.)

YOU: Is there anyone here who feels differently?
(No hands are raised.)
Well, then why don't we just stop the trial right now? Why don't we just forget about any trial, any evidence, any proof, and simply convict him and sentence him?
(Wait for it . . .)

JUROR: I'd like to see the evidence.

YOU: Why? He confessed. What's the point?

JUROR: Yeah, but maybe that's not all there is to it.

YOU: What do you mean?

JUROR: I mean. Maybe there's more to the story.

YOU: Like what? What more could there be?

---

[37] You must tell the jurors about this evidence in voir dire. This is the only time and place you can effectively control that kind of devastating information.

JUROR: Well, I don't know . . . maybe his confession is no good. I mean, maybe he was forced into it against his will. Maybe he was tricked into confessing, or something like that.

(This is what you've been waiting for—a juror to say just that. But a juror is making the argument for you, and not you yourself. The juror has given voice to your theory of the case. The jury now owns it.)

YOU: Thank you. Thank you very much for saying that. You will see evidence that indicates that's exactly what happened.[38]

(The juror just gave you the gift. We do not continue without fully acknowledging the gift with genuine gratitude.)

YOU: How many of you feel the same way?

(There will be several tentative hands. Now a discussion can follow between the jurors themselves and with the attorney. Keep your ears open. You will learn much about the jurors as they discuss this point among themselves, as you lead it. Make sure and note which jurors raised their hands in support of and in opposition to your theory of the case.)

See what has happened? By simply switching roles with the jurors who are against you, and letting silence do its work, it enabled the other jurors themselves to frame your case and argue it for you. We never want to be at odds with the jury, and we always want to avoid any arguments.

Note that at all times you thanked the "bad" jurors for their honesty. You also did not attempt to argue with them or manipulate them into changing their beliefs. You showed respect and accepted their feelings in their entirety. You never asked the juror why he felt that way, for that would suggest that you didn't understand what he was saying or that you couldn't understand it, or might allow for the possibility that he had a valid point. You also enabled him to own his feelings honestly

---

[38] Be prepared for an objection here, on the grounds that you are improperly arguing your case in voir dire. Your response is that you are not arguing the case; you are merely telling the jurors that they will see evidence that supports that conclusion. Besides, once again, you are an advocate. Let them object.

and publicly, and not be ashamed of them. The other jurors do not reject him because you didn't and because they know and understand why he feels the way he does. They respect him for being honest about it. And they respect you for enabling him to do it. They see you as someone who will stand by them and support them, no matter what they say. They see you as a person who honestly accepts them *as they are*. They trust you. You are well on the way to winning your case.

i. The Sexual Assault Accuser

In a sexual assault case, what we are most afraid of is the accuser and how to cross-examine her.[39] The worst approach to cross-examination of an accuser of sexual assault would be to attack her without provocation in front of the jury. It would be akin to publicly shaming her and blaming her—in essence assaulting her all over again—for being an alleged victim. The jury would never forgive us and would punish our insensitivity and arrogance in their verdict. However, it is a sad truth that not all accusers of such a despicable act are telling the truth. Victims do lie and for any number of reasons. So how do we cross-examine such an accuser effectively without alienating the jury? How do we confront any problem in our case? We start with voir dire.

When we have a fact problem in our case that we are worried about, no matter what it is, we must first discuss it with the jurors to see how they feel about it. By doing so, we learn how best to approach the problem during the evidentiary phase of the case, and also identify who on the jury panel is with us and who is against us. And the best way to address any problem is head-on.

In order to set up the best cross-examination of the accuser, we must begin by finding out how the jurors feel about her and, more importantly, *how they want us to cross-examine her*. This will lay the foundation for an in-depth and honest dialogue with them regarding how they feel about victims of such crimes, and what kind of

---

[39] Prosecutors love to refer to the targets of the assault as "victims." It is perfectly understandable why they do. We should always object, however, on the grounds that it is a grossly and unfairly biased term, and the court is buying into it improperly. After all, persons are not *victims* until the jury says they are. I prefer to use the term *accuser*. It strikes a much more neutral and acceptable tone, and in fact it subliminally suggests that whether or not the person is in fact a victim is open for debate. Which it certainly should be.

variables are important for them to determine how far they feel our cross-examination should go in any given situation. In essence, we will be seeking the jury's permission *up front* to allow us to do what we have to do to learn the truth.

Voir dire regarding how to cross-examine the sexual assault accuser is not unlike approaching a mine field on a moonless night. As the Wicked Witch of the West said, "These things must be handled *delicately!*"

Approach the subject gently but honestly. Consider using the following to generate a discussion:

> *Now, there is one final thing I need to talk with you about. And this is the most important thing of all.*
>
> *A young girl has accused Johnny of sexually assaulting her.*
>
> *What concerns me is how I am going to have to question her when she takes the stand to testify. I don't know how I am going to do it because I am afraid of what you might think of me if I don't do it in a way that you approve of.*
>
> *You see, both you and I need to get at the truth of what really happened here, and I don't know at this point how difficult a process that might be.*
>
> *How do you feel about the manner I may have to use to uncover the real truth in this case? In other words, I need to know how far you will allow me to go in my cross-examination. How do you feel about that?*
>
> *I may have to ask some pretty tough questions. How do you feel about that?*
>
> *May I have your permission to ask those tough questions? Will you allow me to do that?*
>
> *Thank you. One more thing . . . Will you give me the freedom to decide when I feel I need to ask those tough questions?*
>
> *Thank you all very much. You have all been very helpful and kind.*

By approaching the voir dire in this fashion, we accomplish several critically important things:

- **We build our credibility and trustworthiness with the jurors by revealing to them what we are most afraid of in our case.**

We trust the jury to receive that information as a sign of good faith in our relationship and not to use it against us. They will not use it against us, for by presenting it in the manner we did, we are revealing our vulnerability and thus we are no threat to them.

- **By telling them we are very concerned about what they might think of us if we do something to offend them, we show great respect and honor for them. We want them to know we value their feelings.**

We acknowledge them as the most important persons in the courtroom. The ones most deserving of our respect.

- **By telling them that "you and I both need to get at the truth of what really happened here," we send the message that they are ultimately going to have to decide whether Johnny is guilty and that it is a quest that we are both critically invested in.**

We are therefore a team, we are on the same side—on a quest for the "real" truth. It is a very true statement, and they know it. They have been chosen to find the truth. They don't want to make a mistake. They will see us as assisting them in their quest, and by doing so, they will empower us with the ability—and their authority—to do it. We become their subcontracted agents to carry out their mission.

- **By asking them how they feel about our specific fear, we are asking for their permission up front to do whatever we have to do in order to find the real truth.**

We no longer fear what to do—or what the jurors will think of us—when we rise to begin our cross-examination. We will still have to sense that the time is right before we can knock out the witness, but our dialogue with the jurors will reveal to us whether they will question our decision once we make it. If we secure beforehand their permission to knock out the witness if we need to, then that decision becomes much easier to make when the time comes. We are also securing their permission for us to use our best judgment as to *when* to knock out. They will trust us to know when the time is right.

j. Flexibility

One of the most important keys to a successful voir dire is flexibility. The ability to change gears and turn on a dime is a skill usually associated with Formula 1 drivers, giant slalom ski racers, and fighter pilots. However, it is a skill that is also of great importance in voir dire.

In voir dire, you never know with certainty where the next answer will take you. You must therefore be ready to go with that juror immediately and make it appear as smooth and seamless as if you were waiting all day for the juror to say just that.

Many lawyers aren't flexible in voir dire because they are too busy arguing with the jurors, trying to get them to change their minds and say what the lawyer feels they *should* be saying. We have learned that this is the wrong way to do it. We have instead learned that we welcome whatever the jurors say, and we accept it totally and thank them for their honesty. For one of our goals in voir dire is to identify those who are against us. And we cannot do that effectively if we are not flexible.

We must develop flexibility because the road to a successful voir dire is not smooth—it is filled with potholes. While some are merely annoying or amusing, others are potentially crippling. We must know how to steer around them in order to avoid being stranded.

Here are some examples of voir dire "potholes" that jurors can create for you:

- I don't agree with that at all.
- I don't understand your question/what you mean.
- I think that anyone who did what your client is accused of doing is guilty. No victim could make that up.
- I was put in a life-or-death situation once, and I didn't need to use deadly force. I retreated. I believe there is always a way out, and I don't believe in self-defense. I believe people who resort to self-defense are just trying to find an excuse for killing someone.
- A person who is charged with a crime and is innocent should always testify at trial. If they don't, it means they're hiding something. They're really guilty.
- I can set aside my strong personal feelings and consider the evidence fairly and impartially.

- I feel you're manipulating me.
- I believe in Jesus Christ as my Lord and Savior. He tells me what is right and wrong, regardless of what the law says.

As you can readily see, many of these responses from jurors can easily derail your carefully planned voir dire if you are not trained to steer quickly around them to avoid damage. The most important thing to remember in your answer is to meet all issues, no matter how potentially dangerous, head-on without flinching. The jurors are being honest. It's a gift to you. Rejoice. There are no brick walls or dead ends. Think of each response as opening a door or a window to another route that will get you to where you need to be. *Find it.*

Here are some suggested methods to avoid disaster:

- First and foremost, ALWAYS expect the unexpected. Drive defensively and keep your eyes on the road and both hands on the wheel at all times. Always listen to a little voice in the back of your head that says, "*Could this next stretch of road contain some hidden dangers? What are they likely to be? Get ready.*"
- For such generally benign potholes as "I don't agree with that at all" and "I don't understand your question/what you mean," here are some reliable responses:
    - Tell me more about how you feel.
    - I'm sorry. I apologize if I didn't make myself clear. Let me try again.
    - What I hear you say is ________. Am I understanding your feelings correctly?
    - I'm sorry. You're absolutely right. That question didn't make any sense at all. Let's try it again.
    - I'm not sure I understand your answer. Tell me more about that.

For more problematic challenges, here are some effective methods to handle the more dangerous "potholes" listed above:

JUROR: I think that anyone who did what your client is accused of doing is guilty. No victim could make that up.

YOU: Thank you very much for being honest. Johnny is charged with a terrible crime, and many people no doubt feel the same way you do. In fact, when I first read the file that was my exact response. I, too, couldn't believe anyone could make that up. Who here feels the same way? *(Identify hands.)*

So let's talk about that. Let's talk about things that we know can be 'made up.' Can anyone here think of a crime that can be made up?

(Accept and clarify all answers. Eventually, direct the conversation to the point where most jurors will admit that just about any crime can be made up—including this one. A good follow-up question might be, "What type of evidence would need to be fabricated in order to make up a crime?")

(Once the jurors have identified your case as an example of a fabricated crime, confirm it with: "Can we all agree. . . . " *The real issue therefore is not the claim that the accuser is making, but her* **credibility**. *The real question is whether we can tell truth from fiction; the honest person from the liar. See if you can get the jurors to agree with that statement. They all should.)*

(Now, you might want to consider talking about how we can tell if someone is lying in a case like yours.)

How can we tell if someone is not telling the truth in a case like this?

(Call on jurors. Various ideas will be suggested. Accept all of them. Eventually, someone might suggest a person might be lying if they have something substantial to gain from it, or would lose something of great value if they revealed the truth, which of course might be your theory.)

Thank you. Who here agrees with that? Will you allow me to show you in this case that that is in fact what has happened here? Can you all allow me to show you that? Thank you very much.

(Now you'd better be able to deliver on that promise!)

JUROR: I was put in a life-or-death situation once, and I didn't need to use deadly force. I retreated. I believe there is always a way out, and I don't believe in self-defense.

I believe people who resort to self-defense are just trying to find an excuse for killing someone.

YOU: Thank you very much. That must have been a terrifying situation. Would you mind telling us more about what happened?

(Get the juror to agree that she was placed in a life-or-death situation but that she was fortunate enough to have a way to retreat to safety. Then probe to find out if she had a weapon available, and if so, would she have used it? How about if there had been no way to safely retreat? Ask her to imagine any scenario where she would not have a safe retreat. If she can, then ask her if she would then feel compelled to use deadly force. If not, then fine. Get her to commit that there is absolutely no situation where she could envision herself using deadly force. How about other people? Could she make room for the fact that others may feel differently about that? If she can, then fine. See if she will agree that she could allow that there are facts in this case that would show that Johnny was put in that situation and had no alternative but to use deadly force. Then ask her if she will allow you to show her those facts. She will. Thank her.)

Then: Who else here feels the same way? That you personally may not ever feel the need to use deadly force *yourself*, but that you can imagine a situation where others might be forced to use it. (*Finish the same way.*)

(If the juror says that she cannot imagine a scenario in which anybody *would ever have to use deadly force, then shore her up on that ("set the hook") and identify her as a juror you would seek to challenge for cause or strike with a peremptory. You are done with her. Thank her for her honesty.)*

Then: Who else here feels the same way? *(Same process for them. Presumably any jurors who do not raise their hands feel that self-defense is okay in the right situation. Confirm that presumption.)*

For those jurors: Those of you who feel that way, will you allow me to show you evidence in this case that Johnny was in fact placed in the type of situation where he believed he had no choice but to use deadly force to save his life?
(*They'll all agree.*) Thank you.

JUROR: A person who is charged with a crime and is innocent should always testify at trial. What are they afraid of? If they don't testify it means they're hiding something. They're really guilty.

YOU: Thank you. A lot of people no doubt feel exactly the same way. Who else here feels that way?

Johnny hasn't decided yet if he will testify. How do you feel about that?
(Accept all responses.)

Can anyone here think of a reason why an innocent person would decide not to testify?
(*Accept all responses. At some point, someone will say*, "Maybe because he's scared." or "Why would he be scared? If he's innocent, what does he have to be afraid of?"
(*Accept all responses. Someone will say*, "Because he doesn't think anyone would believe him.")

Why would an innocent person believe that?
(*Accept all responses. Someone will say something like*, "Because he might not speak very well, or he might appear as if he's lying.")

Thank you all for those wonderful answers. I believe that if Johnny decides not to testify, it will be for exactly those reasons—that he doesn't speak very well, he's extremely frightened, and he doesn't believe anyone will believe him.

How do you feel about that?

If Johnny decides not to testify, will you allow room for the possibility it is for those reasons we just discussed, and not because he has something to hide?

Is there anyone here who does not feel that way?

(*Accept and explore. Either way, shore them up.*) Thank you.

JUROR: (*The juror has indicated he is against you.*) But I can set aside my strong personal beliefs and consider the evidence fairly and impartially.

YOU: Thank you. Let's all talk about that for a minute. I believe we can all agree that no one ever wants to admit that he or she has a bias or prejudice that can't be set aside. I know I feel that way. Like most people, I have many biases and prejudices, some of which could disqualify me from sitting on certain juries. Can we all agree that that is how we all feel?

But here's what I wonder about. I wonder if, even when we say we can set aside our personal feelings, we really can't. They're just too deep. They're such an integral part of who each of us is as a person that no matter what we would like to believe, at the end of the day—or if we're in a jury room deliberating on the fate of another person—in our deepest heart of hearts, we really can't set them aside. That no matter what we see or hear, we filter it through our biases and prejudices and cannot ignore them. They're part of who we are. We cannot ignore them any more than we can ignore who we really are as persons.

I feel that way about some things. (*Give a relevant example—a personal one if possible—of our own bias or prejudice that we would like to say we can ignore, but we really cannot.*)

How do you feel about that?

(*Now back to addressing the juror.*)

If the judge were to tell you that regardless of how strongly you feel, you must set aside those feelings and be fair and impartial, how would you feel about that?

(*The jurors will indicate whether or not they are likely to be bullied by the judge. If the jurors are not likely to be bullied, then shore them up on that and see if they will admit that, in this case, their personal feelings are simply too strong and that they would judge all of the evidence and the testimony through those feelings and beliefs. They could not be fair or impartial in this case, even if the judge told them they must. They can now be successfully challenged for cause.)*

(On the other hand, if they can be bullied by the judge (or anyone else) and would agree that they are completely capable of setting aside their personal feelings, then:)

Thank you. What I hear you say is that the personal feelings and beliefs you have expressed in this case (*reiterate them*), are not strong enough or deeply held enough to cause you to keep them or believe in them enough to prevent you from ignoring them in *every* case. Would that be fair to say?

How do you feel about that? *(Have the juror tell you. Don't suggest anything to them.)*

(The juror will have to agree, or else they're admitting they can't ignore them. But the problem is this: they're still lying. They cannot be trusted. You'll have to use a peremptory challenge to strike them.)

JUROR: I feel you're manipulating me.

YOU: *(Sincerely)* I am so sorry I made you feel that way. I have no intention whatsoever of manipulating you. I'm merely trying to find out how you feel about certain aspects of this case that are important. Obviously, I've not done a very good job of that, and I apologize.

Is there now a trust issue between us?

How are we going to deal with that, you and I?

I believe that when you tell me that you are feeling manipulated that you are being honest with me and telling me how you truthfully feel. Am I correct?

I trust your feelings and accept them absolutely and unconditionally.

At what point do you feel you began to feel manipulated?

(Go back to that point and start again. Then once things get back on track):

(Smiling): Are we OK with each other now? Do you still feel manipulated? Will you tell me if you do? Thank you

(To panel): Anyone else here feel manipulated? Do you feel as if I am honestly hearing and responding to your feelings? That I'm listening carefully to what you're telling me and being honest with you? Thank you.

JUROR: I believe in Jesus Christ as my Lord and Savior. He tells me what is right and wrong, regardless of what the law says. Christ is the ultimate authority.

YOU: Thank you very much. I understand and deeply respect your feelings about that. I can imagine that it goes without saying that that is an absolutely fundamental bedrock belief and that no one could ever change your mind. Am I correct?

And that if there was any part of the law in this case that the judge will give to you that you would not agree with, or that conflicted with your deeply held religious beliefs, that you simply would not be able to follow the law, as you have stated, am I correct?

It would be *asking too much of you* to do in this case.

Your spouse couldn't change your mind? The other jurors? The prosecutor? And I couldn't? And certainly the judge couldn't, could he?

You likely have now successfully challenged this juror for cause to be struck from the panel.

k. Know When to Shut Up

Once you have the jury talking to you, you must then do something that nearly every lawyer finds virtually impossible to do: shut up and listen. Why is that difficult? Lawyers do not like feeling vulnerable—we want to control. We are afraid to lose control. Silence infers that we no longer control the situation, and we feel we must continue speaking so that we remain in control. We are afraid to have the spotlight move away from us. But we can help ourselves more by listening, in order to find out how people feel about our cases and the characters and events therein.

The whole point of this exercise is to get the jury talking to you. If you are talking, then you are not listening, and you don't have the time to waste.

l. Going "Off Road"

While you may wish to have notes or an outline as to where you want to go with your voir dire, never be afraid to deviate from the script. You never know where a juror will take you. Since you are exploring and you are willing to accept whatever the jurors present you with, look forward to the opportunity to go "off road" with a juror, to go off on a tangent that may not appear at first to be relevant to the discussion at hand. But you don't know that. Sometimes going off road with a juror can reveal an immense and priceless treasure trove of information that you would have never thought possible. Be open to that possibility. And if it doesn't pan out, you've lost nothing in exploring. You've respected the juror and listened to him. After going off road, you can always return to the main highway.

m. Individually Sequestered Voir Dire

In cases involving high emotional content, where a large number of jurors would be uncomfortable discussing their feelings openly before the others, you should request that voir dire be conducted in chambers with jurors individually. This will allow you to voir dire the jurors about certain sensitive topics in an environment where they can feel more comfortable revealing their honest feelings. As with any voir dire, be sure to have the court reporter present to preserve the testimony.

n. Final Thoughts

Listen carefully to what the jurors say in response to your opponent's voir dire, but don't ever worry about what your opponent is doing. Who cares? Whatever it is, it is not going to be anywhere near as good or as interesting as what you are doing.

Don't fall into the trap of reacting to what the other side is doing. You'll end up playing their game instead of yours. Create your game plan and stick to it. Have faith in it and in your ability to drive it home. Let your opponent worry about what *you're* doing. If you give the impression that you are in total control and utterly confident in your ability to present your case, you will be. Your opponent will pick up on that vibe and will be rattled. It's all psychology. Be yourself, be honest, trust the jury, always tell the truth, accept the jurors unconditionally for who they are and listen.

VOIR DIRE DIAGRAM

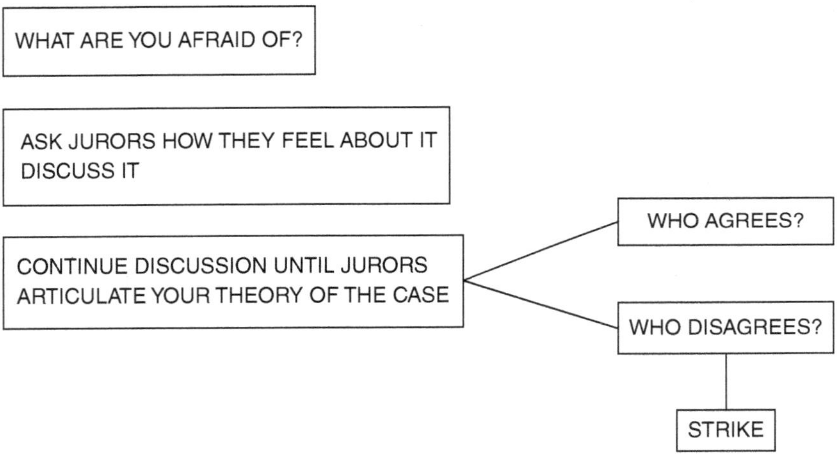

13
Opening Statement

If you can't explain it simply, you don't know it well enough.

—Albert Einstein

The importance of a well-delivered opening statement cannot be overstated. If voir dire is the most important aspect of a trial, the opening statement is nearly so. Following up an effective voir dire with an equally effective opening statement is the equivalent of delivering a devastating one-two knockout punch. Studies have shown that by the end of the opening statement, the majority of jurors have already made up their minds as to who they believe should win the case. The great trial lawyers will agree that if they have an opportunity to accomplish these two things, the case is, for all intents and purposes, over. The battle for the hearts and minds of the jury is finished, and, as they say, "It's all over but the shouting." Your opponent is done, the case is over, and it hasn't even started.

This is because the credibility-building process begins in voir dire. By establishing your credibility with the jury in voir dire, you don't have to jump over that hurdle either in your opening statement or at any later point in the trial. They will automatically be receptive to you as a trustworthy person, and you are then free to concentrate exclusively on your client's story, as will the jury. Your opponent, on the other hand, will be struggling with trying to secure the jury's trust while he's trying to sell them on his case.

The opening statement is where you introduce the jury to your client's story of innocence by presenting the theme of your case that you introduced in voir dire. Opening statements are not intended to be arguments; rather, they paint an overview of where the case is going and what evidence the jury is going to see.[1] One should not overdo it, however. The best opening statements are relatively brief and illustrate critical highlights. Think of them as a movie trailer. Show just enough to tantalize the jurors and leave them wanting to see more.

If the prosecutor makes a statement regarding the evidence that is not substantiated at trial because of a subsequent ruling by the judge, it may or may not be considered misconduct. Comments made by counsel during an opening statement regarding evidence to be introduced at trial are not improper if made in good faith and in the reasonable belief that the evidence is admissible, even if the proof referred to is afterward excluded. Statements will be considered misconduct only when the subsequently excluded evidence is so patently inadmissible as to charge the prosecutor with knowledge that it never could have been admitted.

Although we might be tempted to not pay much attention to the prosecutor's opening statement, it is a good idea to do so for a couple of reasons. First, he may say something in violation of the rules, thus giving you a perfect reason and opportunity to object.[2] Second, though unlikely, he may admit facts that preclude a conviction, in which case you should immediately move to close the case and seek a judgment of acquittal for your client.

---

[1] It is not uncommon for opposing counsel to object during an opening statement and claim that we are "arguing" our case. The general rule is that counsel shall not argue the case during opening statement, nor make statements that cannot be supported by the evidence. Such behavior is viewed as improperly influencing the jury and is considered professional misconduct. Many times, however, your opponent may simply be testing you to see how well you recover when interrupted. Remember, trial is combat. What may be permissible under the rules does not always mean that it is fair. Keep in mind that you are an advocate and consider returning the favor when the need arises.

[2] It could even be egregious enough to justify moving for a mistrial.

Many attorneys fall into the trap of standing up in front of the jury and saying something like this:

> "*Good morning.*" (Check off "Say Good Morning" on your legal pad with a colored pen.) "*Well, folks, you've been listening to me drone on all morning in voir dire, and now you have to endure me for another hour or so.* (Ha! Ha!) *Try to bear with me, and I'll try to be done as quickly as I can.*" (Check!)
>
> "*Ladies and Gentlemen, this is the part of the case where the defendant* (points to his hapless client sitting all alone across the room) *presents an opening statement.* (Check!) *An opening statement is like a roadmap. It will tell you how we intend to prove our case and the evidence you will see along the way. At the end we will ask that you find the defendant not guilty.*" (Check!)
>
> "*It's important for you guys to remember that an opening statement is not an argument, and nothing I say is to be considered evidence in the case.*" (Check!)

All of that is absolutely correct. And it is absolutely deadly in its effect on your case. You are about as interesting as a bag of wet mice, and it would be entirely understandable if, at that point, a juror raised his hand and said, "Shoot me now."

This is what you have just done:

1. In essence, you have just told the jury not to pay any attention whatsoever to anything you say during the trial, starting right now.
2. You have objectified and dehumanized your client by literally distancing yourself from him and referring to him as "the defendant." You have sent the message that you don't care for him at all, to the point where you can't even bring yourself to utter his name.
3. You have also reminded the jury of how long and excruciating your voir dire was and that they now have to listen to you some more.
4. You are also abstractly describing what an opening statement is, rather than simply presenting the jurors with it. The result is

a colossal waste of time and a missed opportunity to sell your case to the jury.

5. You have insulted the jurors by referring to those distinguished and honored citizens as "you guys," as if you were a server at a fast-food restaurant wanting to know if they'd like fries with your opening statement.

The best opening statements are dramatic and powerful. They grab the jury's attention right off the bat and let them know that they're in for a treat. An effective way to begin is to simply and dramatically repeat the theme of your case. It can—and should—be boiled down to one sentence. Be clear and confident. Walk purposely to the podium, settle yourself, look the jury square in the eye, and let them have it. Send the message that you are not messing around and not wasting their time. You are here to take care of business, and the business of the day is the acquittal of your client.

Using the earlier example of Charlie Williams (the homeless veteran who broke into the pickup truck), you might start by saying something like this:

Ladies and gentlemen, Charlie Williams didn't burglarize anything because he didn't steal anything. The only reason we're here today is because the prosecutor has overcharged him. Charlie has wanted to accept responsibility and plead guilty for breaking into that truck since the moment the police arrested him. But he's not going to plead guilty to something he didn't do. That's not right, and we're going to ask you to fix that by finding him not guilty of burglary.

In the twenty seconds or so it took you to say that, you have:

- Stated the theory and theme of your case;
- Clearly told the jury what was wrong with the case; and
- Told the jury what they need to do to fix it.

The jury now knows exactly where you are going and why. By framing your case this way, you are sending the message to the jury that the case is not about what your client did but about how unfair the state is in its prosecution of him. At a stroke, you have changed the focus of the case from your client to the prosecutor. The "vibe" of the trial has suddenly and dramatically changed. You are now on the offensive, and the prosecutor is now backpedaling. Moreover, by telling the jury you're going to ask them to "fix" the problem, you have "called them to action."

Jurors have a strong belief in the American justice system, and, to a larger extent, the "American Way." They believe in playing fairly—by the rules—and not acting like a bully. Americans don't like bullies. That's why the Declaration of Independence was created. Americans also don't like it when the government overreaches or is overly heavyhanded with people who are easily taken advantage of. It flies in the face of fairness. For that reason, jurors are very receptive to the notion that they have the power to correct a wrong and to hold the government accountable. It's a muscle Americans love to flex.

Once you've stated your case theme, pause; then set the stage for what the jury is to see and hear throughout the trial. Highlight the important themes and points. Avoid getting bogged down in details. Do not mention times of day or dates or weather unless those particular details are pivotal to the case. Remember, an opening statement is an overview, it is not a blow-by-blow breakdown of the entire case. It is a summary of what the case is about[3] and why the jury must find your client not guilty. There is no ambiguity, no doubt, no hesitation. It is "as clear as an unmuddied lake."[4]

It should also not take very long. Some attorneys believe that the longer they speak, the more impressed the jury will be. This is not necessarily the case. Less is often more.[5] You want to tease the jurors with what they are about to see and hear. Give them a glimpse of some dramatic highlights, and relate some tidbits of what some of the witnesses are going to say. Then sit down. Keeping it short also forces you to make it powerful. Leave the jury thinking: "*Wow! This is going to be good. I can hardly wait!*"

---

[3] The case is never about the facts. The case is about your client's story and its emotional content.

[4] As uttered by Malcolm McDowell in his role as "Alex" in *A Clockwork Orange*.

[5] One of the best movie trailers I ever saw was for the original 1979 film *Alien*. All it showed was an egg, then the title of the film above it. The egg then cracked open, and at the bottom of the screen appeared the now famous phrase: "In Space, No One Can Hear You Scream."

A. Use of "First Person"

A very effective technique to use in an opening statement is to give part of it in the "first person." In the right case, rather than simply stand at the podium and describe your case to the jury in the narrative fashion of the "third person" (*e.g.*, "*You will see* . . .," "*You will hear* . . .," "*The evidence will show* . . .", "*This is what happened next* . . . "), consider whether the impact of your opening statement would be enhanced by telling your client's story from their point of view in real time as they experienced it.

Assume, for example, that you represent a homeless man who lived in a small, abandoned, rusty, 8 × 11 foot garden shed in the back of a trailer park. He has been charged with attempted first-degree murder for shooting another man who confronted him in the shed and assaulted him. In the ensuing scuffle, your client fired a pistol, seriously wounding his assailant. Obviously, the question of self-defense is at issue. Consider how much more effective your opening would be (with permission of the court beforehand, of course) if you used masking tape to outline the exact dimensions of the shed on the floor in front of the jury box and then stood in the middle of the tiny square and began quietly:

> *Hello. um . . . my name is James Smith. My friends call me "Smitty." This is where I live. It's my home. It ain't much, but it's warm and dry, and it's all mine. On March 15, 2018, when "Big Ed" came at me with that knife, I had nowhere else to go.*

You can see and feel the visceral impact such an opening can have when you do it in the right case. And you don't have to deliver the entire opening in the first person. But as my father would often say with a sly grin, "Do it *just a little bit* and see what happens."

Finally, call the jurors to action by telling them that not only is there a problem with the state's case, but that you are going to ask them to correct it with their verdict. Remember, the jury is not simply sitting there passively listening to you tell a good story—they have a role to play. It is the most important role in the entire case. They have to determine *justice, and it requires the acquittal of your client.*

14 Cross-Examination

When you have to kill a man, it costs nothing to be polite.
—Winston Churchill

A. Introduction

The criminal defense attorney lives for cross-examining the state's witnesses. It is often the only substantive part of the defense case, other than voir dire, opening statement, and closing argument. As critical as cross-examination is to any trial attorney, it is particularly so for the criminal defense attorney; it is the very essence of life itself.

Before diving into cross-examination, however, it is important to take a moment and consider some basic principles regarding the presentation of the government's case as a prelude to it. The prosecutor's presentation of her case-in-chief may give you significant opportunities to object and inflict some damage before you launch your cross-examination. And as noted later in this chapter, one of the best ways to neutralize your opponent's introduction of lay or expert opinion testimony is to prevent it from being introduced in the first place.

1. Limitations on Lay Witness Testimony

Generally speaking, in addition to testifying about what they personally observed or experienced, a lay witness may offer opinions on a variety of subjects, including:

a. The mental or physical conditions of persons
b. The character and reputations of persons
c. The emotions manifested by a person's acts
d. The authenticity of handwriting
e. The speed of moving objects (including collateral observations such as height, weight, color, shape, distance, and odor)
f. Due care and proper conduct
g. Avoidability of an accident
h. Intoxication
i. Value of personal property
j. Physical damage

Any opinion, regardless of the subject, must be based on a proper foundation before it will be considered admissible by the court. Foundation must include evidence that the witness either personally observed the event and/or possesses sufficient personal experience with the subject. Absent the establishment of a proper foundation, an objection should be made to the introduction of any such testimony.

2. Opinions Regarding Truthfulness of a Witness or Guilt of the Defendant

It is impermissible for either a lay witness or an expert witness to offer opinion testimony as to a defendant's guilt. It is reversible error *per se* when such an opinion is elicited by a prosecuting attorney because it is impossible to determine whether the jury may have relied on the expressed opinion in reaching its verdict.

Since the jury determines the credibility and veracity of any witness, opinion testimony judging the truthfulness of a witness should not be admitted, as it is of no assistance to the jury and is harmful error. Typical examples include:

a. A psychologist testifying that a child did not fabricate a story of a sexual assault; and
b. A police officer testifying that, after hearing a victim's account of a sexual assault, he determined that the victim had been raped.

3. Limitations on Expert Witness Testimony

Rules 702 and 703, Federal Rules of Evidence (F.R.E.), set forth the criteria for the admissibility of a professional opinion by an expert witness. Generally speaking, the court has broad discretion in allowing such testimony, and expert testimony is appropriate when the issue in question is one that the average "reasonable juror" would not be able to properly decide without specialized technical knowledge. However, the jury must determine the weight to give such testimony, and they are not required to accept it if they don't find it credible, as is the case with any witness.

The facts or data in the particular case on which an expert bases an opinion may be those perceived by or made known to the expert at or before the hearing. The facts or data underlying the opinion need not be admissible in evidence and may include hearsay, if it is the type relied on by experts in the field. But, like any opinion evidence, proper foundation for it must be established before it will be admitted.[1]

To be admissible, the opinion should help the jury understand the evidence or determine a fact in issue; it should be based on sufficient facts or data; it should be the product of reliable principles and methods; and the expert has reliably applied the principles and methods to the facts of the case. You should object to the introduction of any opinion evidence offered by an "expert" if you believe that it lacks a proper foundation. If, however, despite your objections, such evidence is admitted by the court, you must neutralize it through cross-examination.

B. Generally

The Founding Fathers considered the right of confrontation and cross-examination so essential that they incorporated it into the confrontation clause of the Sixth Amendment of the United States Constitution. A person's testimony—regardless of the stature and credibility of the individual—can never be taken at face value. The testimony must survive the rigors of cross-examination before it may

---

[1] Do not overlook the opportunity to "head the expert off at the pass" by filing a *Daubert* motion to exclude expert testimony before trial. *See* Chapter 15, Impeachment Method No. 15, "Experts—Qualifications and Curriculum Vitae."

be considered trustworthy. The notion of valuing the search for the truth is ingrained in us from the moment we are born. Even the Federal Rules of Evidence invoke it.[2]

Most attorneys enjoy cross-examination, as it is the opportunity for you to highlight those aspects of your opponent's case that are flawed, and in so doing you are showing the jury why your case is correct. It provides the defense attorney a chance to regain and exercise a bit of the control that he has up to that point had to relinquish. He gets to attack the state's case and try to inflict as much damage as possible. In Hollywood (but very rarely in real life), it can occasionally lead to "Perry Mason moments," which are always entertaining. However, effective cross-examination is a skill that, like every other aspect of trial, must be carefully understood and practiced in order to be mastered. Absent extensive preparation, a great cross-examination is far more often fantasized than it is conducted.

Part of the problem is the attorney's anxiety over what he believes the jury expects of him, that is, something dynamic and dramatic. Compounding this is the attorney's own unrealistic expectations. All of these elements combine to hamper our efforts to reach realistic and effective goals.

We sometimes hear of cross-examination being described as an "art." Historically, it was considered such, and a number of highly regarded legal works were held up as the "Bibles" of cross-examination which declared it to be an art form. The problem is that the methods put forth in such texts described a system of cross-examination that cannot be taught, as they rely too much on the particular skills possessed by the authors.

As discussed in Chapter 12(C) regarding voir dire, cross-examination is not an art; it is a science that can be taught to any trial lawyer. Great cross-examiners are not born; they are trained, utilizing the same methods that are set forth in this manual. What makes them great is that they have studied and practiced these techniques so that

---

[2] **F.R.E. 102:** "These rules should be construed so as to administer every proceeding fairly, eliminate unjustifiable expense and delay, and promote the development of evidence law, *to the end of ascertaining the truth and securing a just determination.*" (Emphasis added.)

they become second nature, and they never deviate from them. They are then free to apply them in an artistic way.[3]

It is essential to understand that a successful cross-examination is rarely, if ever a one-shot proposition, the one brilliant, massive, "mother of all bombs" fatal blow that obliterates the witness entirely and reduces him to a quivering mass. Rather, it is a methodical, calculated, workmanlike, and surgical process. It is akin to a boxer winning a fight not because he landed the one big knockout punch but because he consistently and relentlessly used short, powerful jabs, the cumulative effective being to dismantle the witness's defensive armor, thus leaving him exposed to injury or death "by a thousand cuts."

What many attorneys don't understand about cross-examination is that the goal is not necessarily to score points against the opponent's case, *but to avoid having points scored against you.* Attorneys tend to believe that unless they're ripping and slashing away, tearing the witness to shreds, they are not conducting a good cross-examination. As a result, they approach it as if they're launching an all-out frontal assault at dawn in a go-for-broke effort to wipe out the witness. When the smoke and dust have settled, what remains is that the assault has expended a great deal of effort and energy, often accompanied by much loss of life, with little, if anything positive to show for it.

The key to a great cross-examination is this: a calculated, steady, precise, relentless, and consistent attack. Your goal is not necessarily to inflict any fatal blows. But because cross-examination is so dangerous and exposes the examiner to such potential for reciprocal harm, if it can be accomplished with no points being scored against the examiner, then it is a "great" cross-examination. You have emerged from the battle unscathed.

This is not to say that one must never administer the fatal blow if the opportunity arises. Perhaps the most difficult aspect of cross-examination is determining at what point to switch from being

[3] The methods utilized here are adapted from those taught by the "Zen Master" of cross-examination, Terry MacCarthy, in his excellent book, *MacCarthy on Cross-Examination.* T. F. MacCarthy, *MacCarthy on Cross-Examination* (ABA Publishing, 2007). Terry is the former federal public defender for the Northern District of Illinois in Chicago and is considered one of the greatest trial advocacy instructors in the United States.

the delicate examiner to the hardened inquisitor. The line is never clearly marked. One must sense it more than see it. If there is one principle I have learned about cross-examination it is this: We cannot "knock out" a witness unless the jury gives us permission to do so. If we do it prematurely, without permission, the jury will become angry at us and hate us. We will be seen as heavyhanded brutes. If, however, we have the jury's permission, we may pick the time and the place to do it at our discretion. And the better the timing, the more satisfying the knockout, for both us and the jury. After all, they enjoy the spectacle of a bad character getting his or her comeuppance just as much as any audience. And we often do not need to be barbaric about it. When retribution is due, more often than not it is the subtle unexpected insertion of the knife that is more keenly experienced and enjoyed by the audience than a brutal bludgeoning.

Effective cross-examination rarely requires an aggressive demeanor. One can get nearly everything one needs from an adverse witness by taking the high road and treating the witness kindly. That is because the key to extracting information from a witness relies not on intimidation but on *control*: control over the material, your emotions, your questions, and, most importantly of course, the witness.

As someone once said, "A true mark of character is how you handle power when you have it." Power wielded seamlessly and without being overbearing is the most effective and persuasive use of the power of cross-examination because *you look good using it.* Those who know how to use power effectively do not need to raise their voices, use a biting tone, or employ any other disrespectful tactic. Letting the cross degenerate into arguing, bickering, and quibbling is disastrous, for it sends the message that you have lost control.

Cross-examination is the unique opportunity for you to argue your case to the jury, while diminishing your opponent's, using the witness as the conduit. You become the real witness, and the witness on the stand becomes merely a tool—a broadcasting transmitter pointed at the jury. You are essentially speaking directly to the jury through the witness's mouth. Whatever you say is true thus becomes true. It is a tightly scripted process that is strictly adhered to. The witness has no role to play other than to agree with you. He is asked nothing else and says nothing else.

The witness may or may not present a sufficient reason to knock her out. If not, so be it. Accept the fact that it was enough to simply diminish her credibility and not destroy her entirely. Then sit down. You have done all you can. You conducted yourself with integrity and class. The jury will now have to determine the depth of the witness's credibility and truthfulness. But they will also rely a great deal on your proven credibility and trustworthiness when it comes to arguing what the "real truth" of the case is.

It is for this reason that we are once again reminded that cross-examination, like all other aspects of a jury trial, is theater. Form is far more important than substance. Therefore, the true objective of cross-examination, above all else, is to look good. You want the jury to like you. You want to look good in their eyes. Thus, the form of your cross-examination is more important than the substantive points you seek to make.[4]

C. The Rules

There are just three simple rules for a great cross-examination:

1. *Rule No. 1:* You Become the Witness

As the cross-examiner, you have a story to tell. It is your client's story. Your goal in cross-examination is to have the witness help you tell that story. The challenge is to limit the damage that such an adversarial encounter can inflict on your case. The key, therefore, is to "look good" on cross-examination.

The best way to look good is to tell your client's story in as complete and powerful way as possible. The only way to do that is for you to become the witness and testify yourself. If you are cross-examining the witness, however, how can you also become the witness?

In a nutshell, you tell your client's story through a series of declaratory statements to which the witness must respond with "yes." The witness is limited to that answer only. He is then reduced to the role of mouthpiece—*your* mouthpiece. You therefore become the witness in that you are testifying to the jury through the witness

[4] MacCarthy (2007), p. 39.

you are cross-examining. By limiting the witness's response to "yes," you control him. And if you control the witness, you control the story.

The reason that you ask only those questions to which the witness must agree is that the last thing you want to occur on the stand is for you to engage in an argument with the witness. You are not there to debate the witness; you are there only to have that witness confirm unequivocally the fact or facts that help your case. Leave the argument for your closing to the jury. Therefore, the only words you want to hear out of that witness's mouth are "yes," or "that's correct." Craft your questions so that that is the only response possible.

The way to do that is to make a list of each and every single fact, no matter how detailed, that supports your story. Then simply have the witness confirm each fact. Ignore any fact that does not contribute in some way to your story.

2. *Rule No. 2:* Leading Questions Only

We were taught in law school that a good cross-examination is composed primarily of leading questions. However, in the "real world" of trial cross-examination that is not true. A great cross-examination is not composed primarily of leading questions; it is composed *entirely* of leading questions.

Effective cross-examinations should never be presented in the form of open-ended interrogatories. In fact, they are not questions at all. Rather, they are declarative statements of fact with which the witness must agree. They often end (or begin) with "Correct? . . ." or "Isn't it true . . . " or "We can agree . . . " or something similar. More often than not, the mere declaration of the sentence is sufficient ("The car was green. . . ."). The factual statements are designed to support only your evidence and theory of the case and should be derived from evidence in the case which the witness is forced to agree with. Any questions that are not supportive of your position should not be asked. Period.

Since you are essentially testifying directly to the jury, it is critical that you prepare your questions very carefully with the jury in mind. Put yourself in their position and ask yourself what kind of testimony you would want to hear if you were a juror. Thanks to Hollywood, the jury expects the cross-examination to be dramatic and powerful. This is your opportunity to ask the kinds of pointed questions the jury would ask if they were given the opportunity to do so. They therefore don't want to see that opportunity squandered.

Some lawyers believe that asking an open-ended question is acceptable if the answer cannot harm you. That is a very dangerous habit to fall into, for that line can be easily blurred. You must never forget that whenever you cross-examine a witness, that witness is almost always looking for a way to kill you; a chink in your armor; an opening to thrust the dagger straight into your throat. All it takes is one split second and a poorly worded question. Never, ever, give any witness the chance to do that. Therefore, *there are no safe open-ended questions. Period.* You are in a street fight to the death. Consider what a devastating lethal weapon a leading question is. Why forfeit the enormous advantage that gives you?

3. *Rule No. 3:* Short + Statements = Control[5]

Cross-examination is all about controlling the witness. More specifically, it is about controlling the witness in order to maximize the amount of favorable testimony you put in through the witness, while simultaneously limiting the witness's ability to insert unfavorable testimony. This is accomplished through factual statements with which the witness must agree. The shorter the better. It makes the statements punchy and easy for the jury to grab. More importantly, it gives you total control over the narrative and leaves no "wiggle room" for the witness. Hence the equation:

Short + Statements = Control.

Let's assume that you want to prove that the witness saw Larry Liar enter the bar at 1:30 a.m. on Saturday. Larry arrived in a green convertible and stayed at the bar for about thirty minutes. He left with a blond-haired woman in a red dress. They were picked up by three people driving a white SUV. The witness saw all of it. Rather than ask cumbersome questions cluttered with facts, break it down

---

[5] *Id.*, at 65.

into a series of jabs that drive home the points clearly. It would go something like this:

YOU:	Now I want to ask you some questions about when you were standing across the street from Clancy's Bar early that Saturday morning, you understand?[6]
WITNESS:	Yes.
YOU:	It was about 1:30 a.m.
WITNESS:	Yes.
YOU:	It was dark.
WITNESS:	Yes.
YOU:	A car pulled up.
WITNESS:	Yes.
YOU:	Convertible.
WITNESS:	Yes.
YOU:	Green.
WITNESS:	Yes.
YOU:	A man got out of the car.
WITNESS:	Yes.
YOU:	You recognized him.
WITNESS:	Yes.
YOU:	It was Larry Liar.
WITNESS:	Yes.
YOU:	He walked into the bar.
WITNESS:	Yes.
YOU:	You continued to stand around across the street.
WITNESS:	Yes.
YOU:	After about half an hour, you saw a man leave the bar.
WITNESS:	Yes.
YOU:	You recognized him.
WITNESS.	Yes.
YOU:	It was the same man who had arrived half an hour earlier in the green convertible.
WITNESS:	Yes.

[6] Always begin your cross-exam, as well as a new topic, by telling the witness where you are going. It puts you in the driver's seat. It is called a "transition." (*See* MacCarthy [2007], p. 68.)

YOU:	Larry Liar.
WITNESS:	Yes.
YOU:	He left with a woman.
WITNESS:	Yes.
YOU:	She was wearing a red dress.
WITNESS:	Yes.
YOU:	She had blond hair.
WITNESS:	Yes.
YOU:	They were picked up by some people in an SUV.
WITNESS:	Yes.
YOU:	White.
WITNESS:	Yes.
YOU:	There were three people in the SUV.
WITNESS:	Yes

You are not asking questions; rather, you are telling your story. The witness is merely agreeing with you and is the conduit through which you are speaking directly to the jury. It is a tightly controlled script with no deviations. There is no argument.[7]

An effective drill for learning this method is to simply imagine any activity you do on a daily basis and create a declaratory sentence out of each separate act. For example, go through your routine every morning when you wake up:

You awoke.
You looked at your alarm clock.
It said 7:00 a.m.
You got out of bed.
You put on your robe.
It was blue.
You walked out of your bedroom.
You entered the bathroom.
You brushed your teeth.

[7] Even though you are theoretically "asking questions," you may state them as facts, thus avoiding the raised voice inflection caused by the presence of a question mark. If you feel more comfortable, throw in an occasional "Isn't that true?" or "Correct?" Don't overdo it, however. Less is more.

You took a shower.
You combed your hair.
You got dressed.

You get the idea. Use short, declaratory sentences that the witness must agree with. The reason you want to use many detailed statements is because the more times you have the witness responding "yes" to your questions, the more control you appear to have over the witness, and therefore the better you look.

D. Primacy and Recency

Another technique that effective cross-examiners use is "primacy and recency." Studies have shown that the first words a listener hears will be the words that the listener remembers. This concept is called "primacy." Studies have also shown that the last words a listener hears will also be long remembered. This is called "recency." Always start with an important and positive theme and, likewise, end with one. These will be the things best remembered.

One of the best ways to begin a cross-examination and establish primacy (not to mention asserting your control over the witness from the outset) is for the witness to have a felony conviction. You want to impeach the credibility of the witness. There is no better way to do it than to establish that you are in control from the get-go and will take no prisoners. I liken it to getting the witness's attention by laying a 2 in. x 4 in. lovingly across their forehead:

YOU: Mr. Smith, I'd like to ask you some questions regarding your background, you understand?
WITNESS: Yes.
YOU: We can agree that you are a ***convicted felon.***

Talk about "impactive primacy!" You cannot improve on this.[8]

As we want to start on a high note, so also do we want to end on one. This is what we mean by recency. A good technique to use

[8] *Id.*, p. 50. For further examples of how to impeach a witness with a criminal history, see Section E in Chapter 15 (Impeachment), page 247.

is to prepare a strong final question, preferably one that echoes or even restates your opening theory. When you have completed your examination, you can then wrap it up with that final question, which essentially sums up the gist of the entire examination.

There is, however, a caveat: *Do not attempt to get the witness to admit to the ultimate fact in dispute.* No matter how brilliant you have been and how badly the examination has gone for the witness, he will have been coached never to admit the "Big Question" in the case. You will then end up in a fight that you will lose, which could easily neutralize, if not nullify completely, an otherwise effective cross-examination.

E. The Big Question

We are often tempted during cross-examination to ask the witness the single pivotal question in the entire case in the hope that he will admit it. ("Isn't it true you were the second shooter on the grassy knoll!" or in a civil case, "Isn't it true you were negligent!")[9] This is nothing more than a fantasy triggered by our impatience and ego, as well as our fear that we're not striking big enough blows. There is nothing to be gained by asking the witness the Big Question.

If you want to prove that a witness is not credible, or did something wrong (e.g., was negligent in the performance of a duty of care, or didn't properly investigate the case, or was on the grassy knoll), you will get nowhere by asking her directly if she did it. The witness will never admit it. And once she has denied it, you have nowhere to go. You're stuck.

Instead of asking the witness to agree to a detailed series of facts that cannot be disputed ("*Short + Statements*"), you are attempting to force the witness to agree to *your subjective and argumentative conclusion that the witness is at fault in some egregious way*. Since it is a *conclusion*, the witness will never agree with it.

[9] For those readers unfamiliar with the details of the assassination of President John F. Kennedy, it has been often alleged by conspiracy theorists that the accused killer, Lee Harvey Oswald, did not act alone. There must have been a "second shooter" hidden on the "grassy knoll" located just ahead and to the right of the motorcade as it made its way through the plaza. Such a person was never seen by any witness, however, and there is no known evidence that such a person ever existed.

The best way to prove such a conclusion is to focus on all of the questions that touch on the *individual factual evidence surrounding the conclusion* and try to get the witness to admit his involvement in those individual facts. Then, your argument to the jury is simply to point out that the witness admitted doing all of the facts supporting the conclusion, thus enabling the jury to draw the same conclusion. The fact that the witness denies that conclusion becomes irrelevant and, of course, makes the witness appear noncredible.

For example, when trying to prove that a law enforcement officer did not conduct a proper and thorough investigation, question him on each and every aspect of the case that he did *not* investigate, evidence he did *not* seize, witnesses he did *not* interview, scenes and locations he did *not* visit, and so on. Then simply use these admissions to later argue to the jury that the officer did not conduct a proper and thorough investigation.[10]

F. Know When to Shut Up

Part of a good cross-examination is knowing when to shut up and sit down. A short, powerful, razor-sharp cross-examination that lasts only a few minutes is far more effective than one that drones on and on, meanders all over the place, is unclear, generates numerous objections, and confuses the jury as to what point you are trying to make.

It goes without saying that each witness can only testify about those things over which he has knowledge and to which he can only respond "yes." That means that in your preparation you must clearly establish where you want to go with each witness. There must be a certain destination in mind. Once you have made the points you seek, then you have "arrived" and are finished with the examination of that witness. You must then sit down. Do not be tempted to "play with" the witness thereafter. Nothing good will come of it. Remember, witnesses are looking for that one shot to hit you when you aren't looking. And all it takes is one fumbled question, one question too many, one momentary lapse of focus, and it will all come apart before your eyes. It will happen so fast you won't even realize it until it is too late. Remember, the goal of a great cross-examination is not

[10] For examples of this technique, see Chapter 15, Section 6.

necessarily to harm your opponent but to keep your opponent from harming you.

That being said, not every opposing witness needs to be cross-examined. In many instances, the witness may not have testified to anything that hurts you. A cardinal rule should therefore be that if the witness hasn't harmed you in any way, why cross-examine him? They are, after all, your opponent's witnesses. They are not testifying because they want to help you. If the witness has not harmed you, then why risk harming yourself by cross-examining him and giving him another chance to do it?

The longer you linger with a witness in cross-examination, the greater the chance that you will be hurt. Besides, the shorter the examination, the punchier (and safer) it is, and the jury will remember the points you made.

G. Know When Not to Be Aggressive

Never begin a cross-examination with an aggressive attitude, even with an anticipated hostile witness. You will appear to be a bully if you do, and juries don't like bullies. It also sends the message that you are afraid of the witness. If you are asking him only those questions he must agree to, there is no reason to attack him. Besides, the witness may actually agree with you and give you what you need without coercion.

Sometimes during the course of a cross-examination things might turn ugly. But don't be the one who starts it. Let the witness start the fight. You must remain the picture of reasonableness and fairness at all times, no matter what. Let the jury get the impression that it's the witness, and not you, who's being a smart ass. Keep a close eye on the jury as things continue to deteriorate. It won't be long before you can sense that the jury gives you permission to go in for the hard punch. *You must wait for permission from the jury before you can knock out the witness, however.* If you knock out the witness without the jury's permission, they will not forgive you, and they may punish you with their verdict.

Another point that many attorneys misunderstand is to never rehash your opponent's direct examination testimony: "*Now, on direct examination you testified that. . . .*" Why emphasize it? It certainly wasn't uttered to help you. It's also a waste of time. Never do it. Also, your opponent's witnesses do not "testify." They "claim" or they "give their versions" or "tell their stories," but they never testify. The only witnesses who testify are your witnesses. Why? Because "testify" carries with it the weight of sworn truth.

One more word about beginning a cross-examination. Many lawyers introduce themselves to the witness in some fashion before beginning ("*Good morning*").[11] If for no other reason, it would seem to be good manners. However, some courts frown on such a practice, if not outright ban it. Moreover, studies have shown that jurors are understandably turned off by meaningless salutations. It sounds phony. There is no need to introduce yourself. You are there for a purpose—to inflict damage on your opponent's case. The witness knows precisely who you are. Don't do it.

H. When a Witness "Runs"

What do you do when the witness refuses to be limited to a "yes" answer? In other words, you ask a simple question, and the witness decides that he's going to answer the question in a long, rambling narrative, which doesn't respond to the question at all. He, in essence, "runs" on you:

> *Q:* You saw a car.
>
> *A:* Well, I was standing on the corner and it was raining. I was afraid that if I got too close to the street I'd get splashed by a passing car, and then the light turned green and I dropped my umbrella.

Many attorneys might try to interrupt the witness in midsentence, which usually ends up with both of you talking at the same time, with you becoming increasingly louder and the court reporter finally shouting, "*Counsel, one at a time, please!*" You then ask the question

[11] Or, as Terry MacCarthy whimsically demonstrates: "*Good Morning, Mrs. Jones. I hope you had a pleasant trip to the courthouse this morning. Let me introduce myself. I am Terry MacCarthy. Now, if you do not hear or understand me, you just stop me and let me know. This will not take long. I just have a few questions. Would you like some coffee and a donut before we get started?*" He is being facetious, of course. As he points out, "OK, *this last one we do not use, probably because we never thought about it.*" MacCarthy (2007), p. 47.

again, only more pointedly this time: "*You saw a car, yes or no?*" Again the witness runs on you. What do you do then?

At this point, some attorneys might turn to the court and ask for help. "*Your Honor,*" they whine, "*I respectfully ask that the court order the witness to answer the question.*" The court may look at you, and with blank, dead eyes say, "*Counsel, the witness has answered the question. Ask another one.*" Now what do you do? Call your mother?

Asking the court to assist you in examining the witness is tantamount to throwing your hands in the air and exclaiming, "*I don't know how to control this witness! I have no power! I need help!*" This is certainly not the way to obtain the information you need, and it most definitely does not make you look good. You clearly have lost control of the witness. You must never ask the court for help. It instantly weakens you in the eyes of the jury. You are handing control to the witness and to the court. The jury will lose respect for you.

The best way to handle a witness who runs on you is to "break him to lead."[12] Let the witness ramble on and calmly wait for him to finish. Then ask the same question again. The witness may run again. Wait for it. Perhaps turn your back on him while he continues to talk. Pick up a piece of paper and give the appearance of reading it. Look at the jury. This time, turn to him, look him in the eye, address him by his name, and slowly ask the question again while lowering your voice slightly. Keep asking the question until he finally answers it:

YOU:	The car was green.
WITNESS:	*(Blah, Blah, Blah, Blah, Blah.)*
YOU:	The car . . . was **green.**
WITNESS:	*(Blah, Blah, Blah, Blah, Blah.)*
YOU:	***Mr. Jones,*** the . . . car . . . was . . . ***green.***

---

[12] This is a technique used by those who train horses. It is not in the horse's nature to follow wherever you lead it. It is a process that requires the horse to trust the trainer in order to follow him. The horse must be made to understand that the trainer will not give up and will not accept any response other than the correct one. The trainer will continue to bring the horse back with the lead rope every time he runs. Eventually, the horse understands that running will only result in his being brought back and forced to respond the way the trainer wants it to. It takes a great deal of patience, time, strength, and more patience.

In some cases, you may want to pursue the game a bit and have some fun:

WITNESS: (A couple of "*blah, blah, blah*" responses.)
YOU: Mr. Jones, perhaps the question was too difficult for you to answer. Let me simplify it for you. The car . . . was . . . ***green.***[13]

Eventually, the witness will realize the futility of running on you and will answer the question. You have successfully broken him to lead. It is very important that you do not attempt to control the witness through aggression or abrasiveness. This includes interrupting the witness. Never do that. It leaves a bad impression on the jury. It is rude and constitutes bad manners as well as a lack of common sense.

Looking good means being in control of the witness at all times. You must control the witness by not appearing that you are punishing him, even though in a sense you are.

I. Police Officers

For the most part, law enforcement officers are accustomed to testifying at trial. They understand the fundamentals of direct examination and cross-examination. They have attended seminars, and they have also been trained by the local prosecutors to respond on cross-examination by revealing as little information as possible. In other words, they are trained to severely damage your case if given a chance. Do not give them that chance. Structure your cross-examination of a law enforcement officer in such a way that the officer has no choice but to admit to your questioning, and you should also avoid any kind of opportunity for the officer to engage in a subjective debate.

Many defense attorneys fall into the trap of believing that the police officer will "crack" under the intense pressure of their withering

[13] You might also write the question in large letters on a white board, point to it, and ask, "Can you answer my question?" This is usually followed by, "Well, maybe you just aren't capable of answering that question." This is a technique often employed quite effectively by Gerry Spence. His tone was always friendly, but the underlying threat was clear.

cross-examination, as long as they keep talking and asking questions in an aggressive manner. This is the "Neanderthal" method. Repeatedly banging a stick against a rock will likely accomplish nothing more than breaking the stick, while inflicting precious little damage on the rock.

A more effective technique is to start on the "outskirts" and work your way in, being more specific each time. The "outskirts" are the questions that establish the nature of the officer's job and training (specifically, his training as a *professional* criminal investigator), emphasizing that a *professional* criminal investigator is specially trained to observe certain things and to look for places where evidence could be found, etc., and that the *best investigators* go the extra mile and look everywhere. An investigator who fails to perform all these duties is not thorough, and his conclusions are therefore untrustworthy. The criminal investigator, of course, will certainly agree to all of that. He is, after all, *a highly trained professional* who knows what he is doing. He is proud of it. Play to his ego. Then, begin to draw the noose a little tighter by slowly but surely establishing all of those things he did or did not do in the case which reflect the fact that he did not follow his training or that he did not know what he was doing. He will never admit it if you ask him directly. But you won't ask him the "Big Question." As we discussed earlier in this section, the evidence will be clear, as you will later argue.

Assume, for example, that your client has been charged with conspiracy to possess and deliver a large package of drugs. The package was sent to your client's home address but was intercepted by postal authorities before it could be delivered. The officer has testified on direct examination that his investigation revealed that the package was purportedly shipped from New Orleans by someone else in the conspiracy. Your cross-examination might go something like this:[14]

YOU: I would like to ask you some questions regarding your background and training; you understand?

WITNESS: Yes.

YOU: You have been employed as a detective with the police department for six years.

[14] Based on an actual examination, though edited here for instructional purposes.

WITNESS: Yes.

YOU: You are a sworn law enforcement officer.

WITNESS: Yes.

YOU: You are trained in accordance with applicable policies and regulations pertaining to law enforcement officers.

WITNESS: Yes.

YOU: You received that training and certification in 2010.

WITNESS: Yes.

YOU: Part of your training included instruction on how to investigate a criminal case, did it not?

WITNESS: It did, yes.

YOU: That instruction included such topics and areas as how to follow leads and locate and interview witnesses.

WITNESS: Yes.

YOU: You were taught that the more detailed information you uncover in your investigation, the more accurate and trustworthy your results.

WITNESS: Yes.

YOU: In other words, the more effort you put into a case, the greater the likelihood of solving it.

WITNESS: Yes.

YOU: You would agree with me that your job is to solve crimes. Correct?

WITNESS: Yes.

YOU: Identify persons who might have committed criminal acts, and discover evidence of their involvement in those criminal acts.

WITNESS: Yes.

YOU: And present your findings and conclusions to the local prosecuting attorney's office for review and filing of criminal charges.

WITNESS: Yes.

YOU: You understand that the filing of criminal charges against a citizen is an extremely serious matter.

WITNESS: Yes.

YOU: It impacts their lives?

WITNESS: Yes.
YOU: It often changes their lives.
WITNESS: It certainly can, yes.
YOU: Sometimes forever.
WITNESS: Yes.
YOU: So as a law enforcement professional, you want to make sure that you do the very best job that you can, correct?
WITNESS: Of course.
YOU: You want to uncover every fact, follow every lead, interview every witness, consider every possibility, right?
WITNESS: Yes.
YOU: You consider yourself a professional, do you not?
WITNESS: Absolutely.
YOU: You often have people's lives and futures in your hands.
WITNESS: Yes.
YOU: You therefore want to be absolutely certain that you get it right, don't you?
WITNESS: I want to be as accurate as I can, yes.
YOU: And ***thorough,*** yes?
WITNESS: Yes.
YOU: Leave no stone unturned?
WITNESS: That's right.
YOU: Because if you make mistakes in your line of work, the consequences can be severe, can't they?
WITNESS: Yes.
YOU: Innocent people can be charged and even convicted of criminal acts they didn't commit?
WITNESS: Yes.
YOU: So, we can agree that the most important thing you can do as a professional law enforcement officer and criminal investigator is to investigate and study each and every case, and to invest whatever time and effort may be necessary, to obtain all of the facts that you possibly can, correct?
WITNESS: Yes.

YOU: To uncover the truth.
WITNESS: Yes.
YOU: You considered this an official criminal investigation.
WITNESS: Yes.
YOU: And if, as a result of an investigator not carrying out his sworn duties, an innocent person was charged with a crime, that would be a very bad situation, would it not?
WITNESS: Yes.
YOU: Now I'm going to ask you some questions regarding your official investigation in this case, you understand?
WITNESS: Yes.
YOU: You were the investigator officially assigned to this case, were you not?
WITNESS: Yes.
YOU: During your official investigation, you developed information that led you to believe that additional information and persons of interest were in New Orleans, Louisiana.
WITNESS: That's correct.
YOU: Pursuant to your official investigation, you believed that you needed to travel to New Orleans to obtain further information from these individuals.
WITNESS: Yes, that's correct.
YOU: You flew to New Orleans at the expense of the Police Department.
WITNESS: Yes.
YOU: You arrived in New Orleans on Wednesday, March 15th of last year.
WITNESS: Yes.
YOU: You stayed at the Omni Hotel.[15]
WITNESS: Yes.

[15] The details regarding the name of the hotel, who he called and didn't call, or whatever else he did or didn't do, were all discovered by you in your cross-examination of the officer at the preliminary hearing. Those detailed open-ended questions which comprised your "fishing expedition" early in the case now pay off.

YOU:	That's a four-star hotel?
WITNESS:	I don't know.
YOU:	It was a very nice hotel.
WITNESS:	Yes.
YOU:	You didn't call anyone connected to the case that evening.
WITNESS:	No. I arrived late in the evening and I saw no point in doing so.
YOU:	You began your official investigation bright and early the next day.
WITNESS:	Yes.
YOU:	You made a number of telephone calls.
WITNESS:	That's correct.
YOU:	But you met with exactly no witnesses that day.
WITNESS:	Uh, I don't recall meeting with any witnesses that day, no.
YOU:	They were "unavailable" according to your official investigation report. *(A copy of which you hold up for the jury to see, but you do not introduce it.)*
WITNESS:	That's correct.
YOU:	So that takes us through Thursday, the 16th, correct?
WITNESS:	Yes, I believe so.
YOU:	So, Friday the 17th, you continued your official investigation?
WITNESS:	Yes.
YOU:	After breakfast you attempted to actually call some witnesses?
WITNESS:	That's right. I made some calls.
YOU:	You were once again unsuccessful.
WITNESS:	I, uh, wasn't able to locate anyone, no.
YOU:	And you didn't meet with any witnesses on Friday?
WITNESS:	No. I couldn't locate anyone.
YOU:	You flew out that afternoon and returned to your office, correct?
WITNESS:	Correct.
YOU:	You spent a total of two and one-half days in New Orleans.
WITNESS:	Yes.

YOU:	Officially investigating this case.
WITNESS:	Yes.
YOU:	You were on official police business?
WITNESS:	Yes.
YOU:	And your business was to investigate this case, call and meet with witnesses and other persons of interest.
WITNESS:	That's right.
YOU:	And you submitted your official report of your investigation to the prosecuting attorney containing all of the information you have just testified to to this jury?
WITNESS:	Yes.
YOU:	And that report contains not one summary of any interview you conducted with witnesses because you never conducted any interviews while you were there, correct?
WITNESS:	Yes.
YOU:	And that is the information upon which this prosecutor has based his entire case against my client.
WITNESS:	Yes.
YOU:	Your Honor, I have no further questions for this . . . "Detective."

Note that no questions were open-ended. Note also that at no time did the examiner argue or engage in a debate with the witness as to whether the investigation was worthwhile or even professional. Clearly, it was not. That is argued to the jury in closing.

J. Expert Witnesses

Cross-examining experts requires a great deal of preparation, both mentally and academically. Whereas it might be possible on occasion to conduct an effective examination of an ordinary witness with just a handful of well-thought-out questions, an effective cross-examination of an expert is rarely, if ever, so easily undertaken.

For one thing, you are not as knowledgeable about the subject matter as the expert is. Another thing is that he is often being paid for his opinions, which means that he has a vested interest in being somewhat of an advocate for his employer's point of view. He will therefore be much less likely to be swayed in those opinions, unlike an ordinary witness. All of this means that when you take on an expert, you know you are in a fight. However, the smart defense attorney will realize that successfully cross-examining an expert is more about avoiding being hurt by him and less about defeating him. You must not try to obliterate the expert. Your goal is to simply show the jury that he can be wounded, and you then run away as fast as you can and live to fight another day.

The best way to handle the cross-examination of an expert is to treat him like a mad dog. Keep him in his cage and avoid getting into the cage with him altogether. When you have to jab at him, use a long pole and plunge it between the bars, then move quickly out of the way and approach him from a different position. Never attack him head-on. Instead, concentrate on a specific area where he is vulnerable and keep attacking it. Then run like hell.

An effective technique is to try and disable the expert before they have a chance to offer any opinions. When the prosecutor calls his expert to the stand, wait for him to establish his identity and why he has been called to testify. Then stand and ask the court for an opportunity to voir dire the witness as to his qualifications to testify as an expert. This is particularly important if you did not have an opportunity prior to trial to hold a *Daubert* hearing to test the expert's qualifications.

Cross-examine the expert carefully regarding all aspects of the foundation for his opinions pursuant to *Daubert*, but do not have him state those opinions. When finished, move the court to disqualify his testimony on the grounds that it lacks sufficient foundation pursuant to *Daubert.*

If you are on a case where the issue requires the testimony of experts (other than a drug case where the state chemist merely has to testify that the suspect material is in fact a controlled substance), you should make every effort to obtain the very best one that money can buy.[16] When you obtain through discovery the materials submitted by the state's expert, review those carefully with your expert and

---

[16] *See* Chapter 10(D)(2) "Expert Witnesses."

identify those areas where the two experts differ. Work with your expert to determine why they disagree, and have your expert help you fashion a line of interrogation designed to highlight why it is that the state's expert is wrong. When you have completed your cross-examination of the expert, then sit down. The less time you expose yourself in combat with an expert, the better off you will be.[17]

Another very effective technique is to make the opposing expert "your" expert. In other words, focus on those things that are universally true to all such experts in her field, and which help your case. She must agree to them, or she risks losing her credibility with the jury.

Assuming the opposing expert is credible, she will necessarily agree with your expert up to a point. The more she agrees the better. At some point the opinions differ, however. Try to establish that the point of divergence is due to additional information she was unaware of, or an interpretation based upon incorrect assumptions. Had she been provided that information or the correct assumptions, as your expert was, she would have actually agreed with your expert's conclusion.

K. Being Held in Contempt

One of the questions which always lurks at the back of a trial lawyer's mind is "How far can I go with this?" We must always abide by the rules of ethics and courtroom behavior, and should never be seen as having run amok in the courtroom.[18] On rare occasion, however, the court may threaten us with being in contempt of court. Depending upon one's age and experience, such a threat may or may not carry much weight. While we must never misbehave in the courtroom, we must likewise never be afraid to stand our ground for our clients.

As has been pointed out repeatedly in this manual, as a trial lawyer you are a warrior, and as such you cannot be afraid of being held in contempt if the situation warrants it. While you never want to purposely place yourself in harm's way, if you believe in good faith that the law is on your side, and you are acting ethically and respectfully to the court, when the chips are down you must be willing to risk

[17] See also Chapter 15, Sections 15 and 16, regarding how to impeach an expert.
[18] Like Al Pacino's character in the film *And Justice For All*.

being held in contempt of court for the sake of your client. As an advocate for those who have no one to speak for them, you are not there to make the court's life easy. As Gerry Spence said, "I push my cases as hard as I can and I think it's my duty and my job to do so—to the edge. I don't think I should leave a margin."

There are two types of contempt: civil and criminal, and they can be in the form of either direct or indirect (constructive). Direct contempts are those committed in the court's presence, and constructive contempts are those committed outside of the hearing or view of the judge.

A civil contempt is generally intended to compel a party to comply with a lawful court order, while a criminal contempt is punitive in character and is enforced so that the authority of the law and the court will be vindicated.[19] To determine whether a particular act is contemptuous, courts consider the following:

> [Wh]ether the complained-of acts actually obstructed the proceedings, and it has been said that: ' . . . An attorney possesses the requisite intent only if he knows or reasonably should be aware in view of all the circumstances, especially the heat of the controversy, that he is exceeding the outermost limits of his proper role and hindering rather than facilitating the search for truth.' *Hawk v. Cardoza,* 575 F.2d at 734-735, *citing In re Dellinger,* 461 F.2d 389, 400 (7th Cir. 1972).[20]

If you are threatened with or held in contempt, don't panic. Any discomfort or inconvenience you suffer will be temporary. Remember, you are in this to win it. And also remember, at the end of the day when the smoke all clears, they can damage you, but they can't eat you.

---

[19] *Horn v. District Court, Ninth Judicial District,* 647 P.2d 1368, 1372-73 (Wyo. 1982). *See also Swain v. State,* 220 P.3d 504, 507-08 (Wyo. 2009) (*citing Bloom v. Illinois,* 391 U.S. 194, 201, 88 S.Ct. 1477, 1481-82, 20 L.Ed.2d 522 (1968): "While a judgment of civil contempt is conditional and may be lifted when the disobedience ends, punishment for criminal contempt is unconditional and fixed. In essence, criminal contempt is 'a crime in every fundamental respect,' and a conviction for criminal contempt is indistinguishable from an ordinary criminal conviction."

[20] *Horn,* at 1375-76.

To help you get your head around this, perhaps this will put things in perspective:

> Law enforcement officers have the obligation to convict the guilty and to make sure they do not convict the innocent. They must be dedicated to making the criminal trial a procedure for the ascertainment of the true facts surrounding the commission of the crime. [Footnote omitted].
>
> To this extent, our so-called adversary system is not adversary at all; nor should it be. But defense counsel has no comparable obligation to ascertain or present the truth. Our system assigns him a different mission. He must be and is interested in preventing the conviction of the innocent, but, absent a voluntary plea of guilty, we also insist that he defend his client whether he is innocent or guilty. The State has the obligation to present the evidence. Defense counsel need present nothing, even if he knows what the truth is. He need not furnish any witnesses to the police, or reveal any confidences of his client, or furnish any other information to help the prosecution's case. If he can confuse a witness, even a truthful one, or make him appear at a disadvantage, unsure or indecisive, that will be his normal course. [Footnote omitted].
>
> Our interest in not convicting the innocent permits counsel to put the State to its proof, to put the State's case in the worst possible light, regardless of what he thinks or knows to be the truth. Undoubtedly there are some limits which defense counsel must observe [footnote omitted] but more often than not, defense counsel will cross-examine a prosecution witness, and impeach him if he can, even if he thinks the witness is telling the truth, just as he will attempt to destroy a witness who he thinks is lying. In this respect, as part of our modified adversary system and as part of the duty imposed on the most honorable defense counsel, we countenance or require conduct which in many instances has little, if any, relation to the search for truth.

United States v. Wade, 388 U.S. 218, 256-58 (1967) (Justice Byron White).

15
Impeachment

For the trial lawyer, impeachment goes hand-in-hand with cross-examination. While cross-examination is the process that enables us to probe for and expose weaknesses in the state's case, impeachment is the device—the weapon, if you will—by which we inflict the most injury.

In a nutshell, impeachment is the process by which we attack a witness's credibility. Is he lying or is he merely mistaken? Does he possess a bias that affects the veracity of his testimony? Is he a "bad person?" These questions can become pivotal in a trial. Impeachment is also one of the most confusing and misunderstood parts of a trial, for a number of reasons as will be seen.

There are sixteen recognized methods to impeach a witness.[1] Some are more widely used and thus more practical than others. All sixteen

---

1 The sixteen methods set forth here are incorporated and adapted from those taught by Terence F. MacCarthy and presented in his outstanding book, *MacCarthy on Impeachment*. T. F. MACCARTHY, SEAN P. MACCARTHY, & HON. TERENCE F. MACCARTHY, *MACCARTHY ON IMPEACHMENT HOW TO FIND AND USE THESE WEAPONS OF MASS DESTRUCTION* (ABA Publishing, 2016). (They are used here with the kind permission of Mr. MacCarthy Sr.)

While the materials have been summarized for this chapter, the reader is strongly encouraged to obtain MacCarthy's book, as it contains valuable examples of line-by-line examination, as well as pertinent authority and citations, that the professional must become familiar with.

are summarized here, although many are set forth in an abbreviated fashion owing to their limited applicability and use in a typical criminal trial.

The Sixteen Ways to Impeach a Witness

1. Inconsistent Statements (Rule 613)
2. Contradictions—Contrary Evidence
3. Motivation
4. Truthfulness (Rule 608)
5. Convictions (Rule 609)
6. What the Witness Could Have Done But Did not Do
7. Capacity
8. Bad Acts, Crimes and Wrongs (Rule 404(b))
9. Habit (Rule 406)
10. Writing Used to Refresh Memory (Rule 612)
11. Admissions (Rule 801(d)(2))
12. The Hearsay Declarant (Rule 806)
13. Character Witnesses (Rule 404(a))
14. Certain Evidence of Sexual Behavior by Alleged Victim (Rules 412, 413, 414, 415)
15. Qualifications and Curriculum Vitae (Rule 702) *(Experts Only)*
16. Learned Treatises (Rule 803(18)) *(Experts Only)*

A. Use of Inconsistent Statements

1. Introduction

Impeaching a witness with inconsistent statements is the most important method of impeachment, primarily for the reason that it is the method most used by trial lawyers. It is used to establish that the witness is either a liar or at least mistaken.

2. Relevant Federal Rules of Evidence

Rule 607: Who May Impeach a Witness

> Any party, including the party that called the witness, may attack the witness's credibility.

Rule 613: Witness's Prior Statement

(a) Showing or Disclosing the Statement during Examination

When examining a witness about the witness's prior statement made by the witness, whether written or not, a party need not show it or disclose its contents to the witness. But the party must, on request, show it or disclose its contents to an adverse party's attorney.

(b) Extrinsic Evidence of a Prior Inconsistent Statement

Extrinsic evidence of a witness's prior inconsistent statement is admissible only if the witness is given an opportunity to explain or deny the statement and an adverse party is given an opportunity to examine the witness about it, or if justice so requires. This subdivision (b) does not apply to an opposing party's statement under Rule 801(d)(2).

3. How to Use This Method

Impeachment by use of inconsistent statements is fairly easy, as long as the following limitations are understood.

Use of inconsistent statements is subject to the "collateral" limitation. This means that if the prior inconsistent statement concerns a subject that is *immaterial, or of little or no importance to the issue in dispute*, then it is considered "collateral" to the subject of the witness's testimony, and thus its existence cannot be proven by extrinsic (outside) evidence. It is being used only for purposes of attacking the credibility of the witness, and it is not being introduced as "substantive evidence."

The exception to that is if the prior inconsistent statement was made *under oath* (*e.g.*, trial, deposition, or grand jury testimony). If so, then the statement may come in not only to impeach the witness, but as *substantive evidence as well.* (See Rule 801(d)(1).) In such a situation, you want to request that the judge instruct the jury that the evidence is also being admitted for that purpose.

4. What Is an "Inconsistent Statement"?

A "statement" can be either something spoken by the witness or something written, or it may also be in the form of nonverbal conduct intended as an assertion.

There are three types:

1. Obviously, if the witness has made a statement on a prior occasion that is inconsistent with what he is saying now, that is an "inconsistent statement." For example, if the witness stated earlier that the car was "green" but now claims it was "red," he may be impeached on that inconsistency.
2. It can also occur in a situation involving an "omission," where a witness who made a statement (or did not mention) on a prior occasion that a thing had not occurred or had not existed is now testifying that it did. For example, if a police officer testifies at trial that the defendant admitted at the time of his arrest that the leather bag containing drugs belonged to him, and the report the officer filled out at that time says nothing about such a statement being made, he may be impeached on that omission. As you can see, however, impeachment by omission is not as powerful as impeachment by inconsistent statement.
3. The third example is where a witness testifies that he "doesn't know," "doesn't remember," or "doesn't recall." These are considered "evasive responses." These types of inconsistent statements can usually be handled short of impeaching the witness. They include:
   a. Simply repeat the statement. (Perhaps he didn't hear you, or perhaps he needs to be reminded of the gravity of the moment.)
   b. If that fails, *"refresh his recollection."* Using a document containing the original response to the statement you have just put to him:

Q: You gave a statement to the detective?
A: Yes.
Q: You represented to the detective that it was true and correct?
A: Yes.
Q: You wrote it out?
A: Yes.
Q: You signed it?
A: Yes.
Q: You know what this is? *(Show the witness the document.)*
A: Yes. *(No need for him to explain what it is.)*

Q: Read the highlighted portion to yourself, and not out loud. *(After the witness reads it, take the document back and simply renew your "question.")*

c. Should that fail, and the witness persists in his evasive answer, then impeach him with the statement.

CAUTION! **Allow for the possibility that the witness is being honest but simply mistaken. Attacking such a witness would be in bad form.[2] Instead, you should try the following:**

1) Simply correct the witness: "Actually the car was green and not red."
2) Refresh his recollection.
3) Finally, use the "short version" of impeachment. Simply mention the earlier statement and the fact that the witness then said the car was green.

5. The General Rules of Impeachment with an Inconsistent Statement

There are six general tules of impeaching a witness with an inconsistent statement:

1. Disregard small inconsistencies.
2. Commit the witness to his testimony.
3. Showcase the truth of the impeaching statement.
4. Show the witness the impeaching statement.
5. Read the impeaching statement.
6. Do not revisit the impeaching statement.

Rule 1: Disregard Small Inconsistencies

If the witness you seek to impeach is unimportant or the inconsistency is of little or no consequence, do not worry about it. It's not important enough to waste time on.

Assume the witness's prior statement was that she left the bar at "around 3 p.m."

Q: You left the bar?
A: Yes.

---

[2] As with everything concerning a trial lawyer, you must above all "look good."

Q: It was around three in the afternoon?
A: No, counsel. I left at exactly 2:58 and 30 seconds. I remember I looked at my watch, and it was exactly 2:58 and 30 seconds.[3]

You can impeach this witness, but why would you, unless something important happened in that last minute and 30 seconds. A witness such as this will not come across well to the jury. Knowing that, we refrain from impeaching her on her inconsistent statement. It's not worth the trouble, and it will make you appear petty, and not able to distinguish what is important from what is not. Plus it wastes the jury's time, and, most importantly of all, it does not make you look good!

Rule 2: Commit the Witness to His Testimony

You "commit" him to his testimony so that he is locked in and you can impeach him.

> ***CAUTION!* You *do not always* want to commit the witness. It depends on whether the impeaching statement concerns an issue that is *collateral* or *noncollateral.***

If the statement is *collateral* (unimportant), then *you will not be permitted to use extrinsic evidence* to impeach with it (but you will want to set the hook). If it is *noncollateral* (important), then *you will be permitted to use extrinsic evidence* (but you will not want to set the hook). The extrinsic evidence is, of course, the actual document that contains the original impeaching statement

An example of committing the witness by using a collateral (non-important) impeachment:

Q: You saw a car?
A: Yes.
Q: Green?
A: No, it was red.
Q: You are telling the jury the car was definitely red?
A: Yes.

---

[3] MacCarthy (2016), p. 16.

Q: You are telling them that the car was absolutely not green?
A: Yes.[4]
Q: In your sworn deposition, you told us the car was green?
A: No. I said, as I am now, that the car was red.[5]

End of impeachment! The witness has been given the opportunity to either admit and explain the inconsistency or deny it, pursuant to Federal Rule 613(b). He has denied it. You therefore cannot use extrinsic evidence (the deposition) to impeach the witness. You have scored whatever points you're going to score on that inconsistency. You must accept his answer and move on.

Here is why you do *not* want to commit the witness if the impeaching issue is noncollateral: In a noncollateral situation, you are not merely pointing out that the witness is inconsistent—you also want the jury to believe the original statement is true. In other words, if it is important that the color of the car was actually green instead of red, you do not want to create a situation where you have locked the witness in so tight to his testimony that the car was red, that you are sending the wrong information to the jury. You never want to send the jury the wrong information.

But if you don't commit the witness, couldn't he change his answer back to "green"? Yes, but in order to send the right information to the jury, you will let him do it. You therefore want to allow the witness to change his answer to "green," if it is important for the jury to believe that was in fact the color of the car.

If the witness at some point realizes his peril and changes his answer to "green," has he also escaped being impeached? In other words, haven't you failed in your objective? No. In a noncollateral situation, mere impeachment of the witness is not the most important objective (as it is in a collateral situation). Although he might "get away," his duplicity will not be lost on the jury. And we will have accomplished our most important objective: The car was green and not red.

Assume, however, that the witness does not realize the danger he's in and chooses to fight. An example of a noncollateral impeachment is explained in the next rule, as follows.

---

4 *Id.*, at p. 17.
5 *Id.*, at p. 18.

Rule 3: Showcase the Truth of the Impeaching Statement.

Remember that your objective at this point is to ensure that the jury believes the truth is found in the original statement the witness made, and not the one being presented on the witness stand. Second, but no less importantly, you want them to know that the witness made contradictory statements, thus branding him, at the very least, untrustworthy and not credible.

You do this by showcasing the impeaching statement.[6] You want to assign as much significance and credibility as possible to the original statement, giving it all the indicia of reliability and truthfulness as if it appeared to be coming from "the burning bush." It is the most important purpose of the impeachment process.[7]

The setup:

Q: You saw a car?
A: Yes.
Q: Green?
A: No, the car was red.[8]

Remember, you are in a noncollateral impeachment. You may use extrinsic evidence to impeach the witness. You have the deposition, or sworn statement, to the police, or the FBI "302" statement of the witness where he said the car was green.[9]

You start with a *transition.* Whenever you switch gears or change the focus of your examination, you start by using a *transition:*

Q: I want to ask you some questions about the official deposition / the official police statement / the official statement to the FBI you gave on June 10 of last year, you understand? (*Nodding your head affirmatively as you speak.*)
A: Yes.[10]

---

6 *Id.* at p. 21.
7 *Id.*
8 *Id.*
9 Some courts have held that "302" reports are not "statements," and therefore you cannot impeach a witness with an inconsistent statement in such an event.
10 MacCarthy (2016) at p. 22.

Use of the word "official" is crucial here. It drapes the statement in credibility and truthfulness. You now begin by getting the witness into the all-important "yes" answer mode. In doing so, you then begin your "storytelling mode." The story you are telling through the witness's "yes" answers is the story of your client's innocence which you began in your voir dire.

Q: You went to your attorney's office that day?
A: Yes.
Q: You got there a little before 2:00 in the afternoon?
A: Yes.
Q: You told the receptionist who you were?
A: Yes.[11]

You are now in "storytelling mode." You are also getting the witness into the all-important "yes" answer mode. The more details, the more "yes" answers, and the better you look.[12]

You want to craft your impeachment in the form of your story, or theory of the case. You want the jury to hear the response "yes" to every fact that supports your case. Examples here of points you wish to highlight through your questioning would include:

- You gave a sworn statement to a court reporter.
- You told the truth.
- You knew that others would rely on the truth of that statement.
- The events were fresh in your mind at the time.
- You later made a couple of corrections to ensure it was a truthful statement.

You would fill in the spaces between these points with assorted additional "yes" questions confirming the other myriad details present, including what the room looked like, what the furniture consisted

[11] MacCarthy (2016), at p. 22. See also pp. 22–26 for a detailed example of the "yes" answer mode.

[12] The more often the witness answers "yes," the more powerful you appear. You are controlling the witness, and he is not contradicting you. Ideally, "yes" is the only response you want to hear.

of, who was present in the room, the fact your attorney told you to tell the truth, and so on.

When you have completed this setup by using the "yes" answer mode, you are ready to impeach the witness with the prior statement.

Rule 4: Show the Witness the Impeaching Statement.

When impeaching with an inconsistent statement, you must show or read the statement to the witness.

The vast majority of us have been trained, either in law school or by watching others do it (or even in movies or on television), to show a statement to the witness in the following manner:

> *Mr. (Witness), I now show you what has been previously marked as defense exhibit three for identification, which purports to be the deposition you gave on or about June 10 of 2017, and I ask you sir, do you recognize it?*[13]

This is the wrong way to do it. Here are a few reasons why:

1. First of all, you sound like a goon. You DO NOT want to talk like a lawyer. You want talk to the jury like you would speak to your best friend at a bar.
2. It asks an open-ended question, thus giving the witness an opportunity to play games with you, none of which are good for you. This is cross-examination. Don't give him any wiggle room.
3. You sound like a *stupid* goon. Why tell the jury you're showing the witness something when they can obviously see that is exactly what you are doing?
4. Telling the witness what the exhibit "purports to be" is improper.
5. "Do you recognize it?" is simply wrong. If asked on direct examination, ask: "Do you know what this is?" If on cross-examination, ask (more accurately, you *state*): "You know what this is."[14]

---

[13] MacCarthy (2016), at p. 29.

[14] *Id.*, at pp. 29–30.

This is how to show a witness a document. First, make sure your opponent has a copy of the exhibit.

> ***Q:*** Your honor, may I show the witness Defense Exhibit No. 3?
> *(Turning to opposing counsel.)*
> Counsel, Defense Exhibit No. 3, page 11, lines 14 & 15
> *(Approaching the witness. Show him the exhibit.)*
> You know what this is.
> ***A:*** Yes.
> ***Q:*** This is your *official deposition where you told the truth.*[15]

The witness is now primed for impeachment.

Rule 5: Read the Impeaching Statement.

You are going to use the inconsistent statement. But who will read it? The witness or you? You know the witness is no good at reading anything, let alone such an important document. How about both of you?

(The witness is holding a copy of the impeaching statement.)

> ***Q:*** Please read to the jury what you said you saw when you left the bar.
> ***A:*** "I saw a green car." *(Reading from the document.)*
> ***Q:*** You said you knew the driver of the green car?
> ***A:*** Yes.
> ***Q:*** You said Clancy was driving the green car?
> ***A:*** Yes.
> ***Q:*** You said the green car was going west?
> ***A:*** Yes.[16]

For added dramatic effect, you might want to consider writing "green car" in big block letters on the whiteboard or the big pad of paper propped on the easel in front of the jury.

(CAUTION! **This is not the time to "publish" or move the impeaching statement into evidence. Wait until you have**

---

[15] *Id.*, at p. 31.
[16] *Id.*, at p. 32.

completed your cross-examination. If you do it during your examination, the jurors will be distracted by looking at the document instead of watching you impeach the witness. In some courts, the judge may stop the examination to allow the jury to examine it. But why do that? That interrupts the flow of the drama. Simply finish with the witness before moving to introduce the document.)

What happens if the witness refuses to cooperate and insists on fighting your efforts to impeach him?

> *Q:* Please read to the jury what you said you saw when you left the bar.
> *A:* Well, what it says here is "I saw a green car," *but that's not what I said. I said I saw a red car.*[17]

If the witness refuses to let you impeach him, then so be it. You simply have someone else impeach him later.

You finish with the witness (without argument) and proceed with your cross-examination of any other state witnesses. Then you call the "impeaching witness" on direct examination. It will most likely be the law enforcement officer who took the original impeaching statement from the witness.

The officer takes the stand, and you spend a few minutes having him tell the jury who he is and what he does for a living. The examination will then go something like this: *(Remember, this is direct examination, not cross-examination.)*

> *Q:* Did you talk to [the witness]?
> *A:* Yes, I did.
> *Q:* I want to ask you some questions about the official FBI statement you took from the witness on June 10 of 2017, do you understand?
> *A:* Yes.
> *Q:* Who else was with you when you took this statement?
> *A:* Special Agent Jones.

[17] *Id.*, at p. 33.

Q: Was this an official statement?
A: Yes.
Q: Was this official statement what you call a 302 statement?
A: Yes, it was.
Q: Did you explain the importance of this official statement to [the witness]?
A: Yes, we did.
Q: At any time did he appear to you as not having understood your questions?
A: No.
Q: I want to ask you some questions about what he told you he saw when he left Murphy's bar, do you understand?
A: Okay.
Q: Were these answers important to you?
A: Yes. All of his answers were important to us.
Q: Did you write down what he told you he saw when he left Murphy's Bar?
A: Yes.
Q: Were you careful to make sure you wrote down his facts accurately?
A: Yes.
Q: I want to ask you some questions about what he told you he saw when he left Murphy's Bar, do you understand?
A: Yes.
Q: What did he tell you he saw?
A: A car.
Q: What did he tell you was the make of the car?
A: A Pontiac.
Q: Did you ask him what color the Pontiac was?
A: Yes, we did.
Q: And did he tell you the color of the Pontiac?
A: Yes, he did.
Q: Would you tell the ladies and gentlemen of the jury what color he told you the car was?
A: Green.
Q: Who did he tell you was driving the green car?
A: Ratso Rizzo.
Q: Did he tell you if there was a passenger in the green car he saw?

A: Yes. He said there was blonde woman he did not know in the passenger seat.

Q: Did he tell you what direction the green car he saw was going?

A: Yes. He said it was going west.
(Write "green car" on the whiteboard.)

Q: Did you accurately write down all of this information in your official FBI report?

A: Yes.

Q: Did you specifically and accurately write down the color of the car he saw?

A: Yes.

Q: What did you write down in your official FBI report was the color of the car he saw?

A: Green.[18]

You have now successfully impeached the earlier witness on that particular inconsistent statement, and you may proceed with your examination of the officer, if need be. When you have completed your examination of the witness, you should move to have the original impeaching statement admitted into evidence (since it was in writing). Remember, if the impeaching statement was made under oath, request that the judge instruct the jury that the statement comes in not merely to impeach but as substantive evidence.

Rule 6: Do Not Revisit the Impeachment.

One of the worst habits trial lawyers have is the tendency to "revisit" testimony once it is completed and on the record. It is curiously irresistible, like revisiting an old high school sweetheart. One should never do it, as you cannot improve upon it. You invite disaster by doing so. Nothing good can come of it.

B. Contradictions—Contrary Evidence

1. Introduction

This method of impeachment is often confused with impeachment by inconsistent statement. You have evidence that contradicts something the witness has said either on direct or cross-examination. Someone

---

[18] *Id.*, at pp. 34–37.

is telling the jury that the witness is either mistaken or, more probably, lying. It also is subject to the "collateral" evidentiary limitation. But the difference here is that this method impeaches by using evidence *other than a prior statement.*

In this example, you are not impeaching with an inconsistent statement, but with *contradictory evidence.* That evidence will be in the form of one or two FBI Agents who will call the witness a liar.

Opportunities to impeach by contradictions do not arise all that often for defense attorneys. This method of impeachment is more commonly used by prosecutors to impeach defendants who testify.

2. Relevant Federal Rules of Evidence

There is no specific evidentiary rule pertaining to impeachment by contradictions. But a few courts have suggested that it is most closely associated with Rule 607.

Rule 607: Who May Impeach a Witness

> Any party, including the party that called the witness, may attack the witness's credibility.

3. How to Use This Method

Impeachment by use of contradictions can be used in the following situations:

- The witness testifies he worked on March 17. You have his time card from the factory, and he neither punched in nor punched out on that day.
- He testifies it was a very cold day. You have the day's weather report which shows the temperature was in the 70s.
- He testifies he never left his home all day. You have witnesses who saw him in Murphy's Restaurant and a copy of the credit card bill he signed.[19]

You will notice that these situations set up opportunities for you to impeach by using evidence *other than prior statements* made by the witness. Typically, you would initiate the process by setting up

---

[19] *Id.*, at p. 42.

the impeachment on cross-examination, then follow through later by introducing the contradictory evidence in your direct examination of your witness.

Again, as with impeachment by inconsistent statements, impeachment by contradictions is subject to the "collateral" limitation. This means that if the contradiction concerns a subject that is immaterial, or of little or no importance, to the issue in dispute, then it is considered "collateral" to the subject of the witness's testimony, and thus its existence cannot be proven by extrinsic (outside) evidence. And since it is being used only for purposes of attacking the credibility of the witness, it is not being introduced as "substantive evidence."

And again, as with impeachment by inconsistent statements, the exception to that is if the prior contrary evidence or statement was made *under oath* (*e.g.*, trial, deposition, or grand jury testimony). If so, then the contrary evidence may come in not only to impeach the witness, but as *substantive evidence as well*. (See F.R.E. Rule 801(d)(1).) In such a situation, you want to request that the judge instruct the jury that the evidence is also being admitted for that purpose.

You cross-examine "Mr. Smith" as follows:

Q: I want to ask you some questions about what you told the FBI agents on June 10 of this year, you understand?
A: Okay.
Q: You knew this was an important investigation?
A: Yes.
Q: You wanted to cooperate?
A: Yes.
Q: You talked to them two days after you had been in Murphy's Bar?
A: Yes.
Q: When things were still fresh in your mind?
A: Yes.
Q: You understood their questions?
A: Yes.
Q: They wanted to know what you saw when you left the bar?
A: Yes.
Q: You knew this was important to them?
A: Yes.
Q: You told them you saw a car?

A: Yes.
Q: They wanted to know the color of the car?
A: Yes.
Q: Again, you knew this was important to them?
A: Yes.
Q: You told them the color of the car you saw?
A: Yes.
Q: You told them it was green?
A: No, I told them it was red.
Q: Now, under oath, you are telling this jury that you told the FBI agents the car was red?
A: Yes.
Q: Again, under oath, you deny telling the FBI agents the car you saw was green?
A: Yes.[20]

You have now set up the witness for impeachment, but you have not yet sprung the trap. As we have previously learned, some courts may hold that FBI reports are not "statements," so that you are not permitted to impeach the witness with the document that contains the inconsistent statement.[21]

Assume that is the case here. You are now putting on your case, and you call the FBI agents to the stand as your witnesses for direct examination. Assume you have completed your preliminary questions establishing who the agent is and what he does. Now you complete your impeachment of Mr. Smith:

Q: Were you the agent in charge of this investigation?
A: Yes.
Q: Did you talk to Mr. Smith?
A: Yes.
Q: Where did you talk to him?
A: At our FBI office.
Q: Who else was there?
A: Agent Jones.

---

[20] *Id.*, at pp. 44–45.
[21] *See* Method No. 1: Impeachment with Inconsistent Statements.

Q: When was this?
A: June 10 of this year.
Q: Did you take an official FBI statement?
A: Yes.
Q: Let me ask you some questions about the questions you asked and the answers he gave about what he saw when he left Murphy's Bar, do you understand?
A: Yes.
Q: Were you particularly interested in knowing what he saw when he left Murphy's Bar?
A: Yes, that was important to us.
Q: More specifically, did you want to know the color of the car he saw?
A: Yes, this was important to us.
Q: Did you ask him the color of the car he saw?
A: Yes, we did.
Q: Did he answer the question?
A: Yes.
Q: Did you in some way record his answer?
A: Yes, I wrote it down.
Q: Did you write it down in your official FBI statement?
A: Yes.
Q: Do you remember the color of the car he saw?
A: Yes, I do.
Q: Did you check your official FBI statement to double check what he told you was the color of the car he saw?
A: Yes, although I didn't think it was necessary to do so.
Q: Was it necessary?
A: No, it was not, as both my memory and the official FBI statement were the same.
Q: Agent Black, would you please tell the jury what color Mr. Smith said the car he saw was.
A: He said it was green.
Q: Is there any question in your mind about that?
A: No, there is not.
Q: Are you sure he did not tell you he car was red?
A: Yes, I am positive.

Q: If Mr. Smith, under oath, told the ladies and gentlemen of this jury that he told you the car he saw was red, would he have been correct?
A: No.
Q: Would he have either been mistaken or lying?
A: Yes.[22]

As noted above, if the color of the car was a noncollateral matter, you should request that the court instruct the jury that they may consider the evidence regarding the green car to be used not only to impeach, but also to provide substantive evidence.

C. Motivation

1. Introduction

Motivation impeachment is important and is used by both defense attorneys and prosecutors. Simply put, this is impeachment of a witness by establishing his "bias and prejudice." It is also the term used by the United States Supreme Court in the leading case of *Davis v. Alaska,* 415 U.S. 308 (1974).

We are not proving the witness to be a liar or even to be mistaken. Rather, we are making an issue as to the witness's reliability. There are few, if any, evidentiary limitations on motivation impeachment.

2. Relevant Federal Rules of Evidence

There is no specific evidentiary rule pertaining to impeachment by motivation, but it is mentioned in the commentary to F.R.E. 401, 607, 608, and 611(b).

It should be noted that impeaching a witness's motive also calls into question the witness's credibility. You should not use the word *credibility* when referring to motivation, however. Some judges confuse credibility with truthfulness, which is commonly used in impeachment of a witness's character under Rule 608(b). They are not the same and should not be confused.

---

[22] MacCarthy (2016), at pp. 46–48.

3. How to Use This Method

Motivation impeachment is best defined and explained in three decisions of the United States Supreme Court: *Davis v. Alaska,* 415 U.S. 308 (1974); *United States v. Abel,* 469 U.S. 45 (1984); and *Delaware v. Van Arsdale,* 475 U.S. 673 (1986).[23] From these opinions, the following principles have been established:[24]

1. It does not take much motivation to be impeachable.
2. Motivation impeachment is never collateral. *(This means that extrinsic evidence may be used.)*
3. The "harmless error" rule may become an issue. *(In* Van Arsdale, *the defendant attempted to impeach a meaningless witness with motivation evidence. The trial court refused. On appeal, the court noted that while the trial court was wrong, the witness's testimony was irrelevant to the issue. Thus, the error was harmless.)*

Situations in which motivation impeachment should be considered include:

- Deals with prosecutors
- Past crimes/snitch
- Pending charges
- Arrests
- Arresting officers/lead investigator
- Crimes and no arrests
- Probation
- Potential charges involving family members
- Benefits conferred on witness by prosecutor
- Benefits conferred on family members by prosecutor
- Comforts of living
- Money
- Relationship to witness
- Employer
- Previous contacts/run-ins

---

[23] *Id.*, at pp. 51–55.

[24] *Id.*, at p. 55.

- Experts
- Race
- Decision to speak to both sides[25]

For purposes of this chapter, we will illustrate examples only of impeaching the deal and the arresting/investigating officer, as these are the primary situations that defense attorneys encounter.

4. The Deal

The "ground rules," as it were, for impeaching a "snitch" witness regarding a deal are extremely broad. You are limited not so much by "what" as by "when." Although there are no time limits on what can be used, courts will often employ a common-sense approach. For example, a 20-year-old uncharged felony could not be used, but a recent minor misdemeanor could.

The following list of items can be used to impeach a snitch:

- Any and all bad acts if they are a crime, including minor misdemeanors. (*Van Arsdale* involved public intoxication.)
- Uncharged crimes, even if the prosecutor has no knowledge of them
- Arrests, even if the prosecutor has no knowledge of them
- Crimes without arrests
- Whether the witness:
  - is on probation,
  - is a paid informant,
  - was intensively coached,
  - misrepresented his dealings with the police,
  - gave perjurious testimony that was uncorrected by the prosecutor, or
  - made a deal after being threatened with life in prison if he refused to cooperate.
- Whatever the witness believes, expects, hopes, and desires to come about as a result of the deal.[26]

---

[25] *Id.*, at p. 57.
[26] *Id.*, at pp. 59–60.

A review of this list clearly reveals that the test of what can be used to impeach a snitch on the deal is subjective, not objective. Failure by the state to disclose any of this information is an obvious violation of *Brady v. Maryland,* 373 U.S. 83 (1963), as it pertains to exculpatory and impeaching material.

The Setup[27]

This initial set of questions establishes that the snitch does not like jail and would do anything to avoid going back to it, including lying.

His Problems[28]

Now you are ready to establish his problems as the foundation for his willingness to make a deal. The snitch has problems in that he knows he has committed crimes for which he can be prosecuted and be sent to jail, and he is concerned about how much prison time he is facing.

What He Does[29]

In response to his problems, the witness turns to the prosecutor for help. You examine him about the conversation he had with the prosecuting attorney, and specifically about what the prosecutor told him regarding the maximum sentence he could receive and how he could avoid it.

You may draw an objection that you are imposing on the attorney–client privilege; you are not. The privilege belongs to the witness, and only he can assert it.

Explain to the judge that you have no intention of going into the "actual conversation" between the witness and his attorney. You are simply inquiring about *what he knows.* This is acceptable under *Murdoch v. Castro,* 365 F.3d 699 (10th Cir. 2004).[30]

---

[27] For an example of this examination and the specific sequence of questions, *see* MacCarthy (2016), at pp. 63–64.

[28] *Id.*, at pp. 64–65.

[29] *Id.*, at p. 65.

[30] *Id.*, at p. 66.

His Relationship with the Prosecutor[31]

You focus on the snitch's relationship with the prosecutor. In essence, you establish that there was only one person the snitch could turn to for help—the prosecuting attorney. The snitch would need him in order to keep from ending up in jail serving a lengthy sentence, so he wanted to cultivate his friendship by making a deal with him.

At this point, you are ready to spell out the terms of the deal for the jury. Go to the white board (or the computer display) you have set up for the jury, which contains the details of the deal. Go through the terms one by one, asking the witness to confirm them. You also establish that the prosecutor told him that he couldn't promise him anything and that the extent of his help would depend on the quality of the snitch's testimony. You then lead the snitch to the point where he admits that he would do just about anything to please the prosecuting attorney.

Conclusion[32]

Finally, you wrap up the examination by establishing that since the prosecutor is the only one who has the power to help the snitch, the prosecutor must wait until the snitch has completed his testimony before the extent of his assistance—and thus the extent to which he himself will benefit—can be evaluated. Therefore, the prosecutor must wait to make that decision. That decision cannot be made beforehand because the prosecutor does not trust the snitch, and the snitch knows it.

Keep in mind that in order to amplify the effect of a strong impeachment, you should expose the "deal" to the jury in your opening statement. Get them thinking about it early and mulling over the notion that the state's case is resting on the shoulders of a person with such poor credibility that the prosecuting attorney won't even deal with him up front.

---

[31] *Id.*, at pp. 67–70.
[32] *Id.*, at pp. 70–71.

5. The Arresting Officer/The Lead Investigator

When you are cross-examining the arresting officer/lead investigator in the case, you want to clearly establish that, as such, he has a vested interest in the outcome. He initiated it or at least developed it and has assisted in its prosecution. If the defendant is convicted, the officer will receive praise and the credit for it. Conversely, if he is acquitted, the officer will not be cast in such a favorable light, particularly with his peers or perhaps the prosecuting attorney.

Therefore, it is important to the officer that the defendant be convicted; moreover, he wants him to be convicted (for he believes him to be guilty). In fact, he would do almost anything to achieve that result. The fact that the officer will likely not agree to that on the stand is irrelevant, as you have made your point.

This line of questioning might prompt an objection, and the court may not allow you to do it. However, many Appellate Courts might reverse such a ruling on the grounds that it prohibits you from engaging in legitimate motivation impeachment, which it obviously is.

A situation could also arise where the arresting officer/lead investigator has exposure to motivation impeachment by virtue of certain information contained within his personnel file or information that has been released to the public. Consider the following:

You are in the middle of trial. The state has called its last witness, the arresting officer. The direct examination is completed, and the court adjourns the trial for the day. You will begin your cross-examination the following morning.

Early the next morning you see an article on the front page of the newspaper announcing that the city has recently paid a multimillion dollar settlement in a federal civil rights case involving the wrongful death of a local man who was shot by a police officer during a traffic stop. The suit alleged a number of violations, including police misconduct and falsification of official reports by the officer. The article identifies the officer who killed the man, and it is the same officer whom you are planning to cross-examine later that morning. The article also revealed that the officer was still on "administrative transfer" to a desk position and had not yet returned to street patrol duty. The prosecutor in your case never disclosed to you in pretrial discovery that such a suit had been filed or settled or that the officer was named in the suit.

The failure of the state to reveal to you prior to trial that the civil suit existed and involved the same officer precluded you from preparing an impeachment cross-examination based on motivation, which potentially could amount to a *Giglio* violation.[33] You would be entitled to cross-examine the officer regarding the terms of any agreement he had with the prosecuting attorney in exchange for his favorable testimony, as well as any motivation to attempt to "rehabilitate his reputation" or otherwise curry favor with his employer, the city administration, and the prosecuting attorney, for having caused the city to have to pay a huge civil settlement.[34]

Such an examination might go like this:

Q: You would do *most anything* to get him convicted?
A: No, I would not.
Q: You have been with the police department for ____ years?
A: Yes.
Q: And you have been a street patrol officer for that entire period of time?
A: Yes.
Q: You enjoy that work?
A: Yes.

---

[33] Giglio v. United States, 405 U.S. 150 (1972). The court held that failure by the prosecution to disclose to the defense exculpatory evidence or information regarding witnesses, including evidence of any deals in exchange for testimony, was reversible error. It was an expansion of the landmark ruling in Brady v. Maryland, 373 U.S. 83 (1963). Due process requires the prosecution to disclose impeachment evidence, including plea agreements made with witnesses.

Generally, *Brady* does not automatically require a new trial if undisclosed evidence is discovered in the state's files after trial. The undisclosed evidence must be material. The remedy for a *Brady* violation is a new trial, not dismissal. There is no distinction between concealment of impeachment evidence and concealment of exculpatory evidence. Giglio and United States v. Bagley, 473 U.S. 667 (1985).

[34] Impeaching the officer as to his truthfulness would be slightly different. *See* Impeachment Method No. 4: Truthfulness, *infra*.

Q: You find it satisfying, and it gives you a sense of personal and professional fulfillment?

A: I suppose so.

Q: You would rather do street patrol than any other type of police work?

A: Yes.

Q: As a professional law enforcement officer, it means everything to you to be able to do that work?

A: It means a lot to me, yes.

Q: You could not imagine being a police officer and not doing it?

A: No.

Q: You love it so much, that if you were somehow prevented from doing that, you'd do whatever it took to return to it?

A: I'd do my best.

Q: You were in fact recently suspended from that position, weren't you?

A: Yes.

Q: You were suspended as a result of an incident which occurred while you were on duty on _________ ?

A: Yes.

Q: You shot a man after you pulled him over for a minor traffic violation?

PROSECUTOR: Objection. Improper impeachment. Use of extrinsic evidence.

DEFENSE: Your Honor, the question will show this witness's bias, and it is therefore relevant for impeachment purposes under Rule 402.

COURT: Overruled.

A: Well, he came at me. . . .

Q: Yes, we're all familiar with your "official" explanation, but we can agree that at some point during the traffic stop you shot the driver with your service revolver?

A: Yes.

Q: The wound was fatal, was it not? You killed him?

A: Yes.

Q: And the official investigation concluded that at the time you shot and killed him, the man was unarmed, correct?
A: That's correct. But I believed. . . .
Q: And during the official investigation you were relieved of your duties as a street patrol officer?
A: That's correct.
Q: And the city just paid millions of dollars to settle the lawsuit which was filed by the man's family, correct?
A: I don't know anything about the settlement.
Q: And as of today, you have not yet been cleared by the police department to return to those duties?
A: That's correct.
Q: It would be fair to say that you are worried about that?
A: Well, that's not my call. There's nothing I can really do about it at this point.
Q: Isn't there? A good recommendation from someone in authority and in good standing with the police department would go a long way toward helping you return to that job, wouldn't it?
A: Again, that's not my call.
Q: But you would certainly welcome such a favorable recommendation.
A: I suppose so.
Q: In preparing for your testimony today, you met with the prosecuting attorney?
A: Yes.
Q: The prosecutor knows the chief of police, doesn't he?
A: I would imagine he does.
Q: The prosecutor is relying upon your testimony to convict my client.
A: I really can't say what he's relying upon.
Q: Your testimony in this case would be critical in that regard?
A: How do you mean?
Q: Without your testimony supporting the prosecutor's case, that would have made the prosecuting attorney extremely disappointed and unhappy with you, wouldn't it?

A: Again, I can't say.
Q: Which could adversely affect any positive recommendation he would make to the chief of police on your behalf.

His answer to the last question is irrelevant.

D. Truthfulness

1. Introduction

Every witness who testifies puts his or her character trait for truthfulness in issue. When we talk about truthfulness, we are talking about "lies." The lie must be specific. One cannot simply ask the witness if he or she ever lied. Also, there must be a "good-faith" basis to justify the truthfulness cross-examination.[35]

It should be noted, however, that this impeachment is not limited solely to lies per se. It can include behavior seeking personal advantage by taking from others in violation of their rights: stealing, buying, receiving, or using stolen property; bribery; deceptive practices; failure to file income tax returns; the facts in the case and threats to witnesses in an earlier case. See *U.S. v. Mansky*, 186 F.3d 770 (7th Cir. 1999).[36]

NOTE: The primary limitation of this impeachment method is that all truthfulness impeachment is "collateral." That means that specific instances of untruthfulness cannot be proved by extrinsic evidence.

2. Relevant Federal Rules of Evidence

Rule 608: A Witness's Character for Truthfulness or Untruthfulness

(a) Reputation or Opinion Evidence

A witness's credibility may be attacked or supported by testimony about the witness's reputation for having a character for truthfulness or untruthfulness, or by testimony in the form

[35] MacCarthy (2016), at p. 74.
[36] *Id.*, at p. 75.

of an opinion about that character. But evidence of truthful character is admissible only after the witness's character for truthfulness has been attacked.

(b) Specific Instances of Conduct

Except for a criminal conviction under Rule 609, extrinsic evidence is not admissible to prove specific instances of a witness's conduct in order to attack or support the witness's character for truthfulness. But the court may, on cross-examination, allow inquiry into these instances if they are probative of the character for truthfulness or untruthfulness of 1) the witness or 2) another witness whose character the witness being cross-examined has testified about.

By testifying on another matter, a witness does not waive any privilege against self-incrimination for testimony that relates only to the witness's character for truthfulness.

3. How to Use This Method

The truthfulness trait may be impeached in two distinct ways. The most common method is through cross-examination of the witness. The least effective way is on direct examination of a negative character witness. This second approach is seldom used, however, and so we will focus our attention here on cross-examination of the witness.

Owing to the limitation described above (that all truthfulness impeachment is collateral), there is not much one can do if the witness is confronted with a lie and denies it, thus creating a second lie. There are several things you can do, however.

You may announce to the court, with the jury present, that you intend to use Rule 608 to impeach the witness. You then hand the prosecutor and the court your "basis in fact," a copy of a job application filled out by the witness in which he has lied, for example, about his criminal background. This is called the "persuasive document." The fact that the judge and the prosecutor now have copies of it, and the jury sees that they do, may in and of itself be enough to convince the witness to answer truthfully and acknowledge the lie.

The job application will almost certainly include the question: "Have you ever been convicted of a crime?" Assume the witness lied on the application and answered the question "no." Make an obvious point of holding and reading from the job application while you conduct this portion of your cross-examination. ***(You cannot and will not show or flash it to the jury.)*** You will also turn the pages and conspicuously read from the document, making sure that the jury can see you doing it.[37]

Holding the document in your hands and reading from it, you cross-examine in detail about the document, the date that he filled it out, and what company he was seeking employment with. Then turning his attention to the specific question, you confirm that, in response to the question regarding the existence of a criminal record, he answered "no."

Assuming that was a lie, and he admits that answer on the stand, you proceed by confirming that it was a lie and that he is in fact a convicted felon (or an otherwise admissible misdemeanant). You then make a point of confirming that not only did he lie, but that he lied to help himself (for that's the only reason anyone ever lies). You have now successfully impeached the witness.

If, however, the witness disagrees and again denies that was his answer, then you confirm that he is in fact telling the jury that he answered the question "yes." Now you must use the second method.

You might then ask the court for permission to show the jury the witness's answer to the question. The prosecutor might object, on the grounds that it might be suborning perjury, which objection the court would most likely sustain. You will have gone about as far as you can at this point, but you have still scored big points. First, the jury knows you are reading from the job application, and they know that you were trying to show it to them. Second, even though the prosecutor successfully objected, the jury knows that he was protecting the witness from being revealed a liar. At this point, you should request that the court advise the witness of his Fifth Amendment rights and that he should probably seek advice of counsel if he proceeds further.

---

[37] *Id.*, at pp. 76–77.

E. Convictions

1. Introduction

This method of impeachment is considered by many to address the credibility of a witness. Yet an impeachment for a criminal conviction says much about whether the witness is a bad person and very little about his credibility.

Subject to certain limitations set forth below, a witness may be impeached for having a conviction for a felony that is not more than ten years old, or any crime, felony, or misdemeanor that involved dishonesty or false statement. If the conviction is for a felony and does not involve dishonesty or false statement, a "balancing test" limitation applies. One applies to defendants in criminal cases and is spelled out in Rule 609. The other applies to all other witnesses and is spelled out in Rule 403.[38]

Congress has defined crimes involving "dishonesty" or "false statement" as follows:

> By the phrase "dishonesty and false statement," the Conference means crimes such as perjury or subornation of perjury, false statement, criminal fraud, embezzlement, or false pretense, or any other offense in the nature of *crimen falsi,* the commission of which involves some element of deceit, untruthfulness, or falsification bearing on the accused's propensity to testify truthfully.[39]

This brings up a troublesome point, however. What if the crime itself does not require proof of dishonesty or false statement, but misrepresentation or deceit were involved in the *commission* of the crime? It appears that most courts would permit impeachment on the underlying facts.

---

[38] F.R.E. 403 states:

> **Excluding Relevant Evidence for Prejudice, Confusion, Waste of Time, or Other Reasons.**
> The court may exclude relevant evidence if its probative value is substantially outweighed by a danger of one or more of the following: unfair prejudice, confusing the issues, misleading the jury, undue delay, wasting time, or needlessly presenting cumulative evidence.

[39] MacCarthy (2016), at p. 94.

2. Relevant Federal Rules of Evidence

Rule 609: Impeachment by Evidence of a Criminal Conviction

(a) In General

The following rules apply to attacking a witness's character for truthfulness by evidence of a criminal conviction:

1. for a crime that, in the convicting jurisdiction, was punishable by death or imprisonment for more than one year, the evidence:
    a. must be admitted, subject to Rule 403, in a civil case or in a criminal case in which the witness is not a defendant; and
    b. must be admitted in a criminal case in which the witness is a defendant, if the probative value of the evidence outweighs its prejudicial effect to that defendant; and
2. for any crime regardless of the punishment, the evidence must be admitted if the court can readily determine that establishing the elements of the crime requiring proving—or the witness's admitting—a dishonest act or false statement.

(b) Limit on Using the Evidence after 10 Years

This subdivision (b) applies if more than 10 years have passed since the witness's conviction or release from confinement for it, whichever is later. Evidence of the conviction is admissible only if:

1. its probative value, supported by specific facts and circumstances, substantially outweighs its prejudicial effect; and
2. the proponent gives an adverse party reasonable written notice of the intent to use it so that the party has a fair opportunity to contest its use.

3. How to Use This Method

There is no "collateral" limitation on this form of impeachment. Therefore, should a witness deny the existence of a conviction, you should be prepared to perfect your impeachment with a certified copy of the conviction.

In the vast majority of cases, you will address the convictions of the witness in your cross-examination. Only in rare situations will you find yourself dealing with it on direct examination with your own witness, in which case you are certainly permitted to do so under Rule 607. However, be prepared for the possibility that some judges require a showing of "surprise" before allowing you to impeach your own witness.

Impeachment by use of convictions is one of those areas that we truly enjoy, for it can present opportunities for courtroom drama. Remember, part of your job as a trial lawyer is to entertain the jury and to "look good" while doing so. And few things make you look better in the courtroom than getting the witness to admit on the stand that he is a convicted felon.

Unfortunately, law school pays no attention whatsoever to the training of trial lawyers in the skills of proper and effective cross-examination techniques. Most of us were taught to impeach a witness with evidence of a felony record in the following manner:

> *Q:* Are you the same John Smith who was convicted of robbery in 2000 and received a sentence of five years?
>
> *A:* Yes.[40]

I think we can all agree that that carries all the dramatic impact of a bag full of last summer's buttermilk biscuits.

Being mindful of the concepts of "primacy and recency," we want to take this opportunity to show the jury that we are in control of this witness, and the narrative of this case. A far better technique of impeachment with a felony conviction would be the following:

> *Q:* It would be fair to say that you are a convicted felon?
>
> *A:* Yes.
>
> *Q:* As a matter of fact, you have been convicted of *more than one felony?*
>
> *A:* Yes.
>
> *Q:* You have been convicted of *two* felonies?
>
> *A:* Yes.
>
> *Q:* I want to ask you some questions about your *first* felony conviction, you understand?
>
> *A:* Yes.[41]

---

[40] *Id.*, at p. 98.

[41] *Id.*, at pp. 98–99.

While you are not permitted to dig too deeply into the conviction history, you are usually allowed to inquire into the nature of the crime, the date it occurred, the date of the conviction and the sentence. With the proper attention to detailed questioning, you need nothing more.

As in previous examples of cross-examination, you want to make it as detailed as possible in order to obtain as many "yes" responses as possible. You want to establish that the witness robbed a particular store in a particular town on a specific date. Go into the fact that he was later arrested and charged with the crime.

In addition to delving into this detailed history, recall that this examination also presents an opportunity to inflict further damage on the witness by utilizing *motivation impeachment* covered in Impeachment Method No. 4. When you have established that the witness was charged with a felony, you can lead him through questions regarding his eventual plea of guilty and subsequent sentence. You can then establish that he did not want to go to jail and that he promised the court at the time that he would never again commit another criminal offense. That, of course, was a lie (intended to help himself!), for that is precisely what he did on a later occasion, which constituted his *second* felony conviction.[42] He went to prison on the first offense, which he did not like, and would do anything to avoid returning. After the witness was released from prison, he was assigned a parole officer. He promised the parole officer he would abide by the law and would keep the officer apprised of his situation. That was another lie, naturally, because he was later arrested, charged, and convicted of felony drug possession. You get the idea.

As you work your way through these various impeachment methods, you should be beginning to develop a mindset regarding the impeachment "process."

As an example, consider the following hypothetical scenario:

A senior laboratory analyst with the state division of criminal investigation, specializing in DNA testing, is caught falsifying his pay

---

[42] At some point, the prosecutor might object and claim that you are using improper Rule 609 impeachment. Your response, however, is that while it is not proper Rule 609 impeachment, it is not intended to be. You are introducing it as motivation impeachment as well as truthfulness impeachment.

vouchers. He is alleged to have bilked the state out of many thousands of dollars. Additionally, he has admitted to falsifying some data on various lab reports. Obviously, this will have profound ramifications, impacting the trustworthiness and reliability of his testimony in not only hundreds of cases already prosecuted throughout the state during the analyst's tenure at the division, but also cases that are currently pending.

Prosecutors across the state panic. In a flurry of meetings, e-mails, and letters, they decide that the best way to protect their pending cases is to quickly arrange for the analyst to enter a plea to a misdemeanor and receive a suspended sentence with probation. This, they feel, will protect the analyst from impeachment at future hearings. Indeed, some defense attorneys also feel that absent a felony conviction, they will be prevented from impeaching the analyst.

Neither of these positions is accurate. The knowledgeable defense attorney, having studied these impeachment methods and learning how to "weaponize" the rules of evidence, will realize that the analyst is finished in court, regardless of the nature of his conviction or the resulting sentence, for the following reasons:

1. Under F.R.E. 609, the analyst can be impeached on the misdemeanor conviction, since it unquestionably involves "dishonesty and false statement."
2. Under F.R.E. 608, the analyst can be impeached on his character trait for truthfulness.

The analyst is also subject to impeachment for motivation. As a prosecution witness, the felony charge was reduced to a misdemeanor in order to protect his testimony for the state. Not only is this proper motivation impeachment, but if the defense is precluded from using it, it should likely constitute reversible error.

F. What the Witness Could Have Done but Did Not Do

1. Introduction

This method of impeachment is obviously not found in any formal evidentiary rule. However, it can be a very effective tool, particularly when cross-examining an expert witness or an investigating police officer. It is also among the easiest methods of impeachment. It is one of the forms of impeachment whose basis is established primarily in a thorough cross-examination of the state's investigating officer at the preliminary hearing.

2. Relevant Federal Rules of Evidence

None.

3. How to Use This Method

As any good defense attorney knows, you take every opportunity you can to tell your client's story at trial through the cross-examination of the state's witnesses. As can be seen in other methods of impeachment, this is best accomplished by "milking" the points you make for all they're worth. In other words, why score some points on one single question when you can rack up bushels of points by extending the examination out over a period of time? The remarkable thing about this particular form of impeachment is that it does not require an extensive—or any—legal learning curve. It simply requires an understanding of human nature and common sense.

As mentioned above, an excellent source of material for this type of impeachment can be discovered in a thorough cross-examination of the investigating officer at the preliminary hearing. At that stage of the process, the prosecutor knows little more than you do about the details of his case. He's read the police report at least once, and perhaps he's spoken to the investigating officer briefly before the hearing. In a reasonably busy prosecutor's office, that's about the extent of what is known prior to the preliminary hearing. That works very well to the advantage of the defense.

At the preliminary hearing, the prosecutor is focused primarily on establishing probable cause for the charge. He's not worried yet about whether he can obtain a conviction; his concern is surviving the defense motion for dismissal. He has likely not sat down with the investigating officer and spent a great deal of time probing into what the officer did and did not do with respect to the investigation. He is simply going to offer only enough facts to prove to the court that a crime was probably committed and that your client probably committed it. Whether or not he actually committed it is irrelevant at that point.

That means that the official investigation has probably looked under only those few "rocks" that yielded evidence supporting the charge. Rocks that yielded exculpatory evidence, or none at all, have, at least at that point, been disregarded. That's where you come in.

Once the officer has testified on direct as to what facts were developed which point to your client, you are then free to examine the officer on all of those things that were not done. For example, the items that were not seized, the places that were not searched, the people who were not interviewed, the leads that were not followed, the questions that were not asked, and so forth. It is in those neglected and ignored places where reasonable doubt flourishes at trial. For despite what they did do, they have to admit those things they did not do, and thus they cannot argue that they made no difference because how would they know if they never bothered to find out?

The best part of all is that it costs you *nothing* to find out. For at the preliminary hearing, it is all the prosecutor's show. The defense has the luxury of wading into the state's case and conducting as much of an open-ended fishing expedition as the court will allow. Whereas at trial the cross-examination is tightly scripted with no wiggle room for the witness to say anything other than "yes" or "no" to your "questions," at the preliminary hearing you are under no such restrictions. In fact, you should make it a point of your examination not to be. Your job is to find out as much as possible about what the state does and does not know and what they did and did not do. The only way to do that is to ask as many open-ended questions as possible.[43]

Impeachment by establishing what the witness could have done but did not do can be used in your cross-examination at both the preliminary hearing and trial. You could simply ask a few questions, but as noted above, it would not have much of a dramatic effect:

Q: You did not interview Mr. Jones?
A: No.

---

[43] Remember: Your primary goal at the preliminary hearing is not to impeach. It is to investigate and discover.

Instead, try this approach:

Q: I want to ask you some questions about the investigation you conducted in this case on August 6th of last year, you understand?
A: Yes.
Q: We can agree, this was a major case?
A: Yes.
Q: This case involved the destruction of a large amount of property?
A: Yes.
Q: This case also involved injuries to a significant number of people?
A: Yes.
Q: It was an important case?
A: Yes.
Q: It was a case that you knew the district attorney would be very interested in pursuing?
A: Yes.
Q: It involved the potential charge of arson?
A: Yes.
Q: So there was a need for a forensic investigation?
A: Yes.
Q: There was also the possibility of the involvement of organized crime?
A: Yes.
Q: So you knew at the outset that this case would involve a massive amount of detailed and painstaking investigation?
A: Yes.
Q: As the lead investigator, it was your responsibility to coordinate the investigation in this case?
A: Yes.
Q: And that involved assigning various tasks to other investigators in your office?
A: Yes.
Q: Those tasks included locating and interviewing a number of witnesses?
A: Yes.
Q: Uncovering and handling the evidence of arson?

A: Yes.
Q: Taking photographs?
A: Yes.
Q: You learned later that a number of those interview were not done, correct?
A: Yes.
Q: And a number of samples not preserved for forensic testing?
A: Yes.
Q: That was a major problem?
A: Yes.
Q: It was a problem the district attorney would have liked to know about?
A: Yes.
Q: And it was a problem that you were obligated to tell the district attorney about?
A: Yes.
Q: But you did not tell him about the problem?
A: No.
Q: You did not go to see him to tell him about the problem?
A: No.
Q: You did not call him to tell him about the problem?
A: No.
Q: You did not send him an e-mail to tell him about this important problem?
A: No.
Q: You decided not to let him know about this important problem?
A: Yes.
Q: Up until shortly before trial, he did not know of this important problem?
A: Yes.
Q: He did not know because you did not tell him?
A: Yes.

You can see the difference, and why this technique makes you look good. This technique can be used with anything "not done." The witnesses were not interviewed, photos not taken, forensic samples not preserved for testing, evidence not seized, etc.

Recall that during your voir dire, you made a point of telling the jurors that you both had a similar job—to find the truth of what happened in the case. By establishing through this cross-examination that much of the critical evidence in the case was never uncovered, you are now able to effectively argue to the jury that, in order for them to know the truth, these things should have been done. Since because of what the witness could have done but did not do, they will never know the truth. Accordingly, they cannot convict your client.

G. Capacity

1. Introduction

Once again, this method of impeachment is not found in any formal evidentiary rule. But since you are challenging the witness's ability to *perceive or recollect,* F.R.E. 701(a) is most applicable. Capacity is among the easiest methods of impeachment. You are challenging the witness's senses in that you are suggesting that the witness's ability to see, hear, touch, taste, smell, or feel was defective. Impeachment by capacity can be used to address not only the witness's natural faculties, but also the impairment of those faculties caused by drugs and alcohol, or mental illness.[44]

2. Relevant Federal Rules of Evidence

F.R.E. 701. Opinion Testimony by Lay Witnesses

> If a witness is not testifying as an expert, testimony in the form of an opinion is limited to one that is:
>
> a. rationally based on the witness's perception;
> b. helpful to clearly understanding the witness's testimony or to determining a fact in issue; and
> c. not based on scientific, technical, or other specialized knowledge within the scope of Rule 702.

3. How to Use This Method

In order to successfully introduce such evidence, it is important that the proper foundation be established. You must first show that the capacity problem existed either at the time of the event about which

[44] *Id.*, at p. 111.

the witness testified or exists now as the witness is on the stand. Without these predicates, you will not be allowed to use this type of impeachment.[45] The *collateral rule* does not apply, so you may perfect the impeachment through the use of extrinsic evidence.

You cross-examine at trial as follows:

Q: I want to ask you some questions about what you were doing back in August of 2019, you understand?
A: Yes.
Q: You were suffering from severe headaches at the time?
A: Yes.
Q: You were under the care of a physician?
A: Yes.
Q: The physician prescribed various narcotic medications for you?
A: Yes.
Q: The drugs were very powerful?
A: Yes.
Q: Occasionally, they caused you to hallucinate?
A: Yes.
Q: They also caused memory lapses?
A: Yes.
Q: When you were under the effect of these medications, your ability to recall what had happened was a problem?
A: Yes.
Q: During August 2019, there are things you don't remember?
A: Yes.
Q: These problems were caused by your use of these medications?
A: Yes.

4. Other Opportunities to Impeach

In light of other methods we have learned to date, other opportunities to impeach this witness include:

- F.R.E. 609—Conviction as a drug crime
- Motivation—This would probably be an uncharged crime.
- F.R.E. 608—Truthfulness: If you had evidence he lied to his probation officer.[46]

---

45 *Id.*, at p. 112.
46 *Id.*, at p. 113.

H. Prior Bad Acts—404(b)

1. Introduction

Technically speaking, Rule 404(b) does not involve "impeachment," although it is primarily used to attack and discredit a witness. The difference may be slight but distinguishable in that it may be used in situations other than to directly rebut the witness's testimony.

Rule 404(b) is subject to the balancing test of Rule 403.[47] It also requires the *prosecutor* (and not the defense attorney) to give the defendant "reasonable notice in advance of trial of the general nature of the evidence it intends to introduce," if "requested by the accused." The defense should always demand this disclosure, for without it, you are not entitled to a 404(b) hearing and are walking into trial blind. The defendant does not have a duty to make a similar disclosure to the prosecutor.

Rule 404(b) is among the most litigated of the Rules of Evidence and is used mostly by prosecutors to inflict damage on defendants. However, it is also an important tool for the defense. For that reason, criminal defense lawyers should read and know of *U.S. v. Montelongo*, 420 F.3d 1169 (10th Cir. 2005).[48]

In *Montelongo*, the defendant and his traveling companion were convicted of possession of drugs in their semi-truck. They claimed to know nothing about how the drugs got there. The government called the owner of the truck to testify at trial. The defendants sought to cross-examine the owner about prior cases in which other drivers of his trucks were also convicted of possessing drugs they claimed to know nothing about. The defendants believed that the owner was secretly placing drugs in the trucks for transport, unbeknownst to the drivers. The cross-exam would have been predicated on Rule 404(b). The court denied the request, claiming that Rule 404(b) did

---

[47] F.R.E. 403 states:

> **Excluding Relevant Evidence for Prejudice, Confusion, Waste of Time, or Other Reasons.**
> The court may exclude relevant evidence if its probative value is substantially outweighed by a danger of one or more of the following: unfair prejudice, confusing the issues, misleading the jury, undue delay, wasting time, or needlessly presenting cumulative evidence.

[48] MacCarthy (2016), at p. 117.

not allow for such cross-examination on the grounds that it was not relevant, since the owner was never charged or convicted in the prior cases. The defendants claimed that the court improperly denied them the right under the Sixth Amendment to confront the owner about his involvement in drug trafficking. In reversing the case, the Tenth Circuit Court of Appeals stated:

> Rule 404(b) is typically used by prosecutors seeking to rely on a criminal defendant's prior bad acts as proof of "motive, opportunity, intent, preparation, plan, knowledge, identity, or absence of mistake or accident" in the crime charged. The Rule is not so limited in its application, however, and evidence of a witness's other wrongs, acts or crimes is admissible "for defensive purposes if it tends, alone or with other evidence, to negate the defendant's guilt of the crimes charged against him." * * * This type of evidence is often referred to as "reverse 404(b) evidence."[49]

Subpart (a) of the rule deals with character evidence, and since impeachment of a character witness is covered in Impeachment Method No. 13, it shall not be considered here.

2. Relevant Federal Rules of Evidence

F.R.E. 404. Character Evidence; Crimes, or Other Acts

(a) Crimes, Wrongs, or Other Acts

(1) Prohibited Uses. Evidence of a crime, wrong, or other act is not admissible to prove a person's character in order to show that on a particular occasion the person acted in accordance with the character.

(2) Permitted Uses; Notice in a Criminal Case. This evidence may be admissible for another purpose, such as proving motive, opportunity, intent, preparation, plan, knowledge,

[49] U.S. v. Montelongo, 420 F.3d 1169, 1174 (10th Cir. 2005).

identity, absence of mistake, or lack of accident. On request by a defendant in a criminal case, the prosecutor must:

a. Provide reasonable notice of the general nature of any such evidence that the prosecutor intends to offer at trial; and
b. Do so before trial—or during trial if the court, for good cause, excuses lack of pretrial notice.

3. How to Use This Method

Use of 404(b) evidence is generally defined and limited in accordance with the following:

a. For evidence to be admissible under this rule it must also be relevant under F.R.E. 402.
b. Evidence of prior bad acts must be proven by a preponderance of the evidence, and not by clear and convincing evidence.
c. When the state wishes to introduce evidence of a defendant's prior bad acts, the state carries the initial burden of demonstrating the admissibility of the evidence in the context of the four-part test as follows:
   1) The evidence must be offered for a proper purpose.
   2) The evidence must be relevant.
   3) The probative value of the evidence is not substantially outweighed by its potential for unfair prejudice.
   4) Upon request, the trial court must instruct the jury that the evidence is to be considered only for the proper purpose for which it is admitted.
d. The record is to reflect the trial court's identification of the purpose or purposes for admission of the evidence, the findings and conclusions establishing relevance and probative value, and the factors considered in balancing probative value against the potential for unfair prejudice. While the trial court need not make an express finding on every factor, the record must contain sufficient findings to support the trial court's conclusions.
e. Evidence of other bad acts is admissible if it forms part of the history of the event, or serves to enhance the natural development

of the facts, so long as its probative value outweighs its prejudicial effect.

f. A defendant's prior bad acts may be admitted into evidence if the defense counsel "opens the door" to that line of questioning by making an issue of that aspect of the defendant's testimony.
g. Once the defendant becomes a witness, the admissibility of *prior convictions* is governed by F.R.E. 609, and not 404(b).
h. Improperly admitted evidence is not grounds for reversal unless there is actual prejudice to the accused. That is, a reasonable possibility that in the absence of the error the verdict might have been more favorable to the accused.

I. Habit

1. Introduction

This method of impeachment is used more in civil than in criminal cases. For that reason, it is not worth noting for purposes of this section.

2. Relevant Federal Rules of Evidence

Rule 406: Habit; Routine Practice

> Evidence of a person's habit or an organization's routine practice may be admitted to prove that on a particular occasion the person or organization acted in accordance with the habit or routine practice. The court may admit this evidence regardless of whether it is corroborated or whether there was an eyewitness.

J. Writing Used to Refresh Memory

1. Introduction

A witness whose memory has been refreshed creates a separate impeachment opportunity. This involves "refreshing recollection" and "past recollection recorded."

2. Relevant Federal Rules of Evidence
Rule 612: Writing Used to Refresh a Witness's Memory

(a) **Scope.** This rule gives an adverse party certain options when a witness uses a writing to refresh memory:

1. while testifying; or
2. before testifying, if the court decides that justice requires the party to have those options.

(b) Adverse Party's Options; Deleting Unrelated Matter

Unless 18 U.S.C. § 3500 provides otherwise in a criminal case, an adverse party is entitled to have the writing produced at the hearing, to inspect it, to cross-examine the witness about it, and to introduce in evidence any portion that relates to the witness's testimony. If the producing party claims that the writing includes unrelated matter, the court must examine the writing in camera, delete any unrelated portion, and order that the rest be delivered to the adverse party. Any portion deleted over objection must be preserved for the record.

(c) Failure to Produce or Deliver the Writing

If a writing is not produced or is not delivered as ordered, the court may issue any appropriate order. But if the prosecution does not comply in a criminal case, the court must strike the witness's testimony or—if justice so requires—declare a mistrial.

3. How to Use This Method

There are two ways a witness might refresh her memory. The most common method is to refresh the witness's memory while the witness is on the stand testifying. This can occur on either direct or cross-examination. The witness must show that she does not recall or remember something she once knew and that something would help remind her what it was.[50]

Rule 612 does authorize the opposing attorney to see and introduce into evidence those documents used by the witness to refresh before taking the stand, but only where and if the trial judge finds

[50] MacCarthy (2016), at p. 127.

that seeing and introducing the documents are required by "the interests of justice."

The fact that the document used to refresh is itself inadmissible does not affect its being used to refresh or your right to see and use it, though it will preclude it being admitted into evidence.[51] If a document is used to refresh and it must be turned over, the claim that the document is protected by the attorney–client or, for that matter, any other privilege, will not protect it.[52] Rule 612 also applies to depositions.[53]

Before a trial lawyer is allowed to refresh recollection or memory during trial, the lawyer must, according to some trial judges, have the witness state that she does not recall or remember. The witness must further state that the document would refresh her recollection or memory.[54]

Such an examination would go something like this:

Q: What did the note say with regard to where the automobile parts were located?
A: I don't remember.
Q: Would reviewing the note help you refresh your memory?
A: Yes, I'm sure it would.
Q: Your Honor, may I approach the witness?
COURT: You may.
Q: *(Handing a copy of the note to the prosecutor and the judge.)*
Do you know what this is?
A: Yes.
Q: What is it?
A: It's the note.
Q: Please read it to yourself.
Does that help refresh your memory?
A: Yes.
Q: *(Take the note back.)*
What did the note say with regard to where the automobile parts were located?

---

[51] *Id.*, at p. 128. *See also* United States v. Scott, 701 F.2d 1340 (11th Cir. 1983).

[52] MacCarthy (2016), at p. 128. *See also* Marshall v. Postal Service, 88 F.R.D. 348 (D.C.C. 1980); Leybold-Heraus Tech. Inc., v. Midwest Instrument Co., 118 F.R.D. 609 (E.D. Wisc. 1987).

[53] James Julian Inc. v. Raytheon Co., 93 F.R.D. 138 (D. Del. 1982).

[54] MacCarthy (2016), at p. 129.

K. Admissions

1. Introduction

This particular method of impeachment is usually referred to as an "admission by a party opponent." An opposing party witness has made a statement under certain circumstances, which has the appearance of being or is believed to be truthful and which is considered adverse to the interests of that party.

2. Relevant Federal Rules of Evidence

Rule 801: Hearsay Definitions

(a) Statements That Are Not Hearsay

A statement that meets the following conditions is not hearsay:

(1) An Opposing Party's Statement. The statement is offered against an opposing party and:

a. was made by the party in an individual or representative capacity;
b. is one the party manifested that it adopted or believed to be true;
c. was made by a person whom the party authorized to make a statement on the subject;
d. was made by the party's agent or employee on a matter within the scope of that relationship and while it existed; or
e. was made by the party's conspirator during and in furtherance of the conspiracy.

3. How to Use This Method

Admissions by party opponents are most often seen in civil cases, where they can be used to hold an employer liable for the actions of an employee. For example, the use of the employee driver's statement immediately following the collision: "I'm sorry. I didn't see the stop sign."

In criminal trials, these statements are occasionally used against defendants (particularly in conspiracy cases—see below), but they are seldom used against the prosecution. In fact, that is essentially the only major limitation on the use of such statements by the criminal defendant. This is because some courts take the position that government people are "disinterested in the outcome of cases." As such, criminal defendants are sometimes precluded from using such statements against government employees such as FBI agents and informers, as well as matters contained in government publications.[55]

In a nutshell, the caselaw essentially tells us the following:

1. An opposing party's statement can be of fact, opinion, or conclusions of law or fact and need not be based on personal knowledge.
2. The declarant of the statement need not testify at trial.
3. There is no guarantee of trustworthiness required.
4. Obviously, the statements are subject to relevancy requirements.[56]

4. F.R.E. 801(d)(2)(E) and the Admissibility of Co-Conspirator Statements

Statements of a collaborator in an illegal venture have unique evidentiary value and are rarely capable of duplication in live testimony at trial.[57] Rule 801(d)(2)(E) provides that an out-of-court statement is not hearsay if it is "offered against a party" and is a "statement by a co-conspirator of a party during the course of and in furtherance of the conspiracy." Regardless of a statement's independent reliability or the declarant's availability, co-conspirator statements are not hearsay and are admissible if the government establishes, by a preponderance of the evidence, that:

1. The charged conspiracy existed.
2. The defendants and the declarants were members of that particular conspiracy.
3. The statements were made during the course of and in furtherance of the conspiracy.[58]

---

[55] *Id.*, at p. 134.

[56] *Id.*

[57] United States v. Inadi, 475 U.S. 387, 395–396 (1986).

[58] Bourjaily v. United States, 483 U.S. 171, 175 (1987); United States v. Owens, 70 F.3d 1118, 1124 (10th Cir. 1995).

If the prosecutor intends to introduce such statements at trial, there must first be a *James* hearing, at which the prosecutor proffers the statements to the court to obtain a preliminary determination as to their admissibility.[59]

The standard for admissibility under the rule is "preponderance of the evidence." The court is authorized under F.R.E. 104(a) to consider any evidence whatsoever except privileged material, unhindered by consideration of admissibility. The court can rely on those statements to determine that the conspiracy existed and that the declarant and the defendants were parties to the conspiracy.[60]

Because of the nature of the evidence generally uncovered to prove criminal conspiracies, "wide latitude is allowed [the prosecution] in presenting evidence, and it is within the discretion of the trial court to admit evidence which even remotely tends to establish the conspiracy charged."[61]

The Supreme Court has affirmatively determined that the Confrontation Clause of the Sixth Amendment does not require a court to inquire into the reliability of co-conspirator statements admissible under the rule.[62] The Supreme Court's decision in *Crawford v. Washington*, 541 U.S. 36 (2004), changed much of the law concerning out-of-court testimonial statements, but it did not affect the admissibility of co-conspirator statements.

The principles for determining the existence of membership in the conspiracy are as follows:

1. The conspiracy need not be proved by direct evidence. The elements may be established by circumstantial evidence.
2. The court may consider the proffered statements themselves in determining the existence of a conspiracy.
3. Most courts require some reliable corroborating evidence apart from the co-conspirator's statements before those statements can be used. The direct testimony of a co-conspirator constitutes sufficient independent evidence of the existence of a conspiracy.

---

59 United States v. James, 590 F.2d 575 (5th Cir. 1979).
60 *Bourjaily*, at 180.
61 Nye & Nissen v. United States, 168 F.2d 846, 857 (9th Cir. 1948).
62 *Bourjaily*, at 183–184.

4. The government need not prove that a defendant knew each and every detail of the conspiracy or played more than a minor role in the conspiracy.
5. Once a conspiracy is established, there need only be some independent evidence linking the defendant to the conspiracy.

Once the existence of the conspiracy and membership in the conspiracy is established, statements made "during the course" and "in furtherance" of the conspiracy are admissible pursuant to the rule. A statement is made "during the course" of the conspiracy when the statement "was made while the plan was in existence and before its complete execution or other termination."[63] Statements "in furtherance" of the conspiracy are those that intend to promote the conspiratorial objectives.[64] The focus is on the declarant's intent in making the statement.[65]

L. The Hearsay Declarant

1. Introduction

You can actually impeach someone who may never testify as a witness at trial. Rule 806 allows a hearsay declarant to be impeached as if he were being cross-examined.[66]

The rule is directed at hearsay statements. The statements have come into evidence as an exception to the hearsay rule and have been introduced to prove their truth. The credibility of the declarant is now at issue and should be subject to impeachment as if the declarant had testified in open court. The problem, of course, is that the declarant has in fact not testified.[67]

---

[63] *See* 5 Weinstein's Federal Evidence (Second Edition) § 801.34[4][a] at 801–882—801–883 (2003).

[64] United States v. Reyes, 798 F.2d 380, 384 (10th Cir. 1986).

[65] United States v. Roberts, 14 F.3d 502, 515 (10th Cir. 1993).

[66] While this method has been summarized here, it is strongly recommended that the reader refer to MacCarthy's book (2016) at pp. 135–143 for the full analysis, due to the exceptions and the caselaw annotations.

[67] MacCarthy (2016), at p. 136.

2. Relevant Federal Rules of Evidence

Rule 806: Attacking and Supporting the Declarant

> When a hearsay statement—or a statement described in Rule 801(d)(2), (C), (D), or (E)—has been admitted in evidence, the declarant's credibility may be attacked, and then supported, by any evidence that would be admissible for those purposes if the declarant had testified as a witness. The court may admit evidence of the declarant's inconsistent statement or conduct, regardless of when it occurred or whether the declarant had an opportunity to explain or deny it. If the party against whom the statement was admitted calls the declarant as a witness, the party may examine the declarant on the statement as if on cross-examination.

3. How to Use This Method

The classic case where this rule comes into play is as follows: There are three co-defendants charged in a criminal case. Prior to trial, two of them decide that they have no interest in appearing and so they disappear. The prosecutor then introduces their inculpatory hearsay statements to incriminate the remaining defendant. The defendant's attorney uses Rule 806 to impeach the absent co-defendants' reputations for truthfulness under Rule 608.

Another example is that of a defendant who does not testify at trial and introduces an exculpatory hearsay statement that he himself made. This is often seen in trials involving the insanity defense, where the defendant has made exculpatory statements to the treating psychiatrist and introduces them under the Rule 803(4) hearsay exception for statements made for purposes of medical diagnosis or treatment.

The problem in these situations is that the nontestifying defendant who introduces his own hearsay statement subjects himself to Rule 806 impeachment.[68] As is often the case, a defendant who seeks to introduce such a statement does so in cases where, were he to testify, would be subject to impeachment with a crime under Rule 609 (assuming, of course, he had a record). A prosecutor would typically have little objection to a defendant introducing such a statement if he could impeach him in this fashion. However, a prosecutor may

---

68 *Id.*, at p. 137.

not call a witness for the sole purpose of impeaching the defendant through use of Rule 806.[69]

Another problem arises in that Rule 609 was intended to protect defendants who do not testify from being impeached with criminal convictions. This places Rules 806 and 609 in conflict with each other. Courts have addressed this conflict in several ways. One is to simply disallow Rule 806 impeachment altogether, and another is to allow impeachment with truthfulness under Rule 608 but disallow any impeachment using felony convictions.

Finally, when Rule 806 evidence has been used against you, you have the right to call the declarant as a witness at trial and cross-examine him as an adverse witness.

What methods of impeachment may be used in Rule 806 applications? There are several, as follows, some of which are more successful than others.

(a) Inconsistent Statements

Recall that under Impeachment Method No. 1, when impeaching a witness with inconsistent statements, you must give the witness the opportunity to deny or explain the statement. Since the declarant is not on the stand in this situation, this would be impossible. Note, however, that Rule 806 specifically states that use of the statement "is not subject to any requirement that he may have been afforded an opportunity to deny or explain."[70]

While that problem is alleviated, there still might be the problem of the subject matter of the statement being "collateral." Recall that if it is "collateral," extrinsic evidence cannot be used to prove it. Without it, there can be no impeachment.

The bottom line, then, is that without the declarant on the stand, the impeachment will be less than totally effective.[71]

(b) Motivation

The fact that extrinsic evidence is allowed in motivation impeachment resolves that problem here. However, absent the presence of the declarant, it essentially neutralizes any effect of impeachment.

---

[69] *Id.*, at p. 138.

[70] *Id.*, at p. 141.

[71] *Id.*

(c) Truthfulness

This method of impeachment presents a significant problem. Recall that truthfulness impeachment is "collateral," meaning that extrinsic evidence is prohibited. Thus, unless the declarant is called as a witness and admits to the untruthfulness, it is impossible to perfect the impeachment.[72]

(d) Convictions

Notwithstanding the conflict between Rules 609 and 806 regarding the permissibility of impeaching a *nontestifying defendant* with a criminal conviction, with the declarant absent, the impact of impeachment through criminal convictions is much less dramatic. You may introduce into evidence a certified record of the conviction.[73]

Of course, any and all other methods of impeachment are also available, but without the declarant on the witness stand, the effect of such impeachment is usually less than desired. It is for this reason that Rule 806 is seldom used.

M. Character Witnesses

1. Introduction

Generally speaking, most attorneys rarely—if ever—encounter situations where they must consider impeachment of a character witness. Most defense attorneys are scared to death to use it, and for good reason. They realize that introducing the character of their client into the case presents untold opportunities for the state to introduce all kinds of damaging evidence through cross-examination.

While character evidence can present a good opportunity for prosecutors to impeach, most prosecutors do not know how to cross-examine character witnesses. Due to its propensity for raising

---

[72] *Id.*, at p. 142.

[73] *Id.*, at p. 143. *See* U.S. v. Bovain, 708 F.2d 606 (11th Cir. 1985). Presumably during the cross-examination of a witness who has testified to out-of-court statements made to him by the absent witness. Those statements are hearsay, and even though the declarant was not present at trial, his credibility may be attacked by any evidence that would be admissible for those purposes as if he had testified as a witness. See Rules 806, 608, and 609.

the specter of unfair prejudice, it is extremely dangerous for prosecutors. It must therefore be handled as if it was nitroglycerin. It should never be used unless there is absolutely no alternative. It is so dangerous, so volatile, and so unstable that if mishandled it can blow a prosecutor's case to smithereens, either on the spot or on appeal.

One of the problems with such evidence is that it must be placed in the hands of those who understand it least: the jury. While it is usually accompanied by a "limiting instruction," that is hardly more effective than taping a note to a jar of nitroglycerin that says, "Be Careful!" and handing it to a 12-year-old.

The smart defense attorney will almost never put on a character witness. The benefits are questionable at best and the risks overwhelming. *The defense must tailor the testimony to the particular character trait of the defendant they are electing to portray.* Accordingly, this will dictate the extent to which the prosecutor will be permitted to cross-examine the witness. In other words, the prosecutor's cross-examination is limited to the character trait selected by the defense. Certain character traits are more inclusive than others.

Take, for example, the two most relevant and commonly used traits—honesty and law abiding. If the character trait used by the defendant is "honesty," then the prosecutor will not be allowed to impeach using evidence of the defendant's violent character. In that light, it is therefore easy to see the danger of a defendant using the "law-abiding" character trait.[74] Use of that trait would put few limitations on the scope of the prosecutor's cross-examination.[75]

For these reasons, this section will focus on the methods a prosecutor should be permitted to use to impeach a defense character witness, so that the defense attorney will recognize them and be ready to object if not used properly.

---

[74] Which curiously does not explain why it seems to be the most common character trait used by the defense. Perhaps it is because their clients have talked them into it, thinking it is important.

[75] MacCarthy (2016), at p. 146.

2. Relevant Federal Rules of Evidence

Rule 404. Character Evidence

(a) Character Evidence

(1) Prohibited Uses Evidence of a person's character or character trait is not admissible to prove that on a particular occasion the person acted in accordance with the character or trait.

(2) Exceptions for a Defendant or Victim in a Criminal Case The following exceptions apply in a criminal case:

a. A defendant may offer evidence of the defendant's pertinent trait, and if the evidence is admitted, the prosecutor may offer evidence to rebut it;
b. Subject to the limitations in Rule 412, a defendant may offer evidence of an alleged victim's pertinent trait, and if the evidence is admitted, the prosecutor may:
   i) offer evidence to rebut it; and
   ii) offer evidence of the defendant's same trait; and
c. in a homicide case, the prosecutor may offer evidence of the alleged victim's trait of peacefulness to rebut evidence that the victim was the first aggressor.

(3) Exceptions for a Witness. Evidence of a witness's character may be admitted under Rules 607, 608, and 609.

3. How to Use This Method

As is often the case in this business, there tends to be a wide disparity between the way the prosecutor should properly examine a particular witness and the way that he actually examines him. It is hoped that this example can assist the defense attorney in knowing what to watch out for and when to object.

Consider this scenario: The defense calls a witness to the stand who testifies as to a particular character trait of the defendant. The form of the testimony is limited to either **reputation** or **personal opinion.** Specific acts demonstrating the trait cannot be used.

The prosecutor then cross-examines the witness. Assuming the defense elects "honesty" as the character trait, the witness has testified to the defendant's reputation in the community for honesty. The proper cross-examination would be as follows:

Q: You told the ladies and gentlemen of the jury that you have heard the defendant's reputation in the community was that he was an honest person?
A: Yes.
Q: But you have also heard [**rumors that he ______ [or] that he has a reputation for [having committed certain crimes, bad acts, being arrested]]**?

– *OR* –

Assuming the witness has testified regarding his personal opinion of the defendant's honesty, the cross-examination would be as follows:

Q: You told the ladies and gentlemen of the jury that you personally know and believe that the defendant is an honest person?
A: Yes.
Q: But you also know and believe [**that he ______ [or] that he [has committed certain crimes, bad acts, been arrested]]**?

If, on the one hand, the witness denies having heard that particular rumor or reputation, or denies personally knowing of those specific things, then the prosecutor's examination of that witness is finished. She must accept the witness's answer. She cannot use extrinsic evidence to prove those matters, as they are considered "collateral" (*i.e.*, not material to the issue).

If, on the other hand, the witness knows about or has heard of those things, then the prosecutor may continue to examine the witness as to those matters, as long as she remains within the particular trait at issue.

This impeachment is subject to the following general limitations:

- The prosecutor must have a "good faith" basis for the incidents she is asserting. (They need not necessarily be true, however.)
- The incidents come in only to impeach the witness, and not as substantive evidence.

- She may not impeach with the same crime with which the defendant is charged.
- The incidents cannot be too attenuated in time.

4. The Problem with Character Evidence for the Defendant

To illustrate why it is not wise for the defense to introduce character evidence, let's assume the following factual scenario:

The defendant, a young woman, is charged with the murder of an infant whom she was babysitting. She did not testify. Defense counsel calls a character witness (the defendant's mother) who testified on direct examination that in her personal opinion the defendant was of good character and would never have engaged in the type of behavior of which she was accused in that case (shaking the child violently, resulting in her death). This was obviously the "law-abiding" character trait.

The prosecutor cross-examines the witness. For the most part, the prosecutor is not overly aggressive, and the questioning is generally limited to establishing the witness's lack of personal knowledge of the defendant's behavior on the date in question. Defense counsel is relieved and begins thinking that he is in good shape.

Then things get interesting. The prosecutor pauses momentarily, glances at the judge, and announces, "Your Honor, I just have a couple more questions and then I'm done." The prosecutor turns her head and fixes her gaze directly on the witness.

Q: You have known the defendant all her life?
A: Yes.
Q: You love your daughter?
A: Yes.
Q: You would never say anything that would ever cast her in a bad light?
A: No, but I wouldn't lie for her, if that's what you mean.
Q: It is your opinion that the defendant is of good character and would never do anything to intentionally harm a child whom she was babysitting?
A: That's right.
Q: That she's just not the type of person who would do anything like that?

A: Absolutely not.
Q: *Would your opinion change if you knew that* the defendant had been recently observed reacting angrily and violently shaking the child when removing her from her car seat?

Defense counsel had been half-listening but mostly fantasizing some of the terrific points he was planning to make in his brilliant closing argument. From somewhere in the mist, he faintly hears the words, "*Would your opinion change if you knew that. . . .*"

Suddenly everything is in slow motion, and he hears what sounds like a terrible multiple-car collision with a freight train. He realizes it's his case. He leaps to his feet. As he does, he hears the witness answer with a forceful, "*No.*"

DEFENSE COUNSEL: Objection!
COURT: Yes, Counsel?
DEFENSE COUNSEL: Uhhh. . . .

His mind is a complete blank. He can't think of a thing to say, but he senses he had better say *something*. He feels the blood rushing from his face and senses a terrible dark presence standing close to him. The prosecutor, not taking her eyes off of the witness, says nothing.

COURT: *(Setting aside his crossword puzzle and turning his full attention to the witness.)* Overruled. You may continue.
DEFENSE COUNSEL: *(Mouth open, looks helplessly at the judge. Oh my God—was that actually a smile slowly beginning to form on his honor's lips? Counsel collapses weakly into his chair. The prosecutor continues, clearly relishing the moment.)*
Q: I'm now going to ask you some questions about a different subject.
A: But . . . alright.
(The prosecutor turns and picks up several papers stapled together from her desk and steps over to the defense table and hands a copy to defense counsel

without looking at him. She then walks briskly to the bench and hands a copy to the court. She turns smartly and returns to the podium, holding the papers in her right hand, extending them at arm's length so the jury can clearly see.)

Q: Would your opinion change if you also knew that the Department of Animal Control has been conducting an investigation into claims that your daughter has been torturing and killing pets and other small animals, and burying them on her property? And that animal carcasses have been recovered from that property that were charred and exhibited evidence of horrific physical abuse?

(His senses reeling, the defense attorney sees everything suddenly vanishing into a white fog before him. Suddenly, he remembers something from his Bar Review course.)

DEFENSE COUNSEL: Objection! This is improper cross-examination. Counsel is attempting to introduce improper extrinsic and collateral evidence. It also violates the court's pretrial order *in limine.*[76] Moreover, we were never notified of the existence of this evidence prior to trial, and so it is a *Brady* violation. We move for a mistrial!

(To himself: Please, God, let me out of this mess and I promise never again to fudge on my continuing legal education hours.)

PROSECUTOR: *(Coolly, as if ordering a Margarita poolside.)* Your Honor, the defendant has placed her "law-abiding" character at issue through the testimony of this witness. She has therefore opened the door to cross-examination using specific instances of bad

---

[76] Naturally, a good defense attorney will have filed a pretrial motion *in limine* to exclude improper evidence, including any irrelevant prior charged or uncharged criminal behavior. The court would likely have denied the motion as to "uncharged" criminal behavior, for the reasons illustrated here.

character, pursuant to Rule 608(b), as well as Rule 404(a)(1).

As you can see from this official report, Your Honor, this evidence is based upon a good faith belief in its truthfulness, and it is relevant to the issue at hand, and thus noncollateral. However, we do not intend to introduce this report into evidence or examine this witness with it. Lastly, although we only learned of this evidence one week prior to trial, we were under no obligation to disclose it to defense counsel because it is not exculpatory, and we had no knowledge that the defense would call a character witness.

(Defense counsel is now sweating bullets. His case has just disintegrated into a million tiny fragments right in front of his eyes. His heart is hammering, and he feels faint. His only hope now is that a giant meteorite will suddenly crash through the roof of the courtroom, obliterating everyone in sight.)

COURT: The defense called this witness and has offered opinion testimony regarding the defendant's law-abiding character. The information contained in the report from the Department of Animal Control is relevant and therefore proper cross-examination under Rules 608(b) and 404(a)(1). Furthermore, the state has shown a good faith belief as to its truthfulness.

I also find that the information is not exculpatory and thus is not subject to disclosure to the defense under *Brady*. Not only that, but the state had no reason to believe that it would need this evidence in their case-in-chief, since it would not have been admissible at that point. It wasn't until the defense elected to call this witness and undertake this line of questioning that the information became relevant.

Objection overruled. Motion for mistrial denied. Counsel, you may continue.[77]

---

[77] If only the court's rationale was like this in real life.

Q: I'll repeat the question. Would your opinion of your daughter's ability to fatally harm a child change if you knew that the Department of Animal Control has been conducting an investigation into claims that your daughter has been torturing and killing pets and other small animals, and burying them on her property? And that animal carcasses have been recovered from that property that were charred and exhibited evidence of horrific physical abuse?

A: Oh, my God . . . how . . . (*She begins to sob.*)

Q: No further questions, Your Honor. *(Turning to defense counsel.)* Your witness, counsel.

5. Teaching Points

This is, of course, a stylized graphic example of why it is so foolish for the defense to call witnesses to introduce evidence as to the defendant's law-abiding character. It essentially throws open the door to anything the prosecutor wishes to use, including crimes (including those otherwise precluded by Rule 609), bad acts, arrests, and even rumors.

A smart prosecutor would have thoroughly researched the applicable law and evidentiary rules in the off chance that she would have an opportunity to use the rebuttal character "evidence," even though it was only two questions on cross-exam. They were, however, critical questions and so explosive that even if the defense had been in good shape up to that point, things would likely have taken a turn toward catastrophe immediately thereafter.

a. Question No. 1—The Prior Shaking Incident

When impeaching a character witness's opinion testimony, you must couch your question in terms of whether their opinion would change if they became aware of the new information.

If the witness answers "No," the prosecutor is now done with that line of questioning. She cannot introduce extrinsic evidence to prove it. If the answer is "Yes," then the prosecutor may follow up with how her opinion would change and will likely conclude with her agreeing that the defendant was capable of violently shaking the child on at least one occasion prior to the day of its death.

If the defense counsel had been able to voice his objection, it would have essentially been the same one he articulated in response to the second question. Not that it would have mattered. The question was proper.

Here, the witness answered, "No," and the prosecutor properly moved on to the second question.

b. Question No. 2—The Animal Control Report

The report is obviously being used here for dramatic effect. She should not hand it to the witness and should not introduce it into evidence. However, the jury sees that she (as well as the judge) has what they now believe is the report, and she is ready to establish that she has a good faith basis to believe the information is true.

The defense attorney articulated the best objection he possibly could have under the circumstances. Unfortunately, it was to no avail. He hadn't realized until too late that he should never have called the witness to begin with.

The court's ruling on the objection was correct. And it didn't matter what the witness's answer would have been. The damage was done.

N. Victims of Sexual Assault

1. Introduction

In many states, there may be a specific statute that details or limits the manner in which evidence may be introduced to impeach a victim of sexual assault. Generally, such evidence is limited to the victim's character regarding prior sexual history with persons other than the accused. There is usually no limitation on the evidence regarding the victim's prior sexual conduct with the accused, however.

Some state statutes deal specifically with the introduction of evidence regarding the prior sexual conduct of the victim, as well as reputation evidence or opinion evidence regarding the character of the victim, which would be used in conjunction with F.R.E. 404(a)(2).[78]

2. Relevant Federal Rules of Evidence

In response to the level of national concern regarding these types of cases, Congress has enacted several rules of evidence dealing specifically with sexual assault cases. They are essentially "rape shield laws" and are found in Rules 412, 413, 414, and 415. With the exception of Rule 412, rather than being useful tools for the defendant to impeach witnesses, these rules specify what kind of evidence may be used to impeach the *defendant*.

---

[78] As an example, this is the Wyoming statute:

W.S. § 6-2-312. Evidence of Victim's Prior Sexual Conduct or Reputation; Procedure for Introduction.

(a) In any prosecution under this article or for any lesser included offense, if evidence of the prior sexual conduct of the victim, reputation evidence or opinion evidence as to the character of the victim is to be offered the following procedure shall be used:
   (i) A written motion shall be made by the defendant to the court at least ten (10) days prior to the trial stating that the defense has an offer of proof of the relevancy of evidence of the sexual conduct of the victim and its relevancy to the defense;
   (ii) The written motion shall be accompanied by affidavits in which the offer of proof is stated;
   (iii) If the court finds the offer of proof sufficient, the court shall order a hearing in chambers, and at the hearing allow the questioning of the victim regarding the offer of proof made by the defendant and other pertinent evidence;
   (iv) At the conclusion of the hearing, if the court finds that the probative value of the evidence substantially outweighs the probability that its admission will create prejudice, the evidence shall be admissible pursuant to this section. The court may make an order stating what evidence may be introduced by the defendant, which order may include the nature of the questions to be permitted.

(b) This section does not limit the introduction of evidence as to prior sexual conduct of the victim with the actor.

(c) Any motion or affidavit submitted pursuant to this section is privileged information and shall not be released or made available for public use or scrutiny in any manner, including posttrial proceedings.

Rule 412

This rule attempts to deal with the problems which can occur with "rape shield laws." Generally speaking, these rules specifically exclude impeachment offered to show that the victim engaged in other sexual behavior, or to prove a victim's sexual predisposition. There are exceptions, however, and they are set forth in 412(b)(1):

(a) Exceptions

(1) Criminal Cases. The court may admit the following evidence in a criminal case:

a. evidence of specific instances of a victim's sexual behavior, if offered to prove that someone other than the defendant was the source of semen, injury, or other physical evidence;
b. evidence of specific instances of a victim's sexual behavior with respect to the person accused of the sexual misconduct, if offered by the defendant to prove consent or if offered by the prosecutor; and
c. evidence whose exclusion would violate the defendant's constitutional rights.

(b) Procedure to Determine Admissibility

(1) Motion. If a party intends to offer evidence under Rule 412(b), the party must:

a. file a motion that specifically describes the evidence and states the purpose for which it is to be offered;
b. do so at least fourteen days before trial unless the court, for good cause, sets a different time;
c. serve the motion on all parties; and
d. notify the victim or, when appropriate, the victim's guardian or representative.

(2) Hearing. Before admitting evidence under this rule, the court must conduct an in camera hearing and give the victim and parties a right to attend and be heard. Unless the court orders otherwise, the motion, related materials, and the record of the hearing must be and remain sealed.

Rule 413

This rule expands the impeachment of defendants in sexual assault cases. The types of assaults contemplated are defined in the rule under subsection (d). Rule 413 creates an exception to Rule 404 in sexual assault cases. In these cases, you can now prove propensity.[79] It is evidently not necessary to prove a prior conviction for sexual assault, since the standard is "committed." (Preponderance of the evidence?) Moreover, misdemeanor sexual offenses appear to be included.

(a) Permitted Uses

In a criminal case in which a defendant is accused of a sexual assault, the court may admit evidence that the defendant committed any other sexual assault. The evidence may be considered on any matter to which it is relevant.

(b) Disclosure to the Defendant

If the prosecutor intends to offer this evidence, the prosecutor must disclose it to the defendant, including witness's statements or a summary of the expected testimony. The prosecutor must do so at least fifteen days before trial or at a later time that the court allows for good cause.

(c) Effect on Other Rules

This rule does not limit the admission or consideration of evidence under any other rule.

(d) Definition of Sexual Assault

In this rule and Rule 415, "sexual assault" means a crime under a federal law or under state law (as "state" is defined in 18 U.S.C. § 513) involving:

1. any conduct prohibited by 18 U.S.C. chapter 109A;
2. contact, without consent, between any part of the defendant's body—or an object—and another person's genitals or anus;
3. contact, without consent, between the defendant's genitals or anus and any part of another person's body;

[79] MacCarthy (2016) at 153.

4. deriving sexual pleasure or gratification from inflicting death, bodily injury, or physical pain on another person; or
5. an attempt or conspiracy to engage in conduct described in subparagraphs (1)—(4).

Rule 414

This rule is identical to Rule 413 except that it concerns "child molestation cases" instead of sexual assault cases.

(a) in this rule and Rule 415:

1. "Child" means a person below the age of 14; and
2. "Child molestation" means a crime under federal law or under state law (as "state" is defined in 18 U.S.C. § 513.)

Rule 415

This rule essentially expands application of Rules 413 and 414 to civil cases.

3. How to Use This Method

The extent to which you will be permitted to examine the victim in open court will be determined by the court once it has heard and considered the evidence that you submit in your pretrial offer of proof and any subsequent hearing held in chambers. Be prepared to research how these evidentiary restrictions might be subject to the Confrontation Clause of the Sixth Amendment.

O. Experts—Qualifications and Curriculum Vitae

1. Introduction

The best way to deal with your opponent's experts at trial is to find a way to exclude them from testifying at all. Consider filing a *Daubert* motion before trial to try and disqualify the expert from being permitted to testify.[80] There's no better way to start off the trial than by

[80] Daubert v. Merrell Dow Pharmaceuticals, Inc., 509 U.S. 579, 113 S.Ct. 2786, 125 L.Ed.2d 469 (1993).

cutting your opponent's case off at the knees before you ever walk in the door.

For the most part, impeachment of an expert employs the same techniques described in the fourteen methods of impeachment for all witnesses, set forth above. However, the impeachment of experts also presents opportunities that are unique to that caliber of witness.

2. Relevant Federal Rules of Evidence

F.R.E. 608 (Truthfulness)

3. How to Use This Method

Many resumes list membership in prestigious and high-sounding organizations. They can be effectively and even powerfully used to impeach, in particular to highlight the expert's ego and pretentiousness.

Like any good cross-examination, you start broadly and methodically narrow it down. You establish that the expert prepared his resume and that he wished to list all of his accomplishments that distinguish him and that would impress people. Then you select one or more entries that you have previously researched. You confirm that the expert belongs to an organization or prestigious-sounding academy of professionals, one of which he is proud. You then note that there were no tests to take, or interviews to give, or accomplishments to achieve in order to qualify for said membership. Then you close the noose by confirming that all he had to do to qualify for membership was simply send in an application with the required mandatory fee.[81]

Experts are vulnerable in a variety of ways:

1. They are usually being paid for their opinions, which by necessity colors their opinions with the taint of conflict of interest.
2. Typically, many experts testify for only one side of the conflict, for a variety of reasons. Sometimes it's personal and therefore not objective. For example, some medical experts only testify for the defense because they don't like the plaintiffs' attorneys.
3. They know nothing of the case at hand, other than through the materials they have been given to review by counsel.

---

[81] *Id.*, at pp. 160–161.

Therefore, what they don't know can hurt them or even cause them to reverse their opinions on the stand.

4. They may have never taken courses in the specific subject matter. They may not teach the subject at a university.
5. They may never have examined, tested, or even met the individual involved, or visited the location of the event. They almost certainly were not the treating expert.
6. They may never have written a book or articles on the subject. If they did, it was not peer reviewed nor ever published in a prestigious journal recognized for its academic discipline.
7. They are not certified in the particular field.
8. Since they are usually not the treating expert and have only been retained to offer an opinion, they are subject to impeachment by Impeachment Method No. 6: What they could have done but didn't do.
9. If they have a particularly unique expertise, or if they have developed a national reputation and are used frequently in many cases (in other words, they've become the "expert du jour"), they are vulnerable not as expert in "doing" something but in "testifying."
10. If they have testified before in similar cases for the same side, that testimony is a matter of court record. Look into it. If they have changed their opinions, they may be seen as playing "fast and loose" depending on who's paying them. You are looking for inconsistencies. At the very least, check with other colleagues who may have used them, and find out what their reputation is.
11. Other experts disagree with them.

Generally, the two most common areas of vulnerability are their qualifications to be permitted to testify as experts in a particular field, and the quality and veracity of their resume or curriculum vitae.[82]

[82] Never underestimate the value of thoroughly investigating the expert's background. Sometimes it is not all it appears to be. Here's an actual example: An attorney friend of mine was advised by an opponent in a very large civil case that they had retained an expert witness for trial. A copy of the expert's resume was attached to the disclosure. My friend checked out the expert's stated credentials. It turned out that none of the universities he listed had any record of his having

As noted earlier in this manual, the best way to handle an expert on cross-examination is to avoid climbing into their back yard altogether. Regardless of how smart you think you are or how learned you are in the expert's field, there's a good reason that you are not making a living testifying about it. At the end of the day, you will come out on the short end of the stick.

Study where the expert may be vulnerable and attack those areas only. *Then sit down.* Never engage in a debate with the expert toe-to-toe on his home turf. You will lose. Remember the advice in Chapter 14: The goal of cross-examination is not to inflict damage on the witness but to get through it without having any damage inflicted on you. If you emerge unscathed, you have conducted a great cross-examination.

If nothing else, you can always "look good" to the jury by asking the classic questions:

> *Doctor, you were hired and are being paid by my opponent to present your opinions here today, correct? The information upon which you are basing your opinions was supplied to you by my opponent, was it not? Please tell the jury how much are you charging for your testimony.*

P. Experts—Learned Treatises

1. Introduction

This rule allows you to impeach an expert witness with something the expert did not say and indeed something the expert may not agree with. Although you are impeaching the expert with an inconsistent statement opinion, it is *someone else's* statement or opinion that is found in a printed work—a "learned treatise."

To do this, you must first, to the satisfaction of the trial judge, establish or show that the learned treatise is "reliable authority." It

attended a single class. He had completely fabricated his academic background and possessed none of the degrees or certifications he claimed. In one case, he even invented the name of the school and the address! Needless to say, that information came in handy at the settlement conference. Copies of the investigation file were handed out to opposing counsel. The case settled immediately. The moral of the story? *Never* assume an expert's resume is truthful.

may turn out that the expert does not agree with the reliable authority (you hope he doesn't) and in fact may not have ever read it (you hope he hasn't).

2. Relevant Federal Rules of Evidence

Rule 803(18). Exceptions to the Rule against Hearsay

The following are not excluded by the rule against hearsay, regardless of whether the declarant is available as a witness:

(18) Statements in Learned Treatises, Periodicals, or Pamphlets

A statement contained in a treatise, periodical, or pamphlet if:

a. the statement is called to the attention of an expert witness on cross-examination or relied upon by the expert on direct examination; and
b. the publication is established as a reliable authority by the expert's admission or testimony, by another expert's testimony, or by judicial notice.

If admitted, the statement may be read into evidence but not received as an exhibit.

3. How to Use This Method

You can establish or prove reliable authority in one of three ways:

1. The best and easiest way is through your cross-examination of the expert. Get him to admit that as a professional who is always abreast of the latest knowledge in his area of expertise, he knows of the learned treatise and he considers it one of the leading works in the field. Therefore, he considers it to be reliable authority. A simple series of questions with "yes" responses should handle that nicely. If, for some reason, he denies that it is a reliable authority (or worse, he's never heard of it), so much the better. With a few questions you firmly establish that for the jury.

2. Later, when you are presenting your case, you call a witness to testify about the "reliable authority." The witness should be a person who is well qualified to talk about it and is quite familiar with it and its value to the subject at hand. Have the witness confirm that it is the leading authority in the field and that it is used by other professionals in universities to teach the subject. Finally, have the witness confirm that any reputable expert in the field would be familiar with the work.
3. Get the trial judge to take judicial notice that the work is a reliable authority.

Now that the treatise has been recognized as a reliable authority, there are some limits as to how it may be used. It is admissible as substantive evidence, but it may not be received in evidence *as an exhibit* (since it contains hearsay). Instead, *the relevant portion can be read to the jury.* You should be the one reading the material if you are cross-examining, and your expert does the reading if on direct.

Finally, in addition to reading the material, you may also be able to show the relevant parts of it to the jury in the form of a chart as demonstrative evidence.

16
Putting on the Defense Case

A lawyer's vacation is the time between a question and the answer.

—Garvin Isaacs

If you're explaining, you're losing.

—Bob Rose

A. Motion for Judgment of Acquittal

After the state has presented all of its evidence and has rested, the court will excuse the jury and ask whether the defense wishes to move for judgment of acquittal. The defense will certainly agree, as failure to so move is essentially tantamount to malpractice (regardless of the apparent strength of the state's case). The judge may rule immediately, or take the motion under advisement, and wait until the defense has submitted its case before issuing his ruling.

If the motion is denied, as it is well over 90 percent of the time, the court will then ask the defense whether it intends to introduce any witnesses or evidence, and if so, whether the defendant will be testifying. In the event your client will be testifying, many courts take a moment to advise the defendant directly, on the record, as to his constitutional rights and solicit his response as to whether he agrees to waive his right to remain silent and testify under oath.[1] At that point, the court may take a recess so that the parties may prepare for the next phase of the trial.

B. Direct Examination of Your Witnesses

Many attorneys believe that cross-examination is the more difficult of the witness confrontations to master. However, others believe that a good direct examination is more difficult to do. This is due to several factors: (1) it is so easy to make it boring; (2) you cannot control what the witness says; and (3) there is no guarantee that the witness is going to testify the way you believe he is.

Most direct examinations are about as interesting and uncomfortable as having your teeth cleaned at the dentist. The problem appears to be that since direct examination is to be conducted with open-ended fact questions (who, what, when, where, why, how), lawyers seem to lose all of their imagination—as well as linguistic skills—and revert to: *"And then what happened?"* or its equally titillating counterpart, *"What happened next?"* for nearly every question.

You must understand the difference between a general fact witness, an expert, and your client. Each one is distinct and requires a different examination approach. Since these are your witnesses, you have already interviewed them and know what they are going to say. However, when presenting to the jury, you must not act as if you are disinterested in their testimony. Likewise, you should not hang on every word in feigned astonishment as if they were describing human flight for the first time. Keep in mind that the jury has not heard this witness before, so prepare as if you are a member of the jury and ask questions as if you were wanting to know the answers yourself.

Another good, effective technique, especially with testimony relating to a particularly important fact or event, is to employ "looping." This technique allows you to reincorporate an important fact

---

[1] Keep in mind that while you must advise your client as to the pros and cons of testifying, the decision whether or not to do so is his alone to make, not yours.

or phrase from the previous answer and reemphasize it by weaving it into the next question. For example:

YOU: Mr. Smith, were you at the house on the afternoon of March 13, 2017?

WITNESS: Yes.

YOU: Why were you there that day?

WITNESS: I was attending a birthday party.

YOU: At approximately 3:15 p.m., where were you?

WITNESS: I was walking from the kitchen into the living room.

YOU: What were you doing?

WITNESS: I was bringing my wife a beer.

YOU: As you were walking from the kitchen into the living room, was your attention drawn to anything in particular?

WITNESS: Yes.

YOU: What was that?

WITNESS: I glanced out the window and noticed a pickup truck was pulling up outside.

YOU: Why was your attention drawn to that pickup truck?

WITNESS: It was a red Ford F-250.

YOU: Was the fact that it was a red Ford F-250 mean anything to you?

WITNESS: Yes.

YOU: What was significant about it?

WITNESS: I knew it belonged to David Wilson.

YOU: As the red Ford F-250 pulled up outside the house, did you observe anything else of significance about the truck or its occupants?

WITNESS: Yes. I saw the driver get out.

YOU: Why was that of significance to you?

WITNESS: I recognized him.

YOU: Who was he?

WITNESS: David Wilson.

YOU: Did you notice anything else as Mr. Wilson got out of the truck?

WITNESS: Yes. He had a pistol in his hand.

YOU: What did Mr. Wilson do with the pistol he had in his hand?

WITNESS: He pointed it at the defendant.

Instead of simply droning on, question after question, describing what the witness did "next," you focus the jury's attention on the important facts of the testimony, that is, the color of the car, the fact that it belonged to the assailant, that he got out of the vehicle brandishing a pistol at your client, and so on. The questioning is direct and open-ended, yet it is not boring. It flows naturally, as if you were a member of the jury wanting to know why the witness was doing what he was doing.

Direct examinations are designed to elicit information from the witness, in the witness's own words, and thus are purposely open-ended. Try to conduct the examination as if you were the director of a motion picture and were filming the scene being described by the witness. Make it dramatic and interesting, as if you are describing the scene from different viewpoints and camera angles, and help the jury paint the picture in their minds as if they were seeing it on the screen as you describe it. Your job is to make that event—and the related inquiry—as interesting as possible, thereby ensuring that the jury understands the areas of the testimony that are of particular importance.

Using open-ended questions is primarily what makes a good direct exam so difficult and nerve-wracking for the attorney. You are usually unable to use leading questions, as you are in cross-examination, and so your ability to control what the witness is saying is significantly limited. Therefore, a thorough preparation of the witness prior to taking the stand is crucial to success, but one must be careful not to overdo it. You don't want the witness to sound over-rehearsed with canned responses. Here are some helpful guidelines:

- Make sure that the witness is completely familiar with any oral or written statements previously made to police or others. Provide the witness with a copy to review ahead of time. He will no doubt be examined regarding any inconsistencies.
- Review with the witness those areas that are of particular importance. If the testimony concerns certain elements of the

case that must be proved in order to secure an acquittal for your client, make sure that the witness understands that she must testify clearly about them. Test the witness on the strength of the testimony so that there is no doubt or hesitation.

- Avoid "coaching" the witness on how to state certain things. Her testimony must be her own, in her own words. All you should do is tell her why certain evidence is important, and confirm that it in fact is what occurred. Then simply have her tell the jury about it in her own words.

One more thing about direct examinations: You typically introduce your documentary, photographic, and other exhibits through your own witnesses. After the court has admitted them into evidence, it is a good idea to wait to request that the exhibits be published to the jury after the testimony is concluded, rather than immediately after the court has admitted them. This is because you don't want the jury distracted by examining the exhibits while your witness is still in the midst of giving testimony. Thus, it is better for you to wait to publish the documents until you are finished with the witness, for at that point you want the jury to be distracted from your opponent's cross-examination of your witness. Most courts routinely pause the proceedings to permit the jury to examine evidence, thus avoiding this concern.

C. Direct Examination of Your Expert

You are offering the expert to establish or explain a subject that requires a particular scientific or professional expertise that the jurors likely do not possess. Therefore, you must examine the expert in a special way.

First of all, you should be quite familiar with Evidence Rules 702, 703, and 704, which control the admissibility of expert testimony. You don't want to give the prosecutor any opportunity to limit or preclude altogether the introduction of your expert's testimony because you didn't understand how to establish a proper foundation for it. It is therefore a good idea to prepare a script that you can follow so that you don't miss any critical points. You must also be familiar with the subject, for the effectiveness of the direct examination of your expert depends on the extent of your knowledge of the subject matter the expert is discussing, and your ability to explain it clearly to the jury.[2]

The direct examination of your expert is particularly challenging if you are also using charts, exhibits, videos, and other demonstrative aids. You absolutely do not want to wait until you're standing in front of the jury to try it for the first time. Set aside plenty of time before trial to meet with your expert, and prepare the necessary exhibits and rehearse how best to demonstrate them. When you present the exhibits with your expert's testimony, you want to appear as if you and your expert have been working together all your careers. You don't want to appear anxious, uncomfortable, or uncertain.

As with any witness you call on direct examination, if there are areas of the testimony that are weak or support the state's case, be up front about it. Don't try to hide it. If you address it head-on, you can control the narrative, and have the witness explain why the evidence is that way. Quite often, you are able to smooth it over so that it no longer appears as weak as it was, with the result being that it takes the power out of the prosecutor's cross-examination. If you try and hide it, however, the prosecutor already knows it exists, and thus he will make a huge, dramatic production out of prying it loose from your expert when he cross-examines him.

Here are some guidelines that will help:

- Do not use hypotheticals; they are not necessary.
- Begin the examination by establishing that the witness is qualified in the area he or she is testifying about. This is usually accomplished by having the witness go through his curriculum vitae.
- Be up front about the fact that you are paying the witness for his testimony. What's sauce for the goose is sauce for the gander.

---

[2] Presumably, if you're like me, you have to really simplify it in order to grasp it. That's a good thing, for that's exactly what you and your expert are going to have to do for the jury. This is not a time for you to impress the jury with how smart you think you are. Instead, I take this opportunity to reassure the jury that even someone as dull as I am can grasp the subject. The key is translating it into concepts and language the jurors can easily understand. The more elemental, the better, especially if it involves physical demonstrations and examples. Not because the jurors aren't smart, but because you don't have the time to try and explain complicated academic or scientific concepts. Work with your expert ahead of time so that the two of you function as a team when you present it.

- Once the expert's qualifications are established, you may do one of two things: either ask for the expert's opinions and then establish the foundation for them, or establish the foundation and then ask for the opinions. Either way is acceptable.
- Work with your expert beforehand to ensure that he avoids overly fancy or technical terms. It will not impress the jury. You are trying to educate the jury about your case and why they should vote for you. They are hearing this for the very first (and only) time. You want to make it as clear as possible.
- Avoid agreeing to have the prosecutor offer to stipulate to your expert's qualifications to testify. That is often an attempt to prevent the jury from hearing how eminently qualified your expert is, especially if the state's expert is not nearly as qualified or impressive.
- Have the expert use models or demonstrative exhibits. They are interesting, memorable, and juries like them. Plus, if they are admitted into evidence, the jury will get to play with them while they deliberate!

D. Direct Examination of Your Client

Defense attorneys offer differing beliefs as to whether or not to call the defendant as a witness. Some never do, others always do, and still others do it selectively, depending on the circumstances of each case. Most attorneys adopt the "always" or "never" approach, based on anecdotal experience. It is a decision that must not be entered into lightly.

Your client's decision whether or not to testify in his own behalf is the most important decision your client will ever make in the case and possibly in his life. Your client has lived with the case from the moment it first occurred. It has replayed countless times in his head. He may therefore be emotionally drained, not to mention frightened of testifying. Your job is to reassure him and calm him down so that he can tell his story as if it is fresh. This is the first (and only) time the jury will hear it. It is therefore critical that they get to know your client as the person who not only has the major stake in the outcome of the case, but is also someone whom they like and trust, and deserves the benefit of any "reasonable doubt."

Generally speaking, the client should not testify if there is any other witness in the case who can tell his story. If all your client is going to do on the stand is deny his guilt but offer nothing more, there is no reason to put him on the stand. It is presumed that that is what he will say. After all, the very reason he is on trial is because he entered a plea of not guilty at his arraignment. His denial adds absolutely nothing but instead exposes him to catastrophe on cross-examination. Unless your client is a savvy, experienced criminal trial lawyer, he will likely be at the mercy of one.

If you have a specific defense, you should make every effort to have other witnesses in the case testify about it, and that includes prosecution witnesses. In many, if not most, cases, your client has made some kind of a statement to law enforcement officers, or other witnesses observed him acting in a particular way. Those are the witnesses that very often can tell your client's story.

By using other witnesses to tell your client's story—the story of his innocence—you not only accomplish that goal, but in a way that insulates your client from destruction by effective cross-examination. Even if the prosecuting attorney is a novice, and completely benign and incapable of inflicting any harm whatsoever on your client, do not forget that the jury is using their combined hundreds of years of accumulated human experience to determine whether or not he is telling the truth. They will instinctively be able to sense it. And even a novice prosecutor can get lucky and be lethal given the right circumstances. Why give him that chance?

Encourage your client to put off making the decision to testify until the very last possible moment, typically after the state rests its case. You never know precisely how the evidence is going to shake out at trial, and for that reason you should not commit either way until you are as certain as possible what the state has actually proved. It is important that you prepare your client prior to trial for the possibility that he will need to testify, with the understanding that the final decision will be made at that point. Also, by waiting, you avoid committing your client either way in your voir dire and opening statement.[3]

---

3 Remember, you must address the possibility of your client not testifying in voir dire. *See* Chapter 12(3)(d).

If your client decides to testify, good preparation is critical. Meet with her often, to ensure that she has a clear grasp of the relevant facts. Most importantly, encourage her to tell the absolute truth. The credibility of her testimony may depend on her grasp of the accuracy of the smallest details. Do not "drill" her on her testimony, however, for you do not want to risk her appearing to the jury that she has been "coached." You want her testimony to be natural, in her own words. Practice cross-examining her, so that she becomes familiar with the prosecutor's style and the attacks he will likely launch against her. Pay particular attention to those areas of her testimony that are weak or that she must admit or explain. If there are such areas, it is far better for you to bring them out in her direct examination, when you have an opportunity to explain and control them, than to have the prosecutor expose them for the first time under cross-examination.

The most critical area of preparation comes into play if your client has a criminal record that is admissible, and you know it's coming in. Under no circumstances should you keep that hidden. If the prosecutor reveals that record to the jury for the first time in his cross-examination, the effect can be devastating. Instead, prepare your client to reveal, during your direct examination of her, each and every crime for which she has been convicted. If necessary and relevant, have her briefly describe what happened in those cases. By eliciting the "bad news" yourself on direct examination, you take the "shock value" out of it and thus dramatically reduce its impact. It also helps to present you and your client as credible people who tell the truth, and have nothing to hide.[4]

Here are some helpful guidelines:

- Make sure you have reviewed all of the evidence with your client, including any statements he may have made to the police or other witnesses.
- Anticipate issues that are troublesome and present targets for the prosecutor in his cross-examination. If certain facts exist or your client made statements that are going to be a problem, be up front about them. Take this opportunity to "spin" them in

[4] An extreme (and notorious) example of this can be found at R. R. Rose, *Tales from the Crypt,* Wyoming Lawyer, June 2019, at 36–37.

your client's favor, so that the prosecutor won't be as effective when cross-examining him.

- If your defense requires affirmative evidentiary proof, make sure that your questions cover all necessary areas.
- Make the questions (and hopefully the answers) flow as naturally as possible. Do not simply ask a series of "what happened next?" questions. Use techniques like "looping" to highlight important facts and reincorporate them into the story. Put yourself in the "hide" of the jurors, and ask yourself what responses you would like to hear if you were listening for the first time. Make it interesting.
- If there is an emotional element to the story, then allow your client to let those emotions percolate to the surface naturally, while taking care not to let things spin out of control. Nothing is more powerful than natural and honest emotion.
- Unlike the direct examination of your expert, or the cross-examination of the state's witnesses, you should not tie yourself down to a script when conducting the direct examination of your client. You could easily fall into a rote question-and-answer routine that will bore the jury. This is the one witness where such a result could be fatal to your case. Instead, have a general outline of topics and points you wish to make, but ask questions naturally and go with the flow.

E. Preparing Your Witnesses for Cross-Examination

Preparing your witnesses for cross-examination by the state is crucial. The good news is that many cross-examinations are not nearly as effective as they could be; the bad news is that they can be devastating. A good preparation can therefore go a long way toward saving your case.

The method of preparation varies slightly with the type of witness you are preparing (*e.g.*, lay witness, expert, the defendant). Generally speaking, however, the preparation should cover the following ground:

- As with direct examination, make sure that the witness is thoroughly familiar with all written and oral/recorded statements

previously made. Emphasis should be placed on those areas that differ from other statements or that do not support your case.
- Prepare the witness to acknowledge those areas that are weak or do not support the case. No testimony is perfect, and there are always areas that can be exploited by the state. Usually, there is a valid common-sense reason for them, and the witness should be prepared to answer plainly and affirmatively regarding those reasons. Juries will forgive many witness imperfections as long as the explanation is reasonable.

The best way to deal with your witness having to explain why he did or did not do or observe certain things is to affirmatively bring it out on direct examination first. Have your witness explain in detail what happened and why. This way you can control the answer and tailor it to your needs before your opponent asks. It significantly lessens the impact than if the state forces your witness to reveal it for the first time on cross-examination, when he may be prevented from explaining it. That may force you to redirect and rehabilitate your witness, therefore making it appear as if the witness got caught with his hand in the cookie jar. It might make the jury think that you're trying to hide something from them. And that is precisely what the state will argue.

Prepare the witness to "counterpunch." If during cross-examination the prosecutor scores points on an admission or confirms a bad fact for your case, it is typically in response to a tightly constructed question that leaves no opportunity for explanation. Rather than let that answer lie there for the jury to stare at, train the witness to qualify his answer so that his response includes an explanation. Assuming, of course, that the answer requires an explanation. If it doesn't, then don't offer one. Here is an example:

PROSECUTOR:	You broke the window of the truck, unlocked the door, and entered the truck?
CLIENT:	Yes.
PROSECUTOR:	And you did not have permission or authority from the owner of the truck to do that, did you?
CLIENT:	No. I kept hearing my mother's voice calling to me, and I was trying to find her.

PROSECUTOR: You grabbed the toolbox that was on the passenger seat and removed it from the truck?

CLIENT: Yes, but I didn't take it anywhere. When I grabbed it my mother's voice stopped, so I just placed it on the ground next to the truck and left it there.

As discussed earlier, cross-examinations are not (or should not be) presented in the form of open-ended interrogatories. They usually end (or begin) with *"Isn't it true . . .,"* *"We can agree . . .,"* or something similar. Obviously, if the statement is *entirely* true, that's no problem. But if it is not, then by all means the witness should not agree with it. Instead, the witness should disagree and take the opportunity to explain in detail why the statement is *not* correct. In other words, train the witness to not permit counsel to put words in his mouth that are not entirely accurate.

Do not let the prosecutor "bait" your client or attempt to get under his skin for the purpose of rattling him, all in an effort to try and shake his testimony or make him appear in a bad light. Prepare your client by advising him that such tactics could be employed, and give the witness some examples and how to deal with them. The best response is to be calm and level-headed, answer directly, and ignore any efforts to make him upset. Under no circumstances should he lash out with sarcasm or anger, and he should never attempt to engage in verbal swordplay with the prosecutor. This plays directly into the prosecutor's hand and significantly increases the likelihood that the witness will blurt out something he will regret, or stumble and misstate a material fact that, up to that moment, was considered solid. It is important to trust in the jury's ability to observe what the attorney is trying to do, and as long as the witness is calm and playing by the rules and not falling for it, the jury will like the witness and dislike the prosecuting attorney. The prosecuting attorney will likely be considered a bully, and the jury will instinctively protect your client.

These guidelines are generally applicable to all witnesses but most specifically to your client, and to lay witnesses who may be unfamiliar with the experience of testifying and being cross-examined in open court.

F. Resting Your Case

When you have called all of your witnesses and submitted all of your evidence, you are essentially done with your case. However, before you stand and declare to the court that "The Defense rests," you should take a few moments and review with co-counsel, or your investigator or other trial assistant, to make sure that all of your exhibits have been marked and have been submitted to the court for admission into evidence, and published to the jury. If necessary, ask for a brief recess to review. Unless the court has just taken one, chances are good the court will agree and will take a quick break. You or an assistant should be using a chart prepared beforehand in which you note the introduction of your exhibits as you proceed through the trial, so as to avoid missing any. If you discover evidence that has not been submitted, bring it to the court's attention. Discuss it with opposing counsel to see if there is any objection to you simply asking the court to mark it, and include it without further testimony or foundation. If there is objection (and you have not yet rested), you may have to re-call the particular witness involved with that exhibit so that you may establish sufficient foundation and then offer it. Remember, once you've rested, you are done with your evidence, and you cannot introduce anything further.

G. The State's Rebuttal Evidence

After the defense rests its case, the state is given the opportunity to rebut it through the introduction of additional evidence. Ordinarily, such witnesses or exhibits need not have been listed in the state's pre-trial memoranda, since the prosecutor never knows beforehand what evidence, if any, may be needed on rebuttal. This does not mean, however, that a prosecutor may always rely on the rebuttal phase of the trial to introduce evidence that she has intentionally held back, or perhaps inadvertently omitted in her case in chief.

Generally, evidence introduced by the state in rebuttal is limited to those issues or evidence raised for the first time by the defense in their case. Evidence sought to be introduced by the state which does not rebut such evidence, or which is cumulative and similar to evidence already submitted or which could have been submitted in the state's case in chief, will not be admitted. In a nutshell, evidence that could have been submitted during the state's case in chief, but was not, will likely not be admitted in rebuttal.

H. Objections

Chico: *I object.*
Prosecutor: *Oh, you object! On what grounds?*
Chico: *I couldn't think of anything else to say.*
Groucho: *(Bangs gavel) Objection sustained.*
Prosecutor: *Your Excellency! You sustained the objection?*
Groucho: *Sure, I couldn't think of anything else to say either! Why don't* YOU *object?*

—Groucho Marx
as attorney Rufus T. Firefly in *Duck Soup*.

If the prosecutor attempts to introduce certain improper evidence or behaves in such a way as to invite an objection, you must be prepared to object quickly. The objection must be timely, specific, and on the record. In many instances, failure to object in a timely manner operates as a waiver of the objection.

Many attorneys worry a great deal over whether or not their presentation will draw an objection from their opponent, while others give it little consideration. To a large degree, it comes down to the individual's comfort level. To be sure, certain objections must be taken into consideration as you prepare and present your case. You don't want witnesses attempting to introduce hearsay testimony; exhibits must be relevant and have a proper foundation; witnesses offering opinion testimony should be properly qualified; arguments must be based on facts that are in evidence; each side should have listed in the pretrial memoranda all evidence and witnesses they intend to introduce at trial; counsel should not lead a witness's testimony on direct examination; and so forth. These are common situations that can generate objections and thus are easily anticipated and largely addressed through proper pretrial preparation.

You should be particularly aware of the timing of objections you make. Object as soon as the grounds have arisen; don't wait. Quite often the court will rule that even though your objection was well taken, it is overruled if it was not timely made. Review the rules of evidence prior to trial regarding those items you know are going to be introduced by the state. Be ready to object when the prosecutor moves to introduce or admit them. Be confident, state the grounds for your objection clearly, and, if necessary, cite proper authority. Have notes available in your file for such use. You may be surprised at how often an objection is sustained, not necessarily because you are correct, but because the judge might not know the answer, and if you sound like you know what you're talking about, the court may defer to you.[5]

When your opponent objects to something you do, calmly wait until she has stated the basis for the objection before responding. The court may go ahead and rule on it without seeking your input. If the court solicits your response, be prepared to make it clearly and firmly. In most cases, you will be able to gauge when something you ask will draw an objection, which will allow you to prepare for it ahead of time. Be ready. If need be, include a sheet of anticipated objections and your responses in the particular witness file you are using at the time. It is at your fingertips, and you won't be caught flat-footed. If the court rules against you, don't worry. Do not react. You are in total control. Everything is fine. You are not hurt. Remember, looking good is critical. If improper evidence was admitted and you did not timely object, you should move to strike the evidence.

Most seasoned attorneys don't dwell too much on either drawing or making objections. Too many objections tend to disrupt the flow of the proceedings. It can also appear as if counsel is engaged in a petty squabbling match rather than presenting evidence. This is not to say, however, that one should not make objections. When necessary, a proper objection timely made is appropriate and will be required to preserve the record on appeal. On the other hand, the hallmark of a savvy trial lawyer is knowing when an objection should be made and when it should not. Just because your opponent has created an instance where an objection would be legally appropriate does not necessarily mean that it should be voiced. More often than not, it is best to be sparing in your objections, lest you risk overdoing it. Particularly if whatever you are objecting to is not hurting you.

---

[5] Yet another example of where "perception is reality."

If your opponent persists in acting inappropriately, object immediately. You must not permit improper activity to continue. If the prosecutor's behavior is sufficiently improper, do not be afraid to move for a mistrial. Stand your ground. Do not be intimidated by the court. Even if denied, it should send a signal to the prosecutor that you are being vigilant and will not tolerate improper behavior. Call him out every time he does it. Don't be concerned if the judge disagrees with you. If your case goes up on appeal, the appellate court may think differently.

On a different note, sometimes raising an objection may risk drawing the jury's attention to something that you would prefer they not notice. Moreover, if you object too much, the jury may get the impression that your case is being severely damaged by the witness or the event and that you are desperate to stop it. While that in fact may be the case, it is not wise to let the jury sense your anguish. The old adage "Never let 'em see you sweat" is crucial in a jury trial and should be kept in mind at all times. In those instances, your attention to what the jury is doing and how they appear to be reacting to the testimony will be critical in determining whether to object at any given point.

Finally, a real trial lawyer never worries about whether he will draw an objection from his opponent. As noted repeatedly, being a trial lawyer is not for the timid or faint of heart. You don't care if your opponent objects. In fact, you want him to object. If he doesn't, you are not hurting him. You are a warrior, and you are on the offensive at all times.

1. Forms of Objections

The following are forms of typical objections and how to respond to them:

- Hearsay

The evidence you are seeking to admit may constitute hearsay under Rule 802. Your response is:

a. The statement is not hearsay, as it is
   1) not an out-of-court statement;
   2) not being offered to prove the truth of the matter asserted;

3) non-hearsay; or

b. The statement is admissible as an exception to the hearsay rule (Rule 803).

- **Form of the Question**

The question you are asking is improper in its current form (leading, improper hypothetical, lacks foundation, etc.). Your response is: *"I shall rephrase the question."*

- **Lack of Foundation**

The evidence you seek to admit lacks sufficient foundation (failure to establish a condition of fact).

Under Rule 104 it should be admitted upon, or subject to, the introduction of additional evidence sufficient to fulfill the condition. Your response is: "*Your Honor, I'll provide additional foundation.*"

- **Relevance**[6]

The evidence you seek to admit is irrelevant under Rules 401 or 403. Your response is:

a. It is relevant under Rule 401 as it goes to the probable existence of a material fact in the case; or

b. It is relevant and it is not overly prejudicial, does not confuse the jury, and is not a waste of time.

---

[6] Many years ago there was an attorney I knew who voiced only one objection: "Your Honor, I object on the grounds that it is irrelevant, incompetent, and immaterial." He may have known others, but that is the only one I ever heard him state in all the years I knew him. He was also hard of hearing, and he would rise, stand directly and conspicuously behind his opponent, while dramatically cupping his hand to his ear while his opponent was speaking, then march to the center of the courtroom and shout his objection. There was also a long-time federal district court judge who was trained in the 1930s, long before the federal rules were adopted. He had one standard response to any objection, no matter the issue: "Oh, I'll let it in as part of the *res gestae*." Those were the days.

- Asked and Answered

The question you are asking has already been asked and answered. Your response is: "*Your honor, the question has been* asked, *but the witness has not* answered *it.*"

2. Offer of Proof

If the court excludes evidence you have offered that affects a substantial right of your client, you must make an offer of proof to the court pursuant to Rule 103(a)(2), as a means of preserving your objection on the record. Your offer of proof is essentially your means of making the substance and purpose of that evidence known to the court.

The generally accepted method of making an offer of proof is for you to request that you be permitted to present the evidence (or "proffer" it) to the court, either in a summary fashion or as it would have been offered to the jury. If you are presenting it in a summary fashion, your offer is ordinarily made at a sidebar, on the record, but outside of the jury's ability to hear you. You then simply explain to the court what your witness would have said were he allowed to testify. The court may require you to call the witness for a hearing outside of the presence of the jury, which is then excused.

17
The Home Stretch

It doesn't matter how many laps you lead, as long as it's the last one.

—Richard Petty

A. Jury Instruction Conference

The instructions given to the jury by the court become the law of that case. Therefore, it is critical that the defense attorney has a clear understanding of the law that applies to the facts as presented at trial and that the law is accurately set forth in the instructions. You will only be allowed those instructions that are supported by the evidence in your case.

Avoid building reversible error into the case by ensuring that your instructions are based on the latest Appellate Court decisions. Typically, there will be a set of "pattern" jury instructions for you to follow. However, they are not always current and therefore must be double-checked for accuracy. If for some reason you need an instruction that is not provided in the pattern instructions, it is often good practice to compose the required instruction based on either statutory construction or excerpts taken from current and relevant Appellate Court opinions. Make sure that you submit such instructions with adequate citation to the authority from whence they came. If possible, review it with your opponent prior to the conference so that any objections may be either eliminated or articulated during the conference so as to avoid waste of time. If you object to any instructions offered by the prosecutor, state your objections clearly and plainly at the appropriate time, so that the court may preserve a record of your objections for any appeal.

With regard to preserving the record, always have such hearings as instruction conferences, voir dire, opening and closing statements, motion hearings, and any hearing argued in chambers recorded by a court reporter. If there is a reversible error in the proceedings, it will not be considered on appeal if it does not appear in the record.

B. Closing Argument

Almost all attorneys enjoy closing arguments, for it is here that you may properly make your argument for what you seek as the justice in your case. Finally, you can "let it all hang out." A closing argument for the defense, however, differs in some material ways from that presented by the state.

The defense is permitted fairly wide latitude in its presentation, while the state must be more reserved. The prosecutor cannot be overly emotional, cannot appeal to the "passion or prejudice" of the jury, cannot engage in "victim impact" arguments, and must essentially be limited to commenting on what the evidence has proved, namely, the elements of the offense required for conviction. The prosecutor cannot comment on the veracity of any witness, nor tell the jury what its "duty" to the community is. That is for the court to do. Ample caselaw is available which sets forth the applicable guidelines the prosecutor must follow. Violation of these guidelines may result in reversal of the conviction and remand for retrial. For these reasons, a good defense lawyer should not hesitate to object if the prosecutor appears to be running afoul of the rules. They are there to protect your client.

The defense, on the other hand, is generally free to be as creative and as passionate as you wish to be. Therefore, there is no excuse for you not to be. Push the envelope. Think outside the box. Consider using demonstrative exhibits, models, and blow-ups of important photographs. Use blow-ups of important jury instructions to emphasize to the jury the importance of certain language or what boxes to check on the verdict form. Urge the jurors to examine the state's case carefully and hold the prosecutor's feet to the fire regarding certain promises she may have made in her opening statement. Remind them that this is a very serious matter and must not be treated casually.

Always begin your closing argument by restating your theme. This will tie it into your voir dire and your opening statement and remind the jury what it is they should focus on. Build slowly. Speak clearly and loudly enough for all to hear. Draw together all of the facts and evidence that support your theme. Do not be afraid to use dramatic phrases and language where appropriate. During the trial, pay special attention to certain phrases or quotes from witnesses that have a particularly resonant quality to them or that perfectly highlight and capture the tone or theme you are arguing. You can use them during your closing to accent and emphasize something important. Using these phrases also indicates that you were paying attention to the evidence.

Use whatever dramatic skills you have to physically act out something if it helps to get a point across to the jury. Also, use different dynamic ranges of your voice. If music is important to you or your client, and if it has relevance to your case, then bring in a stereo or CD player and play an excerpt for the jury.[1]

Move with purpose, such as when changing topics or making a particular point. Otherwise stand still. Constant movement is distracting. Maintain eye contact with the jurors as much as possible. Since you know the details of your case intimately at this point, there is no reason you should need to read your argument or even be tied to much of an outline. Reading your closing argument is the worst thing you can do. It destroys any sincerity in your delivery. It makes you appear that even *you* don't believe what you are saying. Don't do it. Use bullet points that you can refer to if need be.

Have passion. Imagine that your client is your child or sibling or parent and that you and your presentation are the only things that

---

[1] One of the great criminal defense lawyers in the country, Dale Cobb, once sang a portion of a country western song in his closing. The lyrics were a perfect fit for his case theme. He won.

stand between them and jail. Because they are. Do not underestimate the power of emotion. As I stated earlier, the emotion of your client's story lies at the bedrock of the decision the jury will make.[2]

Remind the jury of the gravity of their duties as American citizens to the criminal justice process. Show them why your client is innocent, not just "not guilty."

The presumption of innocence has been one of the pillars of our society for 250 years. It is part of what the Minutemen fought and died for. Exhort the jurors to not be afraid to stand and fight for your client during deliberations, and that if they believe the state has failed to prove the defendant guilty beyond a reasonable doubt, to stick to their guns and not be bullied into changing their vote just to speed up the verdict and go home.

One of the techniques I like to use toward the end is the following phrase:

> *Ladies and gentlemen, the state makes a big deal about _______. Now, they can stand here all day long and talk about what it means, but here's the thing, and there's really no getting around it: _______________.*

You then fill in that last blank with the one fact in the case that is in your client's favor that is irrefutable. It is a fact that cannot be argued away or diminished in any way. It is as solid as granite and is staring the prosecutor right in the face, and there's nothing he can do about it. Your job is to discover what that fact is in your case and build your argument around it. That fact could carry the day for you.

Remind the jury that the prosecutor will have another shot at them after you sit down, but you will only have this one last opportunity to speak to them. Tell them that just like you, they only have one chance to get it right. There are no "do-overs."

---

[2] To demonstrate that power, try this technique for practice: Take a few minutes at work and meet with a trusted co-worker. Stand looking at each other, as if you were at a bar. Take 30 seconds and describe your resume. Begin wherever you like, but go for about 30 seconds. Stop. Now, do it again, except this time begin with the following words: "Once upon a time, there was a young couple, (insert your parents' first names). They had a little (boy / girl), whom they named (insert your first name)." Continue on as before. See what happens to your story.

Remember, a jury trial is theater. You are limited only by your imagination. Make the jury's experience one they will never forget.

C. Jury Nullification

Owing, perhaps, to the growing frustration society seems to be expressing with the criminal justice system, we are hearing more about instances of "jury nullification" arguments. It is an argument that urges the jury to arrive at a verdict based on what they believe justice calls for, regardless of whether it is permitted by law or supported by the evidence. It should be noted, however, that while jury nullification is a power the jury possesses, there is no "right" for such a result that exists anywhere in the law, in either state or federal courts. In fact, courts generally frown on such arguments.

While jury nullification exists, it is a defense of true desperation and last resort and should not be used if any other viable defense is available. It essentially requires a defendant to admit his guilt, and yet it argues that "justice" demands that he nonetheless be acquitted by having the jury ignore the evidence. Since a defendant has no legal right to assert the defense, the jury will not be instructed that it may consider it. The "justice" argument must be truly compelling (i.e., the particular facts of the case must be just right), and the jury must be receptive to it. An effective argument to make in this regard is to tell the jury that they are the "third branch of the government," and they alone have the power to decide what is right, regardless of the evidence.

D. Jury Questions during Deliberations

It is not uncommon for juries to have questions during their deliberations. They will usually submit their questions in writing to the court. This is often a delicate situation and must be handled carefully. Whether and to what extent the court responds to a jury question depends largely on the nature of the inquiry. Questions can run the gamut, ranging from "*When do we get lunch?*" to "*What is the meaning of reasonable doubt?*"

Sometimes the jury will ask that certain portions of the evidence be provided or repeated (such as replaying a video tape or requesting a transcript of a particular witness's testimony). Generally, the court will deny such requests, since it is improper for the court to draw the jury's attention to or emphasize a particular piece of evidence over another. Many times the court will simply respond that the instructions are appropriate as written, and the jury is directed to re-read and review them carefully.

Whenever the jury submits a question, the court will notify counsel. You will be required to meet with the court and opposing counsel, review the inquiry, and discuss the appropriate response. Such discussions, and certainly any response made, should be entered on the record. Once the court determines what response should be given, the jury may be called in and have the response read by the court. In the alternative, the court may simply choose, with consent of counsel, to respond to the jury in writing. They are then excused to continue their deliberations.

E. *Ex-Parte* Communication Between Jurors and the Court

It should go without saying that once the jury has been given the case and has retired to deliberate, there should be no *ex-parte* contact or communication between the jurors and anyone not authorized to communicate with them, including the judge. Any such unauthorized contact or communication is almost certain to result in a directed verdict of judgment of acquittal or a mistrial. If not, it is still highly likely that if taken up on appeal, the case may be reversed and remanded for a new trial. This is such a substantial violation of the rules and presents such a significant obstacle to justice that such remedies may be imposed even if none of the parties intended the contact or communication to be improper and even if they took steps to preserve the record of such contact for appeal.

A case in point is *U.S. v. Mehta.*[3] In that criminal case, multiple defendants were charged. Three days after the trial had begun, the court clerk orally notified the judge that several of the jurors wished to speak with the judge about a problem. The judge agreed to meet with the jurors. The judge ordered that the meeting be reported by the

[3] 919 F.3d 175 (2d. Cir. 2019).

court reporter but did not notify counsel and give counsel an opportunity to attend. The jurors told the judge that they felt that two of the defendants were "lingering" and "staring" at them as the jurors entered and exited the courthouse. The judge responded by stating, "That's *disturbing*. I think what I would do, if you don't mind, would be to assign a court security officer to accompany you to your cars."

The judge also said:

> I don't know why they are doing that. I mean, I've been doing this for years and years and once in a while you get somebody that acts inappropriate like that but I think we should have a court security officer there, and I will talk with staff and have somebody ready for you tomorrow.

The judge then met with the attorneys handling the case and summarized what had occurred in the previous meeting with the jurors. But unfortunately, the judge did not provide counsel with a copy of the verbatim transcript of the meeting. Instead, the judge generally summarized his version of the jurors' concerns, as well as his response, but did not mention the specific words he used to characterize the defendants' alleged behavior.

Defense counsel immediately moved for judgment of acquittal. The motion was denied. Defense counsel then moved for a mistrial, which was also denied. The jury later convicted the defendants.

On appeal, the Circuit Court reversed the decision, concluding that faulty jury instructions, combined with the *ex-parte* juror contact, were sufficient to invalidate and overturn the verdict. The court reasoned that had the trial judge followed the guidelines set forth in *U.S. v. Collins*,[4] defense counsel would have had the opportunity to offer an alternative account of the circumstances and one that could well have fully addressed the jurors' safety concerns. Moreover, the judge failed to reduce the prejudicial effects of the *ex-parte* meeting by never discussing it with the *entire* jury panel and by failing to determine (through voir dire of the jury) whether they could remain impartial as a result of the alleged behavior.

---

[4] 665 F.3d 454 (2d. Cir. 2012).

The *Collins* guidelines for handling *ex-parte* requests from a jury are these:

1. The jury inquiry should be in writing.
2. The note should be marked as the court's exhibit and read into the record with counsel and the defendant present.
3. Counsel should have an opportunity to suggest a response, and the judge should inform counsel of the response to be given.
4. On the recall of the jury, the trial judge should read the note into the record, allowing the jury an opportunity to correct the inquiry or to elaborate on it.[5]

In addition to the guidelines, the important lessons of *Mehta* are threefold:

1. Attorneys should never stay silent. Here, the defense attorneys were wise to object and state the reasons for their objections on the record, as well as submit the appropriate motions. Their failure to do so might have significantly reduced their chances on appeal.
2. Attorneys should never pass up an opportunity to interview and/or meet with jurors post-trial. In addition to gaining valuable insight as to the effectiveness of your trial performance, you also may uncover incidents such as the one here. Even though the trial judge preserved the meeting on the record and later informed the attorneys, that is not always the case. Sometimes these meetings go unreported, and the only way to discover them is through post-trial interviews.
3. Finally, judges should never be left alone with jurors during trial proceedings. Even where, as here, the judge acted conscientiously and in good faith, he nevertheless deviated significantly and materially from the guidelines.

F. The Verdict

No trial lawyer, no matter how experienced, ever gets used to waiting for or receiving the verdict. It is often anguishing, for the typical

[5] U.S. v. Collins, at 460.

lawyer does little else during the wait than review in his mind all of the perceived errors he made during trial. You suddenly are aware of how exhausted you are. The words, "*We, the jury, find as follows . . .* " are excruciatingly nerve-wracking. It is, however, part of what makes a trial lawyer's profession unique and also why few in the legal profession become trial lawyers.

Immediately following the reading of the verdict, the court may inquire of the losing party whether they wish the jury to be individually polled. Often the party agrees, but it is not required. Following that, the court then thanks the jury, gives them some parting comments, and dismisses them.

When receiving the verdict, regardless of the time of day or the length of deliberations, the trial lawyer is the consummate professional. Proper attire is necessary. Proper courtroom decorum must be observed at all times. Attitudes are solemn. Great respect is afforded the jury. More likely than not, they have struggled to arrive at a decision that may have been extremely difficult and emotionally wrenching. Win or lose, you do not react, at least until the jury is excused and they have left the courtroom. Never, ever, have anything alcoholic to drink before appearing in court to receive the verdict. There will be plenty of time for drinks and decompressing afterward.[6]

It is always good practice after the jury has received the case and been dismissed to begin deliberations to walk over to your opponent and shake his or her hand. Congratulate your adversary on a hard-fought battle. Being a trial lawyer is hard. You are both gladiators engaged in what few in your profession are trained or willing or able to do. You will not always win. But you can always be respectful of your opponent, even if you don't think he or she deserves it. Always take the high road. You will meet again.

If you lost the case, you may wish to interview the jurors to find out where the problem was. That is entirely appropriate and usually very valuable. However, it is usually a good idea to wait a couple of days (especially if it is over a weekend) in order for the jury to decompress.

---

[6] Any experienced trial lawyer will undoubtedly recall instances of counsel heading to the local bar immediately upon the jury being excused to begin deliberations, only to be summoned a few hours later to receive the verdict, appearing in a less than "professional" state of sobriety or dress.

Be very courteous. Never express your anger or frustration with a juror over the verdict. Remember that it doesn't matter if you had all of the law and all of the facts on your side. Juries decide cases based on emotion—what they feel is the right thing to do. They may not see the case the same way you did. They focus on things that you may disregard as insignificant. This is why voir dire is so critically important. Those are the kinds of things you want to discover when you select the jury.

You are seeking to learn why you failed to convince them. Find out what they liked and what they didn't like about your case, and particularly your presentation. Probe into what they felt was the most important factor in their decision. Insist that they tell you the truth, and not sugarcoat it. You are trying to become better at this. You don't want to make those mistakes again. Thank the jurors sincerely. Then reflect very carefully on what they told you. If they were honest with you in their critique, everything they told you was a gift.

G. Mistrial

Occasionally, circumstances may arise necessitating that you seek a mistrial. Either improper evidence was submitted to the jury, or there was improper behavior on the part of a juror that could not be cured by the substitution of an alternate; the judge or a juror became ill or incapacitated; or the jury became deadlocked in their deliberations and unable to reach a unanimous verdict. In any event, you must move for a mistrial if an event occurred that gave rise to sufficient and actual prejudice to your client, making a fair result impossible or highly unlikely; or if the prejudice cannot be removed or cured by a cautionary instruction or some other remedy.

Either party may move for a mistrial, but as a practical matter the state rarely, if ever, does so. Since there was no finding of guilt, a mistrial is a "win" for the defense.[7] Generally speaking, you should move for a mistrial as soon as it becomes apparent that sufficient grounds exist. Once you become aware of the error, you will not be permitted to await the decision of the jury before making your motion.

7 Remember that in a criminal case, two of the three possible verdicts—mistrial and not guilty—are acquittals.

An important factor to consider in determining whether a mistrial should be declared is whether your client consents to it. The question of a mistrial may arise without your seeking it and could present double jeopardy issues under the Fifth Amendment. In some cases, the granting of a mistrial without your client's consent may completely bar further prosecution for the same offense.

If you move for a mistrial, the prohibitions against double jeopardy don't apply and thus do not prevent a retrial, since the motion is considered a waiver of any double jeopardy claim. The question then becomes whether the state will seek a retrial. In that instance, it will likely depend on what caused the mistrial. Therefore, it is best to make no public comment regarding the refiling of charges at that time. Office policy should dictate the manner and means by which a response is made. The case, and the reasons for the mistrial, will first need to be carefully analyzed.

If, on the one hand, the mistrial was caused by the actions of the prosecutor (particularly if it was intentional), your client would certainly not object to a mistrial, as this particular circumstance would trigger the Fifth Amendment prohibition against further prosecution for the same offense. On the other hand, there may be occasions when you would not want a mistrial declared, even if sufficient grounds exist.

For example, if the mistrial was caused by errors on the part of the state, but they would almost certainly be corrected upon retrial (thus ensuring your client's conviction), you may not want a mistrial but instead may use the *threat* of a mistrial and the ensuing loss of time, availability of witnesses, and so forth, to force the prosecutor to negotiate a plea agreement now and cut his losses. This may be a particularly effective resolution in cases where the prosecutor refused to entertain any plea offers prior to trial.

As noted earlier regarding discovery abuses, and will be noted again later in Chapter 20, prosecutorial misconduct is a fertile area for mistrial motions. One of the most common areas is an improper closing argument. A motion for mistrial should be made immediately, and under no circumstances should the jury be allowed to commence deliberations before the motion is made, as it will not be considered "timely."

H. Adjusting Bond

In the event of an acquittal, the court will simply discharge the bond and, if your client is in jail, will order him released forthwith. Immediately following a verdict of guilty, the court will often declare that the defendant stands convicted and now awaits sentencing. The court may then seek the prosecutor's input regarding whether to confine the defendant in the interim or release him on bond. Often, the court has its own policy regarding such decisions. You should have a well-articulated response ready.

18
Preparing for Sentencing

Preparing for a sentencing hearing can often require as much effort as the trial itself. Witnesses may need to be called, travel arrangements made, and exhibits and examinations prepared. Do not wait until the last minute. There will be no time.

If you intend to rely on professional reports or experts, make sure that they are prepared ahead of time and ready. If you intend to have the defendant's family or friends testify, meet with them beforehand and review their testimony and what they can expect at the hearing. Prepare your argument with great care and thorough, accurate research. If the sentence the state seeks is unusual or controversial, or if it involves an unsettled area of law, take special care in your legal research so that you avoid, or at least minimize, the risk of guiding the court into a decision that results in reversible error.

After a defendant has entered a guilty plea to a felony, the court will likely order that a Presentence Investigation Report (PSR) be prepared by the Department of Probation. It can take many weeks to complete. If the defendant is incarcerated, his interview will be conducted there, of course. However, if your client has been released on bond, the Probation Department will likely request that he not leave the jurisdiction until his interview has been completed. If your client is a local resident, that is ordinarily no problem. However, if your client is from out of state, he may not be permitted to return home until after he is interviewed. That is often distressing news to the defendant after the hearing, when he is anxious to head out of town. If that interview is not scheduled ahead of time, it is not unusual for your client to be forced to wait several days until one can be arranged. In the meantime, he will need a place to live and money for food, often resources he lacks. Therefore, if your client is planning to return home following a felony guilty plea, you should contact the probation office several weeks beforehand to arrange for an interview to be conducted on the day of the plea, so that he may be allowed to be on his way as he had originally planned.

19 Postconviction Motions

Postconviction motions by the defense can take many forms. Some involve renewal of various motions made during trial, particularly the motion for judgment of acquittal and motions to exclude evidence, as well as a motion for new trial. Others may deal with bond or incarceration. The court may direct counsel that in lieu of making oral motions in open court following a guilty verdict, counsel shall be given a certain number of days after the trial within which to file any motions and supporting briefs.

In the event you are a public defender, review with your office's appellate counsel whether any relevant motions need be filed within that time period to preserve certain issues for appeal.

20 Appeal

While this manual focuses primarily on the preparation and presentation of trial, it must be kept in mind that absent an acquittal or mistrial, the only other relief available for your client will be found on appeal. And as anyone who does this for a living will tell you, the opportunities for relief in that realm are slim indeed. That is why effective trial advocacy is so critically important. It is likely the only arena in which your client will obtain real justice. It is also for that reason that any grounds on which relief could be granted on appeal should be carefully preserved on the record. In other words, effective trial advocacy includes being aware of issues that could save your client long after the verdict has been reached and the jury has been dismissed.

Your Public Defender's Office has its own appellate division. Once a trial is completed and the verdict has been reached, if the defendant is convicted and there is a likelihood of appeal, the case will be transferred from the trial division to the appellate division for further consideration. That means that the attorney who tried the case may not be the attorney who prepares and argues the appeal. That is yet another reason why you must be vigilant in the identification and preservation on the record of all issues that may lead to the eventual reversal of your client's conviction. That includes making sure that the proper motions and notices get filed in order for the appeal process to be properly initiated and perfected.

For the private attorney, strict compliance with the appellate procedure is critical. You must thoroughly familiarize yourself with the Appellate Rules so that no deadline or requirement is missed. The smallest details must be attended to, including the size of the paper, the size and style of font, the length of the briefs, the number of words, the manner and content of the argument, and myriad other details. Failure to comply with any of them could result in the dismissal of the appeal.

A few helpful guidelines are included below that will hopefully assist not only in the appellate process, but in the eventual success of the effort altogether.

A. Everything Is on the Record

It goes without saying that anything you wish an Appellate Court to review must be timely preserved on the record. Whatever is not on the record does not exist.[1] That includes any communication with opposing counsel or the court, regardless of whether it is in open court or in chambers. Wyoming is a rural state, and many of the tribunals are located in small communities. It is not uncommon for some judges to encourage counsel to "relax" when in chambers and adopt an air of informality. There is certainly nothing wrong with that, except to the extent that it can lull counsel into the belief that there is no need for certain proceedings to be reported. This is particularly the case if you are trying a case in an unfamiliar jurisdiction and do not wish to "rock the boat."

It is therefore a prudent rule of thumb that in any situation where the parties and the court enter into a communication that affects the course or disposition of the proceedings, you should request that a court reporter be present. If it irritates the judge, so be it. If the judge tells you that it will involve an additional fee because it is not considered a "standard" hearing ordinarily reported, pay it.[2] You are not there to be a "good ol' boy." You are not interested in ensuring

---

1 If there are no transcripts of the District Court hearings, the Appellate Court will assume that the District Court's findings of fact are supported by the evidence presented by the parties at those hearings.

2 Some courts do not ordinarily report pretrial conferences, jury instruction conferences, or other hearings conducted in chambers.

anyone's comfort except your client's. He's counting on you not to drop the ball. Remember, you are at all times a warrior.

B. Stand Your Ground

Sometimes it is hard to stand your ground and make your record, especially when you are a young, inexperienced lawyer and the judge is being difficult. These confrontations can be frightening. But you are in the "pit," and these instances are what test your mettle and forge you into a "steely-eyed trial lawyer." The judge might bark at you and make you feel foolish, but you will have preserved your record and will be a hero to your client. You will have also sent a message to the court and your opponent that you will not be intimidated.

C. Setting Up the Appeal[3]

It's hard enough to try a jury trial and keep everything straight. But while hacking your way through that jungle, be mindful of the second trial that you may have to make—the appeal. Your preparation for appeal does not begin *after* you lose your jury trial. It begins when you sit down to prepare for it.

As previously noted, one of the very first things to do when preparing your jury trial is to determine what jury instructions to use. This will also solidify one of the most common issues in criminal appeals. There are many subtle nuances in the pattern instructions. Take the time to carefully read each instruction you wish to use, and make sure it is still good law.[4] More than one case has been reversed because of faulty instructions, including pattern instructions.

Craft your instructions carefully; then fight for them. Don't agree with the prosecutor's version just because you want to save a few extra minutes to prepare for your closing argument. Make a record of your objections and stick to them. It makes a huge difference in

---

[3] Sections C, D, and E of this chapter were prepared and submitted by Patricia L. Bennett, a good friend, an excellent trial lawyer, and clerk of the Wyoming Supreme Court. (Used with permission.)

[4] Current areas of ongoing developing criminal law are self-defense and second-degree murder.

the standard of review on appeal. And remember, the pattern instructions were written by lawyers, not God. There is nothing wrong with modifying a pattern instruction or even drafting your own as long as it is good law.

Just because you may lose a motion at trial, don't give up on it if you want to address the issue on appeal. If you lose a motion to suppress evidence or a motion *in limine*, you should renew your objection again on the record when the evidence is introduced at trial. It solidifies the issue for appeal and ensures that you are viewed as not having waived your objection. It is worth mentioning again that failure to preserve your objection on the record is roughly equivalent to having acquiesced and conceded to your opponent.

D. "The Big Five"

Although evocative of the "Final Four," the "Big Five" in the world of criminal appeals has nothing to do with basketball (unless your client stole one). They are the primary areas of appeal in criminal cases and are as follows:

- Rule 404(b)
- Jury instructions
- Sufficiency of the evidence
- Ineffective assistance of counsel
- Prosecutorial misconduct

Other lesser issues include hearsay, police interrogations, and expert testimony. Timely objections from trial counsel to any of these will make the appeal infinitely better and significantly improve your chances of prevailing.

The Appellate Court is constrained in every case by the record and the applicable standard of review. The court cannot go outside these boundaries regardless of how much they may personally wish to. And do not count on supplementing or correcting the record on appeal either. While there are methods to do so, they are almost always unavailable except in extraordinary circumstances and therefore should never be counted on as being available at all.

E. Standards of Review

There are several standards by which Appellate Courts review the trial record on appeal. Make sure you understand which standard applies in your situation, then craft your argument to fit the standard.

1. De Novo

This is the best standard of review for appellants. It means the Appellate Court can review the entire record from the same perspective as the trial judge, including reviewing all of the court's rulings and the evidence presented at trial. A de novo standard of review is applied where there is a question of constitutionality or statutory construction.

Typical examples include the voluntariness of a confession and the determination of whether or not a search and seizure was in violation of the Fourth Amendment. In these situations, pretrial motions to suppress evidence are critical. If the motion to suppress is not filed or an objection to the introduction of the evidence is not made at trial, it is probable that the court will not even consider the issue on appeal. The court generally will not consider issues not preserved and raised in the trial court.

The best practice in these situations would be, for example, to file a pretrial motion to suppress the evidence and, if unsuccessful, to object again at trial. An objection at trial, even if defense counsel knows the judge will overrule the objection, will preserve the issue and make it clear that the issue has not been waived. The Appellate Court will review any factual findings of the trial judge for *clear error,* which is exactly what it sounds like. But if properly preserved, the ultimate determination of constitutionality is reviewed de novo.

This also means that if you want the Appellate Court to examine any evidence introduced at trial, such as listening to an interview, watching a video, or considering some other piece of evidence, you must first get it into the record at trial. Just because you received it in discovery does not mean that it is in the record. To be considered as part of the "record on appeal," it must have been admitted into evidence. If you don't want the jury to see it during the trial (e.g., a video of your client confessing to the crime or a child describing a sexual assault), be sure to get it admitted at a suppression hearing, a competency/taint hearing, or in some other manner.

2. Sufficiency of the Evidence

When defense counsel feels that the prosecutor has not presented sufficient evidence to convict, the Appellate Court reviews that claim under the "sufficiency of the evidence" standard. This means that the court will take all of the evidence presented by the prosecution and assume it to be true. The court gives no consideration at all to evidence presented by the defense. Therefore, the most important thing for defense counsel to do at trial is to move for *judgment of acquittal* at the close of the prosecutor's case. Even if defense counsel knows that the judge will rule against him, the motion must be made to preserve the issue for appeal. Since there is some question about whether the argument is waived if the defendant subsequently introduces evidence, the best practice is to renew the motion for judgment of acquittal at the end of the case.

3. Abuse of Discretion

There are several versions of this standard, but generally speaking a trial judge will be considered to have abused her discretion if she makes a decision contrary to the law or exceeding the bounds of reason. This is often a difficult standard to meet. Judges generally have wide discretion in deciding matters before them. Absent a showing that evidence should not have been admitted, along with a proper objection, the Appellate Court will assume the judge acted reasonably.

4. Harmless Error

This is a most daunting standard of appellate review. This standard assumes that even if the trial court committed an error, the error was "harmless" to the defendant. This is often seen in cases where there is a great deal of evidence against the defendant. Notwithstanding the presence of error in the introduction of some evidence, if the Appellate Court determines that the defendant was not prejudiced as a result (in light of all of the other evidence of guilt), the error will not result in a reversal and the defendant will be deemed to have received a "fair trial."

5. Plain Error

This is by far the worst standard of review for the appellant. If there is no objection to the issue at trial, then the standard of review is "plain error." This standard is extraordinarily difficult to meet and is often the death knell to what otherwise might be a valid issue. To overcome this exacting standard, counsel must show four things: (1) the error must appear clearly in the record; (2) the error must violate a clear and unequivocal rule of law; (3) the party claiming plain error must prove a substantial right has been denied him; and (4) he has been materially prejudiced as a result. This is an extraordinarily difficult standard to overcome. To avoid it, trial counsel must object, must not acquiesce, and must make a clear record.

In addition to the general standards of appellate review listed above, there are two additional standards that are unique to the defense situation: ineffective assistance of counsel and prosecutorial misconduct.

6. Ineffective Assistance of Counsel

Thanks to *Gideon v. Wainright*, 372 U.S. 335 (1963), criminal defendants are entitled to effective assistance of counsel. While at first glance it may appear obvious to most practitioners as to what is and what is not "effective assistance," the examples that serve to illustrate the standard have evolved to surprise even the most jaded cynic.

"Effective assistance of counsel" does not mean representation that results in a win or even an acceptable result. In a nutshell, in order to show that counsel was ineffective, the appellant must show that defense counsel's performance was deficient in such a way as to fall below the acceptable standard of care for a "reasonably competent attorney" and that the deficient performance resulted in prejudice to the defendant.[5] In other words, was there a reasonable probability that but for the deficient performance, the outcome of the case would have been different? What does this mean exactly? The critical issue is not the error made by counsel, but whether that error was prejudicial to the defendant. The claim can be determined without considering counsel's deficient performance.

[5] *See also* Strickland v. Washington, 466 U.S. 668 (1984). The defense attorney must be shown to be objectively deficient, and there is reasonable probability that a competent attorney would have led to a different outcome.

7. Prosecutorial Misconduct

The standard of review for prosecutorial misconduct is similar to that for ineffective assistance of counsel; that is, the error must be present and its effect must be prejudicial. If no objection is made at trial, the court considers the alleged misconduct under the "plain error" standard. If an objection has been made, the court employs the "harmless error" standard. The question is whether the misconduct affected the accused's "substantial rights" (e.g., the right to a fair trial). The defendant must show that in the absence of such error, it is a reasonable possibility that the verdict might have been more favorable to the accused.

If a prosecutor is going to commit misconduct, it will most likely occur during closing argument. And it typically involves one or more of the following three areas: (1) Inflaming the passion of the jury; (2) misstating the evidence; and (3) vouching for the credibility of the witness.

Not only are prosecutors advocates for the state, they are also charged with the ministerial duty to seek justice. No wonder they're confused! Perhaps because of this confusion, or simply because they can't help themselves because they can't stand the thought of losing, some prosecutors will, either subconsciously or intentionally, seek to "gild the lily" at trial by "enhancing" evidence they believe isn't strong enough on its own. This, of course, leads straight to prosecutorial misconduct.

While there is a school of thought that cautions against objecting during an opponent's closing argument (because you risk looking like an ill-mannered jerk to the jury), you must object clearly and on the record if the prosecutor crosses one or more of these lines at trial. No one will consider you a jerk for clearly calling out the prosecutor if he or she is trying to cheat. Juries don't like cheaters.

21
Parting Thoughts

Being a criminal defense lawyer is not for the timid, the squeamish, or the faint of heart. You must sacrifice much and be willing to put it all on the line, unblinkingly, and stand in the breach and deliver. You must be willing and able to engage yourself in a manner and to a degree that most others cannot. To many, being a trial lawyer, particularly a criminal defense lawyer, demands an investment of principled conviction such that it transforms a career into a calling.

The following comments by Hon. John L. Kane, U.S. District Court judge for the District of Colorado are worth noting:

> We do know that justice is something most people cannot afford and even fewer have experienced it. . . . Moreover, the decline of jury trials to near extinction is a product of the law itself. . . . It is simply not possible to put their lives back into balance when the gates of justice are only half-open. . . .
>
> I want to offer you what I think is a fresh insight into this situation. The jury trial is vanishing because to a large measure those exercising power, the legislatures and the higher courts, both state and federal, are distrustful of the judgment of fellow citizens. The jury is the very essence of democratic government by the people, and those in power do not trust jurors to render

> verdicts that perpetuate the economic domination of special interests. . . .
>
> . . .
>
> Not only do those with economic power not want to be exposed to the prospect of financial liability for their wrongdoing, I suggest to you that they do not want our society, as represented by their fellow citizens, sitting as a jury, passing judgment on them. It is not just a matter of money; it is also a desire to avoid a moral judgment.
>
> . . .
>
> [T]he value of being a lawyer and the advocate's sense of well-being will not change. When you provide order to families living in chaos, when you afford dignity to those who have been degraded, when you eloquently express the higher aspirations of our culture where otherwise there is greed and corruption, when you take upon yourself the awesome task of ending a person's despair, in sum, when you become another's champion, you succeed.[1]

Criminal defense lawyers are true warriors. They rise to fire when all others with good sense seek shelter. They are not mere "litigators." That is why most attorneys are not trial lawyers. They are indeed a rare breed of cat.

Believe in yourself, believe in your client, and the power of the story of innocence. Hear the bell. Do not be intimidated. Choose not to fail. Stand up for those whose light shines dim and whose voice is heard small.

. . . *and be Chariots of Fire.*

---

1 Keynote address to Colorado Trial Lawyers Association Spring Dinner, reprinted in *W.T.L.A. Coffee House* Magazine, Winter 2016 at 6–7, 27. (Used with permission of Judge Kane.)

Index

Note: Page numbers followed by "n" indicate footnotes.

C